CHAPLAIN

GIL A. STRICKLIN

The scripture references in this Book, unless otherwise noted,
are taken from the New King James Version of the Holy Bible.

Cover Photograph by Jason Janik
Cover Design by Jeremy Culp Design, LLC

Library of Congress Control Number: 2014910619

ISBN 978-0-692-21795-5

RBC Print Services

MMI Publishing
Marketplace Ministries
2001 West Plano Parkway, Suite 3200
Plano, Texas 75075
(972) 941-4400
www.marketplaceministries.com

DEDICATION

Chaplain is dedicated to my personal chaplain, my wife, Ann,
who has been by my side inspiring me to finish the race strong for God's glory,
and
to all our front-line chaplains,
who share these four-letter words,
HELP, HOPE, CARE, LOVE,
with employees in the marketplaces of the world.

CONTENTS

FOREWORD

Chaplain is a must-read book. If you enjoy a compelling story, told in a powerful way, you will love this expression of God's miracles in the marketplace. This is the story of God using one man to build the largest workplace employee care service, provided by chaplains, in the world today.

Your heart will be moved and your spirit motivated by stories of Good Samaritans called chaplains who lift up people, "bandage" their hurting hearts, and get them back on the road of life. These stories happen every day somewhere in the world, while you are asleep or awake, in North America, Central America, Europe, and soon in faraway places like China and South Korea.

This book and its story will motivate you to seek the will of God for your life, to know what you are here to accomplish with His blessings, power, and guidance. You will be overwhelmed by how God makes successful what He decides to do in the life of an individual who is yielded to Him.

I am excited to recommend *Chaplain* for your reading. As a dedicated Christian businessman, I am grateful God impressed me to have chaplains to care for my partners at Pilgrim's Pride Corporation. In fact, we had four hundred chaplains showing God's love to our fifty-six thousand partners, before I sold my company. Marketplace Ministries is still with the company I sold, as well as with my other companies.

The highlight of *Chaplain* is how God has used these care givers to introduce thousands of individuals to Jesus Christ as Savior. I am both proud and grateful that some nine thousand of them were my employees who one day will join me in heaven.

When you read *Chaplain*, it will inspire any believer to be a better Good Samaritan, taking ministry at work and beyond, every day of the week.

Lonnie (Bo) Pilgrim
Former Chairman and CEO
Pilgrim's Pride Corporation
Pittsburg, Texas

PREFACE

For nearly a decade, my dear friend and great encourager Zig Ziglar would tell me I needed to write a book telling the story about God's marketplace miracles and how He created the world's first and largest civilian corporate chaplains' service.

For years, every time I visited with Zig, he would always say the same thing to start our conversation. "Have you started writing that book yet?" he would ask, with that down-home, southern Alabama drawl that had become famous, as he was the number one motivational speaker in the world.

His questioning and prodding on why I should write a book no one else could ever write got so bad, I dreaded to talk to him. However, I began to think about what he said; why I should write it and tell the story of God at work in the marketplace. The more I thought, and heard his words over and over again, the more I began to feel not only my dear brother Zig wanted me to write a book, but that the Lord wanted me to as well.

A book, why, that is a hundred thousand words or more...two to three hundred pages; that would take a lifetime. The desire to write continued, and so did Zig. Finally, late in 2012, I began to plan seriously how I could take time off from my regular duties as chairman and CEO of Marketplace Ministries to write, day after day and week after week until the final word would be written and given to a publisher. Would anyone publish it?

I remember making the book my top priority and telling the staff I was not going to be in the office for several weeks or a few months. I would be in my home office with computer, historic records, notes made over the years, magazine stories, files and files of correspondence and other bits of information, all to be sorted out and put in some form called a book. I was committed to the book project and would not allow anything to deter me until the final word was written.

After I started this project, one of the hardest I have ever undertaken, I could hardly wait to call Zig. He had several health issues and had fallen at home and been seriously injured, but he had not lost his sense of humor or his ability to string words together for life's best wisdom. He had greatly enhanced my motivational speaking career, which allowed me to send my two sons through Baylor University. I loved Zig Ziglar like a brother. He was my example of a good and godly man, a wonderful husband and father and a special friend.

After getting started and realizing I would one day finish the book, I dialed

Zig's telephone number. His "little redhead," his wife, Jean, now had to answer the phone. After a warm greeting, she asked if I wanted to speak to Zig.

"Zig Ziglar here, who has a beautiful red-headed wife," he said as he answered the phone. "Zig," I said, "this is your friend Gil Stricklin, and before you ask me if I have started writing my book, I want you to know I have."

I went on to tell Zig he had inspired and compelled me to begin the task of writing, and writing, and writing until I told the entire story of what God had done with chaplains in the work arena of the world.

"That is great, Gil," I heard him say. "Now you have to make me a promise. I want to be the first person to read it when you finish the first draft. Do you promise?"

There was no one I would rather read my prose than my friend Zig, so I promised. "You will be the first one, Zig," I said, and he was thrilled he had motivated me to begin a difficult task that one day would be completed.

My only sadness is before I finished the book, all one hundred thousand words, our Lord needed a motivational speaker in heaven, so He put out an order to the angels to bring home the best motivational speaker of all, Zig Ziglar, author of many books, and the man who was going to read mine and help make it better.

Even though he will not be the first to read it, I know it will be read, and God will be given all the glory for what He has done in using a redeemed human being to accomplish the Lord's will and tell His story.

Ten years from now, or maybe a hundred, if Jesus tarries His second coming, someone might ask, "How did Marketplace Ministries with all those chaplains get started?" An individual will pick up a copy of this book and say, "Read this, and you will know exactly how it began and how it came to be what it is today."

When people read this book, they may say with me and the psalmist, "This was the Lord's doing; it is marvelous in our eyes" (Psalm 118:23).

Gil A. Stricklin
Dallas, Texas

1

"Hey Chaplain, Do You Have a Minute?"

It was a cold Monday morning, with a strong wind blowing out of the north and clouds blotting out the sun. The day before, I had joyfully celebrated Christmas. But on this day, I walked with sorrow to the graveside of my friend of nearly thirty years, David Worm.

David had battled cancer for more than a year and had been in and out of Dallas hospitals more than a dozen times. He had been pumped full of chemo, which sustained his life for a few months but could not prevent the inevitable.

The graveside tent was closed on the north side in an attempt to block the wind. But gusts still drove through the crowd like a sharp knife. David's wife sat on the front row without a heavy coat, so I gave her mine. I was cold, but my sadness kept me from feeling it much as I looked into the faces of David's family, including his three sons and his brother.

The roar of the Harley-Davidson motorcycles that had accompanied the hearse to the cemetery was silent now. The riders dressed in black leather stood at attention, then moved inside.

As I waited to start the graveside service, my mind wandered back to the first time I met David. It was May 1984, and he was a thirty-two-year-old street salesman for Sysco Food Systems in Dallas. I had recently launched Marketplace Ministries to provide pastoral care in the workplace, doing funerals, performing weddings, making hospital and home visits to the sick and dying. Sysco was our second corporate client, and I was its only chaplain, providing support for Sysco's five hundred employees.

I wasn't surprised that David E. Wicker III, Sysco's chairman and CEO, had asked me to join him in reaching his employees for Christ. He was a good and godly man and my friend since 1970. Why hadn't I talked with him earlier?

I didn't know. I came to Sysco with no other responsibility except to care for, support, encourage, and love workers and their family members, all in the name of Jesus Christ.

Don't get me the wrong. I did not carry an oversized Bible or wear a large cross or a priestly collar. No, I prided myself in being a stealth chaplain, low key, laid back, except when it came to reaching out to people, standing with them in times of loss and sorrow, extending hope for hurting hearts. There would be nothing stealth about my ministry to those in need.

As the wind continued to whip around the tent at the graveside service, I recalled hearing the first words I ever heard from David in the hallway of Sysco, near the sales offices: "Hi, I am David Worm, and you're that preacher."

You might have guessed David was a top salesman with his happy-go-lucky, vivacious, enthusiastic, and positive attitude. He could truly sell ice cream to Eskimos. I liked him the first time I met him, and he became a fast and favorite friend.

But from the way he said the word "preacher" in that first conversation, it was evident David did not have much interest in church or preachers. However, he later shared that he did like the idea that someone was there at work to help employees and their families.

Within forty-five days after we first met, I heard that salesman's voice above the din of activity one afternoon as I made my worksite visit: "Hey chaplain, do you have a minute?"

After we walked to a quiet room, David turned to me with tears in his eyes. "I really need your help," he said. "We have a big problem." David's two-year-old daughter, Jana, had been diagnosed with stomach cancer.

For the next 103 days, the tiny, brown-haired, blue-eyed angel lingered between life and death. And I, as the company chaplain, made 113 visits to Children's Medical Center in Dallas.

David and I shared countless prayers for her healing, two fathers hugging, with tears flowing down our cheeks. I would deliver dinner to David and his wife in the waiting room outside of the intensive care unit, or stay close by Jana's bedside while her parents went to eat.

What I remember most were the things I was never prepared for in graduate school at seminary or Army training, like helping an ICU nurse swab the child's lips with ice or changing her diapers. No professor or Army chaplain taught me how to minister when a little girl is dying and a nurse is weeping.

On the morning of my fiftieth birthday, September 11, 1984, my wife, Ann, surprised me by getting me all dressed up and taking me to an expensive photography studio for one of those executive portraits. Unfortunately, I had been at the hospital with the Worms until 4 o'clock that morning, fearing that Jana would not make it through the night. Needless to say, the picture was horrible; I looked totally beat, red eyes and all. Weeks after, I had it redone for use in Marketplace Ministries.

Then, at about 3 o'clock that fall afternoon, September 13, my pager went off. I recognized the number, Children's Medical Center. I returned the call instantly.

"She has gone home," were the words of her dad.

"I will be right there," I responded, for that is what a good chaplain does, respond now, for now is when needed.

I jumped into my ten-year-old Datsun station wagon, which doubled as Marketplace Ministries' only office, and sped south down Central Expressway toward the hospital. *What can I say to comfort them?* I wondered. *What can I do to help these parents?*

As I drove, I wept and cried out, "O God, help me to help them. I cannot minister to these grieving parents without your compassion, care, and love. God, I need your help."

Finally I drove into the parking lot, jumped out of my car, and briskly walked toward the front door of the hospital. The door opened and out came David and his wife, along with their five-year-old son, John David.

God did not give me any words to say at that moment. I have found that sometimes in life there aren't any words to say, only tears to share, along with loving hugs, more tears and more hugs. That is what we did.

It seemed we lingered a long time in silence. However, I know it was only a few short minutes. During that time all you could hear was weeping, the sound of hearts breaking.

David spoke first.

"We never would have made it without you, Chaplain," were his words through tears that continued to flow.

I could not utter a word. I just stood there and cried like a baby with them. Just like theirs, my heart was broken, for over the weeks and months of seeing Jana almost every day, I grew to love her deeply.

Of course, because they did not have a pastor and I was their chaplain, I would arrange the funeral. Of course, I would write the obituary for the newspaper, contact the church, arrange for music and the funeral bulletin. And now, the funeral home was on the way to pick up the little angel's body.

Three days later, Sysco's chairman, David Wicker, and I would lead a life celebration service, as well as a graveside service. More than four hundred family members and friends attended the funeral at First Baptist Church in Rockwall, Texas, with many of them making their way to the small country cemetery east of town for the burial.

Both services were filled with assurance, celebration, joy, and some laughter, mingled with tears and sorrow. Everyone there knew Jana was not in that small child's casket. Her body was there; however, her spirit and soul were with Jesus in glory, where she would live forever, time without end. She was in that place where there was no more sickness, no more dying or death, no more pain, no more darkness, no more sin, even though this child knew very little about sin and its effect on life. She was in heaven, and there is no sin there, no temptation, and no sorrow. She had really just begun to live, and live on for eternity.

Green is the color that portrays life and living. At the graveside, everyone was given a green helium balloon. At the close of the service, John David stepped out from under the funeral tent to release his balloon, and everyone else joined him to release all the balloons together. The release symbolized letting Jana go to heaven to be with her everlasting heavenly Father.

As David walked away from the grave, he looked up; there was one green balloon, the one his son let go a minute before with a note to Jana tied on it. As David stood there staring, the balloon hovered by itself as scores of the other balloons rose in the distance.

Suddenly, the lone balloon left and took off like a rocket, straight up with accelerating speed. The father watched until the round, green dot was a just a speck in the blue sky, and then nothing. It was gone.

This final event for David is just what he needed and desired, to walk away from the grave with peace in his heart and joy in his spirit. Yes, Jana was home.

Afterward, David shared with me some of his thoughts about his two-year-old little angel. "I still believe Jana was here for a reason," he said. "I look at it as God sending her to us for the short time she was here. I know He did."

God's ways are far higher than ours, and we can't begin to understand His purposes. But I believe David was right; somehow, Jana's life had divine purpose.

One night months earlier as Jana still fought her cancer, David and I sat in the Children's Medical Center. It was one of those sultry August nights in Dallas, when the day's temperature is 105 degrees and the night is not much cooler. It was about 12:30 a.m., when the hospital is quiet, people are asleep in the waiting rooms, and the staff is limited to the must-do medical duties.

Down in the bowels of the building, David and I found a Coke machine and were having a soft drink. Over the months we had talked at various times about death and dying, about whether there is a life after this one. But I didn't push the issue. I just prayed David would have his spiritual blinders removed and one day he would come to Christ, accepting the Savior.

As he took another swig of his Coke, I quietly asked David if he was sure that when he died, he would go to heaven. There was a long silence, and I drank more of my Coke, waiting for a reply.

"I think so," he finally said. "I sure hope so. I try to do my best and treat people right. I think I have done more good things than bad."

"David, if you can go to heaven by being good, and doing more good things than bad, then there would have been no need for Christ to have died on the cross for your sins, in your place, would there?" I asked. "The Bible says, 'For by grace you have been save through faith, and that not of yourselves, *it is* the gift of God, not of works, lest anyone should boast.' " (Ephesians 2:8-9).

Growing up, David had been exposed to a church. However, he did not know if he was in God's family, and he did not know *how* to know. He was ignorant of the knowledge that God offers eternal life as a gift, and all any human has to do is trust by faith what Christ did on the cross—He died for the sins of all people.

I explained to David the Bible tells us very plainly: "But as many as received Him [Christ] to them He gave the right [or authority] to become children of God, to those who believe on His name" (John 1:12).

Then, in the middle of a dark night, with his daughter upstairs dying in ICU, David said he wanted to receive Christ into his life. He bowed his head, closed his eyes, and prayed this simple prayer, repeating after me: "Dear God, I am a sinner; I am sorry for my sins; I am willing to turn from my sins; tonight I accept your gift of eternal life, and you, Jesus, as my Savior. Come into my life and forgive my sins. Empower me to live for you the rest of the days of life, and serve you in the fellowship of a church. Amen."

From that day forward, David's life changed completely; there was assurance he was on his way to heaven. He joined a Baptist church, was baptized into the fellowship, and lived for the Lord God the remaining twenty-seven years of his life.

But by late 2011, that earthly life was coming to a close as David faced his own battle with cancer.

Once as I was visiting him in the hospital, David said, "Gil, you know I want you to do my funeral. I don't want anyone else but you. Will you do it?"

I answered, "Sure I will do that for you, David. However, you may come to my funeral before I go to yours because we all have only one day to live, and that's today. I may be in heaven waiting for you long before you get there. You just can never tell."

"Oh, I know that," he said quickly. "However, some day I am going to die, and if you are still here, I want you to say the final words about me. I really do!"

It was settled that day. I would officiate at David's funeral.

On Tuesday, December 6, 2011, I drove to Rockwall, Texas, to plan David's funeral with him. David lay in his big chair in the living room, where they had put his hospital bed. I had scarcely walked into the room when he declared, "You know, I am ready to go home to heaven, to be with Jesus."

Many would say David was already home. But he knew what many people do not know. That is, his earthly address was only temporary. One day, he would die and go to his real home, his eternal and heavenly home with Jesus Christ and all true believers.

When I was visiting with David that afternoon in his temporary dwelling, I asked him directly if he had any fear as he faced death. He smiled, looked up at me, and spoke slowly. "No, I am not scared of going away," he said with certainty. "The Lord is with me, and God is holding my hand."

I must tell you I have seen a whole lot of people die, and move toward certain death, in fifty-five years of being a minister, with forty of those years as a chaplain in the military and corporate America. I have been there holding that hand when the heart beats for the last time. Yes, I have seen death, smelled death, watched death come in hospitals, homes, retirement centers, and a lot of other places.

You can tell a whole lot about a person's faith by the way he or she dies. I have seen those without faith fighting death, screaming out, tossing and turning, and I have seen those with faith accepting their journey with serene peace and a joyful expression. They quietly slip away as if someone is holding their hand and leading them through the door of death into life eternal. Those with faith in Christ are those who are ready to go from "the land of the dying to the land of the living, forever."

Finally David made that journey. Now it was the day after Christmas, and I stood before family and friends at David's graveside service.

The funeral director waited for everyone to gather before he gave me the official nod to begin.

After the reading of Scripture, a few brief words of comfort and assurance that we would see David again, and a closing prayer, we moved to our cars, and the motorcycles roared to life again as we made our way to the chapel in the funeral home a few hundred yards away.

The room was filled to overflowing, and people were standing across the back of the room and in the hallway. There were all kinds of people from all walks of life and various cultures. Black, brown, white, poor and rich, blue collar and white collar were all present to pay their final respects to a friend, a fellow street salesman, a motorcycle club member, a church member, or a family member.

When it came time for me to speak, I rose and stood behind the white wooden podium. Again, I looked at David's loved ones and felt their pain and sorrow, because I felt the same. I knew everyone present had come because of their love and friendship for David Worm, my friend and theirs.

I began by telling the audience that my friendship with David began out of pain, sorrow, and suffering as I briefly related Jana's story and my role in it with her parents. However, I assured them over the years we often laughed together many times, for we had already cried together.

In Christ, we will join David one day, with all those who have left this temporal world going to the eternal heavenly world and that future reunion in glory. Someone has rightly said, "Christians never say goodbye for the last time."

David always called Jana his little angel, and he had even kept her baby pillow with him all those twenty-seven years since her departure. Before Jana became so ill, every time David would come into the house from work in the evenings, after leaving early each morning before his baby girl was up, she would run to the door shouting loudly: "Daddy's home, Daddy's home, Daddy's home!" and there was hugging and laughter with kisses.

Something like that happened in heaven early Monday morning, December 26, 2011, for Jana, along with Jesus and many others, met David at the gate of heaven. She cried out, "Daddy's home, Daddy's home, Daddy's home," and there was great rejoicing. Daddy was home indeed, and he would never have to leave again.

When I performed Jana's funeral, I had no way of knowing that over the next thirty-plus years more than twenty-eight hundred other Marketplace chaplains would stand in churches, funeral homes, mausoleums, and cemeteries in huge metropolitan cities and small country towns and villages to hold more than ten thousand funerals.

Even though David and Jana were not the only child and parent I buried over the years, I would recall them perhaps more than anyone else, because it is not every day a chaplain is so blessed to bury a little angel.

2

MY ACADEMIC CAREER DIDN'T LOOK PROMISING

I began my academic career by failing the first grade. I celebrated my seventh and eighth birthdays in first grade, and second grade was not much better. Growing up, I was not the smartest boy in my class; however, I was usually the oldest.

My first home had been in Sadler, Texas, a tiny country hamlet west of Denison and Pottsboro, where on a bright early morning, September 11, 1934, the third son of Gilford Lane and Lessie Caroline Watson Stricklin was born. My mother said I was so happy and radiant she called me Sunny, the name I was called until I went to college. That is when I changed it to a more dignified Gil, the first three letters of my legal name, Gilford A. Stricklin. "Gil" sounded more intellectual than "Sunny," and who wants to explain his mother thought he was a "little ray of sunshine"? Besides, "Gil" is the Hebrew word for joy or gladness and fit my personality and smile.

My dad was the railroad agent and telegraph operator in Sadler, Texas. Two Missouri, Kansas and Texas Railroad (KATY) passenger trains stopped there every day, one in the morning and one in the evening, going in opposite directions. The Stricklin family lived in a railroad house close to the side track, not far from the small depot where Dad worked for the KATY.

Most of the town's folks would come down to the station and see if any mail bags were left for the post office. If you got any mail, it came by train, for the railroad was the connection to the outside world.

After moving to Denison, about thirty-five miles to the east, Dad began a new job with the railroad, and we would remain there for many years. Two more sons would join the family, making a total of five; we had our own basketball team. But the mother of those boys was easily the best basketball player in the family, as she was an All-State girls' basketball selection for the Celeste High School Blue Devils and once entertained the notion of playing for a women's professional basketball team in Dallas.

When it came time to choose sides in our family games, everyone always wanted mother. The team that got her won every time. As a 5'3" guard, she was fast and shifty as a water bug. She was already a pro in our eyes.

At first we lived on West Hull Street in Denison, Texas, just a few blocks from the birthplace of General Dwight David Eisenhower, whose dad, like mine, worked for the KATY Railroad. Then my dad found a newer and bigger house over on West Walker Street in a better part of town on the north side. I thought it was a mansion with three bedrooms; one even had a ceiling fan. If the president of the United States and a general in the Army had his start down the block from where I lived, it made me think I, too, could achieve success and stature someday, even living in a small country town like Denison.

I finished my first eight grades at Central Ward Elementary School. I still remember the first loves of my young life: Mrs. Neely, third grade; Mrs. McCoy, fourth grade; and Mrs. Meadows, eighth grade.

Growing up in small-town Denison in the 1940s and 1950s was life at its best. The pace was slow, and you didn't notice much social or moral decay. Almost everyone went to church; alcohol was not prevalent, and you had to drive across the Red River to Colbert or Platter Flats, Oklahoma, to buy even a bottle of beer, and only the bad guys did that. Drugs were unheard of in high school or anywhere else. Not many girls got pregnant out of wedlock, and murder was non-existent. No one locked the doors of their houses or cars, for honesty seemed to override theft.

Church and school were the most important institutions in our family, and in each of our lives. We never missed going to either, school every weekday and church on Sunday and Wednesday night.

Now, unless you wanted to walk near death and come close to a whipping, you could forget trying to skip school. Everyone knew everyone in my town, and surely someone would see you and tell your parents; and if they did, I always hoped they would tell my mother, never my dad. She carried a Bible in one hand and a hickory switch in the other, and she used both to keep her five boys in line, a straight line. But she had a mother's love in her heart, and you could sweet-talk her sometimes.

As much as I hated school and all those studies at home every night, I feared my dad's punishment more. I would never, ever consider playing hooky with some of my buddies. I would tell them they didn't have my dad or they wouldn't dare cut school. He didn't bluff, and I didn't cut.

I did cut church now and again, not often of course. It seems that every time I did, things always went wrong. Even with my best planning, it never worked out very favorably. I remember one time at church camp for the morning service, a friend and I decided we would rather go pick blackberries than hear another boring sermon. Besides, it was too hot to sit in that old wooden tabernacle for an hour or longer.

As the service was about to begin, with the piano and organ already warming up and the youth choir forming, my pal Jerry and I slipped behind the gathering and tried to melt into the tree line and bushes for cover. We had just about made it down the hill when some nosy adult saw us and began to holler for us to come back.

That was my sign to take off in a fast run, going further down the hill, hiding as much as I could. As I ran, I saw a barbed wire fence coming in front of me. It looked the normal size of a cow fence, so I figured I could clear it with one leap in a fast run.

I ran faster as I approached and made that daring leap. I thought I had cleared the top strand of that three-strand fence. However, when I went over the top, I came down on that sharp, rusty barbed wire, and it slit open six inches of the back of my upper leg. Blood went everywhere.

Blood and blackberries don't go together very well, so that ruined the picking session I had planned. The nosy old adult had tracked us down and now was coming upon me as I lay on the ground trying to get the bleeding to stop.

This good churchman was real encouraging. "Good grief, you are going to die," he said. "Either you are going to bleed to death or you are bound to get typhoid or lockjaw for sure."

So much for skipping church.

A trip to Long-Sneed Hospital on Woodard Street in Denison, and the pain of having my leg sewn up with many stitches, brought to an end a very bad morning and my very bad decision. Also, it ended my church camp that year as I lay on my stomach at home trying to explain to my parents what happened.

High school football was the biggest social event in my town, as it was in most Texas cities regardless of size. However, I knew early on that football would not help me get to college. And with my grades, I could forget an academic scholarship. It would take hard work and superhuman determination for me to become a college graduate. It would even take divine intervention.

I did make my high school Yellow Jacket football team; however, Coach Les Cranfield moved me from quarterback to guard. At quarterback I was too slow, too clumsy, and couldn't throw the deep pass or the short one either, for that matter. However, on the line I was 155 pounds of self-described "destructive human dynamite." Still, I was never selected for All-District or All-State honors. I was not a star by any definition of the word.

Even though my parents didn't see all of my game performances in football or basketball, I was on both teams. I remember once going home after a basketball game in the old Denison High gym. Mother always got up when her boys came home at nighttime. It was her kind of late-night inspection.

When she asked me if I got to play, I was so proud to tell her yes, I got in the game toward the end, when the winning outcome was certain. Then she asked if I scored any points. I was pleased to say, "Yes, ma'am, I scored two baskets, four points." She joyfully congratulated me, for that was my high-scoring game of the season.

As I was preparing to leave for another home court basketball game, the approval came quite unexpectedly, just like a bolt of lightning out of a clear sky. I had not been driving long and hadn't taken the car by myself very often. As I got all my stuff together, my mother said she talked to Dad and I could take the car for the evening. "Oh, be careful, Sunny, that's the only car we have," were my mother's final words before I walked out of the house on the side porch.

There sat a gray two-door 1950 Chevrolet. It was the same car my two older brothers Don and Jimmy drove regularly to go hunting. One time when they returned, Mother asked them if they had a good time. We only had to drive three or four miles north to find a lot of Texas jack rabbits, and shooting was good in those days. They both assured her they had a lot of fun.

Then she calmly asked, "What did you shoot?" Don, the older and wiser brother, answered calmly, "The roof of the car." Mother sweetly replied, "Oh, that's nice." Then she screamed, "You shot what? You shot the car; you shot the roof out of the car?"

The boys quickly assured her that neither one of them was hurt, and then told her Jimmy nearly had his head blown off. The 12-gauge shotgun blast missed his head and took out the inside lining and the metal roof of that Chevrolet. Sure enough, she found a gaping, twelve-inch circle that looked like it had been opened up by a dull can opener.

That was all repaired now, new paint, new lining and all. No one could even tell that was the place where Jimmy nearly died when the shotgun went off, even though Don swore he had unloaded it. Jimmy claimed all his life his hearing was damaged by that blast.

Well, I didn't have any shotguns in the car the night of the basketball game, so I didn't have to worry. No, I just had to watch out for those other drivers, those bad drivers, those other teenagers. I was a superb driver, and my parents could trust me with our car, our only car.

I was so proud I had a car for the evening. I walked into the gym twirling the keys around my finger and answering by buddies with much pride when asked if I had the car. I had wheels.

As I sat on the bench during the game, I scanned the crowd for that special girl I could pick up after the game and, perhaps, drive to the Pig Stand restaurant and share a root beer. There she was, that little blonde girl who lived up on Woodard Street, kind of toward my house anyway.

Soon as the game was over, and still in my yellow and black basketball togs, I made my way toward the bleachers and asked if she needed a ride home. Shucks, there was another guy with her, and he had wheels, too.

You know you aren't real popular when you have a car and a little pocket change, and no one will accept your invitation for a ride and a root beer. Oh well, I would just go on home by myself. I had parked right in front of the gym so everyone could see I had wheels for the evening.

As I backed out, with lights on, I started west down Main Street. I thought I would make one last pass by school to see if I could find anyone to take home. So, I looked back and threw a U-turn and started east. I passed the school, and everyone was getting into cars, laughing, talking, shouting, for we had won the game. But the score had been close, so of course, I didn't get to play.

I made a left turn just past the school and headed toward home. As I was making the turn, someone called, "Hey, Sunny!" Of course, when someone screams at you, you automatically turn and look back to see who it is. As I looked back and stuck out my hand to wave, I held the turn a little too long. When I turned back, I heard a big bang. A tree in my algebra teacher's side yard stopped me and that Chevrolet real quick.

As I sat stunned behind the wheel that had rammed my chest (this was long before safety belts), there was a tree implanted in the right front fender.

Would you believe the fellow who hollered at me and caused this disaster didn't even come to see if I was killed or critically injured? I got out and walked around the front of the car. Thank goodness, one headlight was still burning; however, the right front fender was smashed, and so was the headlight.

At that moment I wished I had died in the accident, because now I had to go home and tell my parents I had wrecked the car.

Backing slowly away from the tree and gently maneuvering into the street, I started for home. It was well after ten o'clock, and I knew my parents would be asleep. However, the odds were that Mother would get up to check on me in when I drove into the driveway. I would try to be real quiet, and maybe she would remain asleep.

However, when I tried to make a right turn I made another horrible discovery. The tire rubbed loudly, and I smelled rubber burning. I quickly stopped, got out, and went to the damage zone. With all the strength a sixteen-year-old could muster, adrenaline pumping, I moved the bent metal away from the tire.

I started home again, choosing a route that included only left turns because the tire didn't rub on the frame that way. Finally, I got to my last left turn into our driveway beside the house. I had already turned off the one good light and killed the engine with the car in neutral, using the silent hand brake to stop.

I shut the car door as quietly as I could and took off my shoes as I entered the back porch to go into the house. I prayed my parents would not wake up.

My dad was a good man; however, he was a tough and just man with his five boys. When discipline was required, he knew how to dispense it. I knew he was going to deal with me harshly when he saw the car. However, I deserved it. It was my fault.

Now I heard the back door of the back stairs open. Mother was coming down. Not even my prayers could keep her asleep when one of her boys came home after dark.

She said nothing about the game or the evening. She looked at me, still sleepy in her eyes, and said, "Are you sick? You look sick? Are you OK?"

"Yea, I am OK," I replied, even though that was not the truth.

She then said, "What's wrong, Sunny? Something is wrong."

I then told her I had had a little wreck in the car. But, I quickly added Miss Byers's oak tree was not badly damaged, and I thought it would live. I didn't say it, but I wasn't really sure if I would.

She spoke softly, as if she was with me in some conspiracy. I knew she would be on my side. We will not tell your Daddy tonight, we will wait until in the morning, I heard her say. I thought that was a good idea, a few more hours delay before doom, death, and Dad.

When she said let's go look at the damage, my heart sank further. Now I would have to show her what I had done to the family car. We quietly walked across the back porch with only a dim light shining on the car.

She said, "Oh, Sunny, that doesn't look so bad. That's not bad at all."

"Mother, that is the wrong side; it is over here," I said as I pulled her to the crashed side.

She gasped and said quietly, "Oh, Sunny, that is bad." She spoke as if she was telling me something I didn't know. Of course, it was bad. Anyone could tell that.

We went back in the house, and I turned off the outside light. In the total darkness, the car didn't look quite so bad.

Mother looked at me and said, "Now, I know you are tired. Go on upstairs and get a good night's sleep, and we will tell your daddy in the morning."

That was about like telling a man who was going to be hanged at daybreak to rest peacefully, don't worry, it's going to be all right.

I was awake most of the night, maybe all of it. I heard several freight trains pulling out of Ray Yards heading north or south. I heard a siren sometime during the dark hours and wondered whose house was on fire. I heard dogs barking and the wind blowing. Before long, I saw the first rays of daybreak. Dad was in our one bathroom shaving with his straight razor.

My dad was always up early to go to work, and Mother was up earlier to fix him one of those "country boy" breakfasts with greasy eggs, bacon, fried potatoes, biscuits, and plenty of hot coffee. Dad would pour coffee in his saucer and blow on it to let it cool a bit before downing several cups.

I could smell the coffee and hear the bacon frying. I continued to lie quietly in my bed, without moving. It wasn't long until Dad went down the back stairs, and I knew he was sitting down for breakfast.

I jumped up and dressed quickly. I washed my face, and then told my brothers to stay upstairs. I didn't want them to see Dad's reaction. Also, my two little brothers, Jerry and Charles, were kind of sissies and didn't like seeing blood.

Taking the first step down the stairs was the hardest. But once I started, there was no turning back. As I opened the stairway door into the kitchen, Dad looked up. "Come on, Sunny, breakfast is ready," he said, adding, "You are up early this morning."

I said I wasn't very hungry, as I sat down at the table. Dad had his back to Mother, but I could see her and he could not. She motioned with a twitch of her head toward him for me to tell him.

I opened my mouth to speak, but no words came out. The words were in my mind, but not on my tongue. I just keep opening my mouth and all was silent.

Finally, I heard someone say, "Dad, I had a little wreck in the car last night and I must show you the damage." It was me speaking. He laid down his fork and just stared at me. "Did anyone get hurt?" he asked. "No, sir," I answered, even though that was a lie. I hurt badly.

"We'll look at it in a minute," he said as he drank a sip of coffee that was still smoking.

After a few minutes, which seemed like forever, he pushed back his chair as if to signal that the time had come to examine the damage. We walked out the kitchen door onto the porch and toward the car in the driveway.

I was ready. Whatever he said or whatever he did, I was ready, because I was guilty. It was entirely my fault.

Dad stood there for a long time, surveying the damage.

I started to cry and began to tell him how sorry I was. I knew it was our only car and we didn't have a lot of money for car repairs. I was guilty. I was wrong. I was to blame. I couldn't look at him because I was staring at the ground.

I paused. Then I felt Dad's arm slipping around my shoulder and pulling me toward him, with these words: "It is OK. We'll just get it fixed. You are forgiven."

Surely I didn't hear what I thought I did. He didn't really say that, did he? I must be dreaming.

No, I heard him say again, "It is OK. We'll just get it fixed. You are forgiven."

I began to hug my dad and cry all the more. I could not see him because of tears; however, Dad had a pleasant smell about him, and I could smell that aroma that made me certain he was there.

When I could, I told him I would work and help pay for the repairs, and I would work hard. I would get Miss Byers's tree looked at, too. I couldn't wait to take off for school, walking fast, for my feet were as light as my heart.

Our neighbor, Mrs. Hayes, was out in her front yard, and I yelled, "It's OK. We are going to get it fixed. I am forgiven!"

Another neighbor was getting in his big, bright, new Buick. I cried out, "It's OK. We are going to get it fixed. I am forgiven!"

All the way to school that was my loud slogan for all to hear, "It's OK. We are going to get it fixed. I am forgiven!"

That was the greatest act of forgiveness I had ever experienced. But there would be a far greater act of forgiveness in my future. It would come from a Father, too, a heavenly Father, and it was OK with Him as well, for I was forgiven.

Of all the Stricklin boys, I probably had the most difficulty in school. I could neither spell nor read. But arithmetic was my worst subject. When I was a young kid, my mother and I rode the train to Dallas for an appointment with a brain doctor. There was some consideration that I might be brain damaged. After many evaluations, the tests were inconclusive. The kind, older doctor, trying to encourage my mother (or so I now believe), told her he could not find anything to keep me from learning, and to go home and work hard to help me achieve in my studies.

That's exactly what she did. Every night she would help me and my four brothers with lessons. Every day she would encourage us, pray over us, and ask God to especially help Sunny. She would even call spelling words out to my dad, who had dropped out of school at an early age.

Every Saturday morning, she took me to a retired reading teacher's home for more help. At thirteen years old, I would sit with third- and fourth-grade children on Mrs. Singheiser's front porch on Woodward Street, trying to learn to read phonetically.

Two or three afternoons a week, when football season was over, I would stay after school with Mrs. Meadows to learn math. As my eighth-grade teacher, she would tutor me for an hour, sometimes two, and then she would drive me home out at the edge of town. Never would she accept money from my mother for special help for her most remedial student; however, she always left our house with vegetables, cornbread, and a pie or cookies. That good teacher always said when you go to high school, you need to know arithmetic, and then there would be more difficult math subjects like algebra and trigonometry. She was right.

One day in late 1943, the principal announced that a famous Army Air Force B-25 bomber was going to fly over Denison the next morning. The bomber had made more than thirty bombing runs over Germany, and it had been brought back to the United States to encourage people to purchase war bonds.

Sure enough, the next morning they marched the entire school, grades one to eight, out on the playground, with every kid staring into the sky looking for an airplane. It began with a small whining sound and built up to a deafening roar. Then, out of nowhere, there appeared the Lucky Lady, flying no more than a hundred feet off the ground traveling east to west at a high speed. I could see the co-pilot on the right side of the cockpit looking down at me, and there was a picture of a naked woman brightly painted on the front of the fuselage; she was holding a bomb with black German swastikas on it in her outstretched hand.

The kids on West Walker Street were affectionately known as the Walker Street Rats. The Lilleys' two boys, the Bertis' three boys, the Sneeds' two boys, the Wilsons' two boys, and the Hansons' two boys, plus Bo Brinikie and the five Stricklin boys made for much activity, some of it not really good. Because the Stricklin boys had the largest number of human resources, no one messed with them, at least not without fear of retaliation.

As a twelve-year-old who already had two paying jobs, I was always in church on Sunday morning and evening, as well as Wednesday night for prayer meeting. My mother did not have to make me go to church. I enjoyed going, for I had many friends there, including the Lilleys and the Sneeds. Another friend, Bo Brinikie, was a Catholic. I didn't know how to spell it, and I didn't know what that was. However, I was smart enough to know he was not a Baptist. These high school and neighbor friends would have a lasting Christian relationship with me for sixty-five years and counting, even though Eddie Sneed, Jerry Lilley, and others are now in heaven waiting for us to join them.

Two-week church revivals were vitally important in that small-town culture.

The Baptists had more "protracted meetings" than anyone else. Those big gatherings were conducted in Munson City Park, near the football stadium, where anyone could attend, including blacks. Even though we did not go to school together and rarely attended the same churches, black people did attend revival services with us, especially when the preacher was famous, like the starting point guard on the Phillips 66 professional basketball team from Philadelphia.

I cannot remember talking with my parents about the subject of segregation. I don't recall wondering why we did not go to school together, why black people rode in the back of the bus, why they sat in the balcony of the picture shows, why they had separate drinking fountains, or why they got their hair cut someplace other than where I got mine cut. They had black churches and we had white churches. A wonderful Christian black lady helped my mother when we started taking in boarders. She worked as hard as my mother; we all treated her kindly and with love and respect like all adults regardless their color. That was just the way it was around my house.

Our black friend, Mr. Sid, was known around Denison by all the white folks. He drove the ice truck for the ice company down by the railroad depot and delivered fifty- and one-hundred-pound blocks of ice to businesses and homes. Mr. Sid would bring ice to our house all summer, as my dad thought iced tea tasted best with chipped ice off the big block. Also, Mr. Sid had a unique whistle, and it was louder than a fire truck's siren; every time you saw him anywhere in town and called his name, he would give his famous whistle. My mother always gave Mr. Sid a big glass of iced tea when he made his deliveries to our house. He would sit down on the back porch to visit and rest a minute on the 100-plus-degree Texas summer days, before continuing his ice route deliveries. Mr. Sid was a big man, a friendly man, and as they said back then, "black as the ace of spades." Mr. Sid always liked me, and I always asked him to whistle just one more time before he left. He did, and then we would all laugh.

There was no segregation when it came to play among black and white young people, at least not in my block. We owned the big vacant lot behind our house on Walker Street, and just behind us on Johnson Street lived many black families. We planted a big victory garden on our lot every spring, but when harvest was over and the vegetables were eaten or canned it was the neighborhood football field. We would choose sides, and blacks and whites were on the same teams. I discovered early playing tackle football when a black boy hit the rocky ground, his skinned arm or knee bled bright red just like mine did. The hurt was the same.

When we were not sharing our football field with our Johnson Street neighbors, we would share our home-grown vegetables with them. My mother could grow more food on that quarter-acre lot than even six Stricklin men and one lady could ever eat. Of course she had five boys to do all the work, and Mother was just the foreman, a tough one at that. She always said it was God who made the vegetables grow and we were to share them.

One Saturday night in late August 1946, my mother and her boys were sitting close to the front of the makeshift outdoor canvas cathedral in Munson Park. There were bright white lights strung above the rows of seats. Dad, as usual, was working; he worked hard and was not in church as often as the other members of his family. Big crowds came to those special church events called revivals, so you had to get there early for the best seats, down close to the front. Of course, the preacher hollered so loudly you could hear him just about anywhere in that part of town, or anywhere in town.

I had been attending church services since before I was born, in my mother's womb. That continued all of my life. Consequently, it was not difficult for my life to identify with the man named Jesus Christ. I had known about Him for a long, long time.

The young evangelist was bright, powerful, and humorous. I do not remember his name or the topic of his message that evening; however, I do remember making a new realization: I knew *about* Jesus, but it was through my mother and her faith. My faith in Christ was not that personal; it was secondary. It was my mother's faith that I had inherited.

I did not like the feeling I had that night. I sensed I needed to do something, to make Christ my Savior and Lord, something to make it personal.

To close all the services in the revival and in our church as well, an invitation to trust Christ as Savior was extended to anyone who wanted forgiveness of sins and assurance of the Lord as personal Savior.

I rode home that night with my brothers and Mom. I was quiet, for I felt I missed an important opportunity to settle the question of personal faith. As I crawled into the top bunk above my little brother Jerry, I prayed I would not die until I settled this issue of personal faith in a personal Savior.

Early the next morning, Sunday, I was up and dressed, ready to go to church. Breakfast was quick on Sunday mornings, not like the other days. I could hardly wait until Sunday school was over and we found our pew in the worship service at First Baptist Church of Denison. Dr. Guy Newman, the play-by-play football announcer for the Denison High School Fighting Yellow Jackets, was our pastor.

I knew this day, August 29, 1946, would be my red-letter day to settle the issue with certainty that Christ was my Savior and would always be my Master. As soon as Dr. Newman completed his sermon, which seemed rather long, and as the music began for the invitation, I was moving toward the aisle. I told my mother, then my dad, I was trusting Christ as my Savior. This was my day, my time!

A thousand mules could not have held me back. I knew this was what I must do. It was settled now, and never again would I have to question if my faith was really mine. I knew it was; my name was written in the Lamb's Book of Life and would be there for all eternity.

Baptism was usually in the evening service, but Dad was leaving in the afternoon to drive toward Wichita Falls to fill in for a railroad agent for several days. He would not be there Sunday night; what could we do?

Dr. Newman said we would have a special baptism service Sunday afternoon, before my dad left town. Sure enough, about two o'clock, with the baptism pool ready for the night service, I would be first in the water.

My family was present, along with my favorite neighbor, Mrs. Oliver Hayes, whom Mother called Bess. There were seven witnesses to my expression of obedience to my new Lord. Baptism was a symbol of death to the old life before Christ and rising to walk a new life with Christ. In a moment, Dr. Newman had baptized me, and now I was Christ follower and a member of His church.

Dad left that afternoon, and all was well. He had been one of my witnesses, and I was grateful for his presence.

My personal declaration of faith began my Christian walk with the Lord that has lasted all the days of my life. I have come a long way. However, every time I think I have made some strides upward toward my Lord and His life, He always shows me how far I still need to climb; there is much farther to travel, for I have only begun.

Over the years I have strived to walk in holiness in the lordship of Christ. Twice, I have publically rededicated my life to my Lord. The first came as a junior in high school at age seventeen, five years after I was converted. The next came a few years later as I was working summers on a KATY Railroad signal gang, with tough and sinful men. I wanted to be a witness to my fellow railroaders and everyone else. Moreover, I wanted to help people, the poor, the neglected, the down-and-out, as well as the up-and-out.

God began to do a work in my life really early. I had a feeling He might use me in some way to glorify Him and bless others. I surely hoped so anyway.

3

Paper Carrier, Drug Store Delivery Boy, Landscaper, Ice Cream Maker, Railroader, and Others... in the Making of a Chaplain

For as far back as I can remember, I have had a paying job. Not that it always paid much. Most of my work was not a voluntary effort; almost no work came without a paycheck, except those chores done around home under the supervision of my mother. Payday, which I always looked forward to and still do, was the day "the eagle spit."

Work was inbred in my life, and a strong work ethic was a high priority, along with family and faith. Not one of the five Stricklin boys had the luxury of being lazy, even though I have to admit I tried now and again. It never worked, and I always did.

There were no Saturday or Sunday morning sleep-ins. The first weekend morning, you went to work; the second one, you went to church. All the other days were school days.

Not only did we work during the school year on Saturdays, but in the summer, we worked full-time. Around late April every year, my mother would start the same conversation. "Where are you going to work this summer?" she would casually ask one son and then another. That was a warning sign that I had better begin finding that job, that place to work, starting the first day after school was out.

My brothers and I did not have to find a job. However, we knew the terrible consequences of not getting one: Mother would find us one, and she would accept any job at any hourly rate regardless of how difficult or how low the pay. You did not want Mother to find you a job; she found bad jobs.

We boys laughed and called her a one-woman Texas Employment Commission, for she prided herself in being able to find more jobs for her sons than any employment agency. She had a network of church friends, neighbors, and strangers who owned businesses, and every business needs cheap, hard-working summer help, she thought. This dear lady with all those boys had no reservation about asking anyone if they needed a fine young man to work for them in the summer. She usually had two or three offers for her boys to choose from.

The Horse Apple Tree

The first paying job I can recall was working for Mrs. Oliver Hayes, who lived just one house down the 1100 block on West Walker Street in Denison.

Now, Bess Hayes, whom I always called Mrs. Hayes, had a big old bodark tree that produced a slew of those big green "horse apples," so called because horses are the only ones that could eat them. Horse apples are messy and have a sticky white sap that would run out of them, with hundreds of seeds when a car would run over and smash them in the street. Well, my job was to pick them all up and keep picking them up.

That one tree could sprout more horse apples than any real apple tree could ever produce. It meant I had a regular job, and a hard one for a seven-year-old boy. Those things must have weighed three pounds apiece, and when you got eight or ten of them together in a sack, you had a real load. It was a long trek to the back alley where they would be left and hauled off by city garbage collectors.

I made a whole lot of quarters, and sometimes a half dollar, from Mrs. Hayes, and I just prayed that tree would not die. My prayers were answered, for that tree is still living there today.

The *Dallas Morning News* and *Denison Herald*

It was still really dark at 4:30 in the morning when my brother Jimmy got up to ride his bike to the Texas Interurban Station, down by the Katy railroad depot, to get the fifty *Dallas Morning News* papers he delivered to those rich Denison people who wanted the big-city news, as well as more comprehensive world news. Now and again, Jim would hire his little brother, Sunny, to help him with his early morning paper route, as well as in the afternoons after school, delivering the *Denison Herald*.

Mother made sure he paid me an appropriate amount for my efforts. I could not pedal my bike as fast as he could; however, just to have a newspaper buddy with you on those dark cold streets was worth something. My newspaper career did not last long because I got other jobs, and so did my brother Jim.

Ashburn's Ice Cream, a Fun Place to Work with Tasty Products

Mr. Bill, as he was called, was Mr. William Ashburn, who owned Ashburn's Ice Cream and Dairy Products in the 400 block of Main Street, just down from the high school. He needed a Popsicle wood stick sticker, and I was his man (oops, I mean boy).

Ashburn's was famous for having, during the summer, a cadre of young men, some really young like me at ten years old, to work in the ice cream plant or on the dairy farm out north of town on Highway 91. I was far too young to drive, or help with ice cream making, or the dairy herd.

However, any ten-year old boy who had a mother like mine could hold a handful of those wooden sticks and put them one at a time into sixty holes to make thirty frozen Popsicles. We made all flavors: banana, strawberry, lime, and fudgesicles, of course. I eventually developed the ability and height to stand up on the sacking platform to bag and sack those frozen products ready for the freezer.

I think I started for something like ten cents an hour and was glad to get it. I would work all day, and I felt good about how many packages I had put in the freezer. I knew I might eat one at school the next week or get one from the grocery store when I went shopping with Mom. I could brag I sacked this fudgesicle, and it surely did taste good.

My ice cream profession at Ashburn's lasted several years, and I grew into a teenager working for Mr. Bill. I even got on the ice cream-making team and poured those big black cherries into the mixer. Sometimes I added fresh bananas we had peeled that morning into a vat of heavy cream, milk, and flavoring.

There were some older men working there as I remember, Mr. Earl, Mr. Bonnie, and others whose names I cannot recall. One of the younger ones was drafted and went off to a place called South Korea, where the Korean War was raging in 1950. He was young, always singing country songs. It was a sad day when he came home, because he came back in a flag-draped casket. His body was shipped back from the West Coast on the train. I would see a lot of those returning Korean War soldiers later, when I worked for the Missouri, Kansas, and Texas Railroad that ran through our town.

Kingston's Drug Store Delivery Boy

When I think about the job I disliked most, it would have to be the delivery boy for Kingston's Drug Store on the south side of Main Street in Denison. I did like the soda fountain and a banana split on occasion, when I could afford one. I guess the main reason I disliked that job was fear. Yes, being afraid during those long, night deliveries south of town, the rough part of the city.

I remember praying from after sundown until we closed at 10 p.m. that no one would call in for a delivery at the last minute. However, there were always those occasions when my prayers were not answered the way I asked, for at 9:55 p.m., the pharmacy would get a prescription that needed to be delivered that night.

"Sunny," the pharmacist would call out. "Where is the delivery boy?"

Sure enough, it would be a long way south of downtown, and as the store manager was turning out the lights and closing the front door, I was climbing on my American Flyer bike and pedaling toward Day Street to make the delivery.

I prayed a lot on those dark streets as a young boy, between street corner lights, asking God to protect me and be with me. I would feel better about my duties telling myself I was a hero, saving some sick person's life by taking the medicine he or she needed to live. I am not sure that was always true. However, it made me feel a whole lot better, and I hoped the medicine made the sick person feel better, as well.

I was never physically harmed on those late night runs; however, my prayer life certainly increased, and God was my partner, my fellow Delivery Man. I learned dependence on Him, assurance He was with me and would care for me, with fear defeated most of the time, and what I learned in those pre-adult years has been with me throughout my life.

Even today as I drive by Kingston's Drug Store, I still remember those delivery days and nights. I get some of those same feelings and pray some of those same prayers for God's protection, guidance, and care in my duties now.

Ted the Landscaper

Ted Riffle was the owner of Riffle's Florist and Landscaping. He was the man called on to landscape all the yards of big, expensive homes in my hometown. Needless to say, he never did work in our yard, except after a Stricklin boy went to work for him.

I think most, if not all, of the five Stricklin boys worked for Ted at some time over the years. I know Jerry, Charles, and I did for sure. When you worked for Ted, you worked! That is for certain.

He ran everywhere he went and expected his hired hands to do the same. He could rake faster and better than anyone, plus sketch out a big flower bed and have it planted with flowers, shrubs, and trees before you knew it.

Ted was a master landscaper and always had more jobs of beautifying yards than any one individual could accomplish. He was called on day and night to do something, plan something, and talk about something that would make a home look beautiful.

Remember, this was in the early 1950s before there were the yard crews that can now be found in every city, large or small. It was a different culture at that time in cities like Denison, population twenty-five thousand, with the heart of the economy, the railroad.

Even though the Stricklin boys worked in the landscaping portion of the Riffle's business, our mother was his competition in the floral part of his enterprise. You see, my mother made all of our corsages for all the big proms and other high school or church parties.

There was a huge gardenia bush out front, on the right side of our house, and so, you guessed it, the Stricklin boys' dates always got a gardenia corsage. We gave the same kind every time, and I bet the girls always wondered why we never ordered other flowers.

We had a little secret, too. If you have a corsage, you need ribbon, pins, and something to put it in. So the only "paid business" we did with Riffle's Florist was to pay a few cents for those items and the nice Riffle's Florist box with green tissue paper that always enhanced my mother's artistic work as a corsage maker. Since Ted's florist was the finest one in town, everyone thought those Stricklin boys were rich, for they always ordered their corsages from Riffle's.

KATY Railroad Work—Christmas and Summers

Railroading has been in my blood since I was born. One of my first memories is the sound of a steam engine whistling in Ray Yards, pulling a freight train.

I can still recall the clang, clang, clang of its big brass bell and the huff and puff of steam and smoke as it picked up speed, pulling tons and tons of freight or passenger cars. It was thrilling then, and trains are still a thrill today. I never realized that one day a significant Christian ministry would come to fruition by working for railroads.

My dad worked for the KATY Railroad for fifty years. He started out as a young lad, who had dropped out of formal education at the end of the fifth grade, filling kerosene signal lamps, before electricity came to the rail yard. That was a long time ago, before child labor laws. When you wanted to work, regardless of your age, you could get a job.

He earned his way up, becoming a telegraph operator, a railroad agent in small towns, and finally a dispatcher who directed all the trains across a railroad division. From there he was promoted to an assistant superintendent and finally finished his railroad career as a superintendent, today called a general manager.

My mother dropped out of high school her senior year in 1929 at sixteen to marry an "old railroad man" who was six years her senior. Railroad men did not have a very good reputation in those days. Most of the people in Celeste, Texas, said their marriage would never last, and it did not. They were married only sixty-two years and had five boys and eleven grandchildren before a malignant brain tumor took Mother's life.

So it seemed inevitable that I, too, would become a railroad man, and it was natural that I would work on Dad's Katy. I was fifteen and a high school sophomore when I hired on to handle US mail that was carried in a postal car on the front of every passenger train. Mail was picked up and thrown off at every little town on the line.

In Denison, mail was either picked up at the station by the postmaster or sorted inside the mail terminal at the end of the passenger station and put on the next train going toward the destination. Of course, Christmas was the busiest time of the year for mail delivery with Christmas cards and Santa's packages.

That is when they hired extra hands for the rush of mail and, of course, for the annual Sears and Roebuck catalogues, which I thought weighed one hundred pounds each. They shipped those thick books with all their items in them, from toys to ladies' lingerie and from men's suits to hunting rifles. Whatever you dreamed of one day getting was in that one-volume catalogue.

In fact, each catalogue weighed only about five pounds; however, a whole mail sack full did weigh more than one hundred pounds. I weighed only 155 pounds back then, and I could hardly pick up and carry a sack full of Sears catalogues. I still get tired just thinking about them.

From the time I was a young man, the United States flag meant a lot to me. It had thirteen stripes and forty-eight stars back then. The red, white, and blue are colors, as they say, that never run. My father served in the Texas National Guard as a young man, and when he was promoted to a train dispatcher, he was given a 4-F status as having a job "critical to the war effort," so he was discharged from the Guard.

Uncles Don, Charlie, and Jack all served in the Army and went oversees during World War II, so my family, like most Americans during that war, was a part of the fifteen million US citizens who were involved in defeating Hitler and the Japanese.

Both of my older brothers went into the military after high school. Don joined the Army, while Jim wanted to be a submariner and signed on with the Navy.

I remember going with my mother to take my dad's supper to him when he was working second trick as a train dispatcher during the war. I was only eight years old, and there were tiny American flags at various places on his train order sheet. When I asked Daddy what those flags meant, he told me those were troop trains going to the West Coast, and they had right of way over all other trains. They were "hot shots" and stayed on the main line.

My mother, along with many other church ladies, made sandwiches, baked cookies and cakes, bought whatever fruit they could find, and went down to the KATY station in Denison to meet troop trains and hand out all the food they had. When the Army boys tried to pay the ladies for the food, they always refused to accept even a penny.

War became very personal to me a few years later, after World War II had ended. "Johnny Came Marching Home," and the war effort quickly came to a halt, with American military forces shrinking to only a few hundred thousand, when there had been millions. This had been another war to end all wars.

Less than five years later, the North Korean Army crossed the thirty-eighth parallel to attack South Korea. Of course, America came to the rescue of the South Koreans, and that began nearly four years of a police action. We never declared a war, even though that is what it was. More than thirty thousand of America's finest young men died in frozen rice paddies, defending people half-way around the world they never had met and never would.

"We have a flag on #6 going to Whitewright," our foreman would say as we prepared to meet a passenger train at the Denison depot. A patriotic silence fell on our little group of high school boys and two or three adults. We all knew there was a young soldier going home for Christmas, and he was going home in a flag-covered casket.

All of us had practiced our position for transporting a military casket to the next train. First, we waited for the escort soldier to arrive from back in the passenger cars. Next we removed our hats and gloves as we huddled around the coffin. It was the only time I ever saw a high school boy cry, except when we lost a state football playoff game, or his girlfriend wrote him a Dear John letter.

Two of the crew would be on the ground and six of us around the casket. Taking direction from our foreman, we would lift and move together, gently carrying the coffin to the wide-open baggage car door, carefully sliding the casket onto the mail cart as the others held it steady.

I never dreamed that nearly forty years later I would stand beside other flag-draped caskets at America's most sacred soil, Arlington National Cemetery, as the senior Army chaplain, performing four or five funerals daily. There would be many preparation days before that occurred.

In the 1950s, there were many passenger trains passing through Denison going north to Kansas City and Saint Louis and south to San Antonio, Houston, and Galveston, or west to Wichita Falls and Amarillo. Before airlines became the transportation of choice for most travelers, trains were the preferred way to go, because interstate highways had not been built. Sometimes there would be twelve to fifteen passenger trains a day stopping in Denison in any twenty-four-hour period.

The mail handlers would have to pull the steel-wheeled wagons to the "house," sometimes crossing four or five tracks to make our way to a secure location in the mail house to wait for the next train.

My greatest fear and anxiety on this job was thinking what would happen if I pulled a flag-draped casket out in front of a train, with the coffin and a soldier's body being hit by an engine. I prayed I would be killed if that ever happened. I would wake up at night shaking as I dreamed such a horrible scenario.

I respected the flag and those who paid the ultimate sacrifice for the freedoms we enjoy under it, freedoms bought with the high price of blood. We know now freedom is never free. It costs greatly.

Before I would close out my railroad career, after working on railroads for thirteen years, I logged time with not only the Katy but also the Texas Pacific Railroad, as well as the Burlington, Rock Island, and Chicago Railroad.

I did a variety of jobs, including serving as a laborer on a signal gang for the Katy. A signal gang was just slightly lower than a prison gang and made up of much rougher guys as well. Thousands of miles of telegraph wire was strung from coast to coast and border to border. Also, strong electrical wires were strung on the poles to power the signals that guided trains.

Miles and miles of wire and thousands and thousands of wooden poles, some as high as fifty feet, stood over the roadbeds that supported the tracks. The Johnson grass would grow eight to ten feet high around those poles, with the temperature 120 degrees down in those bottoms.

I had never worked so hard or been paid so well in all my life. A great thrill was to hear a steam engine passenger train approaching the area where we were working blowing its whistle like it was a party celebration. Of course, we had cleared the track and stopped working to watch the train fly by. There to my surprise would be my dad at the throttle of the engine, running the train. He was the one constantly blowing the whistle.

He said more than once he feared hitting a signal crew and killing one of his sons. Thank God that never happened. However, on occasion, going on to heaven to escape the sweat, heat, and blisters from digging pole holes would have been a relief.

One summer I got permission from Dad to see if I could get a job in the car shop, in the south part of our city. The KATY made all its own railroad cars there.

As the new kid on the crew, and the son of a railroad official, I got tagged to see just what I could do as a worker. My dad always told me the other workers would look at me to see if I worked hard and obeyed all the safety and work rules.

"You had better work harder than anyone else," he would say. "And safer, too; don't do anything to embarrass me, for you know the position I am in."

Every day I went to work thinking I had to work harder and safer than anyone else. I could not afford to embarrass my dad or do anything that would negatively reflect on him. That was quite a weight on a seventeen-year-old kid.

The first job I had in the steel shed was the hardest and one of the most dangerous jobs in manufacturing boxcars. I was a rivet catcher. Glowing, red-hot rivets were thrown at me by a pitcher from about thirty-five feet away. I would catch them in a steel cup with my left hand, take a steel twister and grab the rivet, stick it in a hole, and catch the next one, while a bucker would hold the rivet while it was hammered in place.

That was a hard, hot, and sometimes scary job; however, I would not have quit for any reason. I wanted those fellow railroad workers to know I was just as tough as they were, and as determined as any of them. I would work harder and faster, as well as safer, than any of them. Didn't they know who my daddy was? Certainly, they did. Well, I would do it right, the Katy way.

Years later, during theological graduate school in seminary, I hired out as a brakeman on a train crew with the Rock Island Railroad, running north and south out of Fort Worth, Texas. It was a perfect job for a graduate student who had taken a one-year academic delay of entrance in the United States Air Force. I was getting married in May 1958 to Ann March, who was a senior at Baylor University, and I did not want to get too far away from her.

So I decided to study theology for a year, get married, and enter the USAF as a second lieutenant, special staff officer, and general's aide, beginning a thirty-seven-year military career from the beginning rank of second lieutenant to a full colonel.

Since I did not have classes on Monday, I could sign up on the crew board and get out early Friday afternoon for my first train run. If it worked out just right, and it usually did, I could get two runs out and back in four days, Friday through Monday. I would make more in those two trips than most of the other theological students would make at their churches in a month. I could do that sixteen times a month, making a whole lot of money.

The first night I worked as the head brakeman on the Bridgeport local, I did not have a very good start. First, I drew an engineer who was known for his speed, and also for his bottle. It was well known by everyone except the high-ups that this guy had a drinking problem; however, he did not let that get in the way of his running a train, picking up and setting out freight cars, with four other crew members with him.

That night we backed into a huge gravel pit that ran three or four miles down to a massive hole in the ground. The gravel company had a small GE locomotive they used to switch cars around and move them to the top of the dig for the Rock Island to pick them up.

When we hit into the car to buckle up, we were moving a little too fast, and the cars started rolling back down the hill. We tried to stop them, but it was too late as they picked up speed.

After the collision, the GE engine looked like someone had put a big bomb in it, as it was shattered. Also, eight or ten cars of gravel overturned at the bottom of the loading ramp. It was a bad night.

I knew I would be fired on my first night. What should I do? There would be an investigation, a hearing, and I would be laid off until after a decision was made.

"Dad, we had a wreck tonight, my first night on the job," I told my father when I called him in the wee hours of the morning from Fort Worth. "I know I will be fired. We did about $175,000 to $200,000 in damage, I think. What am I going to do? I go before the investigating board next Friday."

I will always remember what my dad said that morning.

"Go in there and tell the truth," Dad said. "That's all you have to do, just tell the truth."

He told me if I did that, all would come out well, and it did. I worked for several months until I had to choose between passing grades or more money. I chose the grades; however, it was only after I had earned enough money to pay for the engagement and wedding rings, the honeymoon, and little bit of cash to start our lives together. It was the right decision. I can still see the Savings Thermometer, stuck on the back of my closet door, as the red ink moved toward the top and overflowing showing I had reach my money goal. That is another reason I love railroads; the railroad pay achieved my financial plan, and I tithed, too.

Work Leading to Chaplaincy

What does work have to do with being a chaplain? A whole lot, and that's certain!

First of all, there are many things that work teaches you, like staying at it when it is difficult, tiresome, painful, and discouraging. Also, regardless of the task or the pay, work can be enjoyable and fulfilling. Doing the work assigned to you by God is deeply meaningful and brings much contentment.

Working shows you how others live, the struggles they face, and the problems they encounter. It helps individuals see a perspective of life from another viewpoint and to realize life is not always easy.

Work teaches you how to achieve under the leadership of bosses of all types, and how to get along with a variety of personalities. It helps you understand the ideas of others and how to go deep inside their thoughts in order to share with them God's love and His desire for fellowship with all people.

Work shows you the lives of people who may not have the material assets you have, and never will. However, they can be poor in this world's wealth and be rich toward God. That is true wealth, lasting wealth, eternal wealth. Working with all types of individuals lets us experience life while walking in another man's shoes, to see how much we have, and to remember, "For everyone to whom much is given, from him much will be required…" (Luke 12:48).

Work emphasizes the cooperation between a human and the Holy Spirit. We know God can do anything and everything; however, as a normal practice He uses us to accomplish His purposes. It is a joint effort, a combination of the divine effort and the human effort, blended together to bring people to Him and to fulfill His purposes.

Being under God's assignment, under God's leading, and under God's provision in a work opportunity brings great joy in this life. When a man is doing God's will at work, the secular becomes sacred.

There is a high calling of work for God's purposes and for His glory. God has ordained each worker to go and bring forth much fruit, and that fruit is to last for all eternity.

Chaplains work, and in doing God's work the eternal lives of many come into a relationship with Jesus Christ as Savior and Lord, to have fellowship with Him now and forever more.

Can chaplains go into the workplaces of the world, beginning with corporate America? I believe so. Let's see what God did by His mercy with one man's faith, mine!

"For assuredly, I say to you, if you have faith as a mustard seed…nothing will be impossible for you." (Matthew 17:20).

4

ROOTS...A LIFE GROWING TO HONOR AND SERVE GOD

The old World War II Army footlocker had a new coat of bright green paint on it along with gold letters spelling "GIL STRICKLIN – BAYLOR UNIVERSITY."

One of my fellow workers at the KATY Railroad box car manufacturing plant in Denison did it for me. A little painting and stenciling made it look brand new. It was a decade old at the time. Although it's much older now, it's one of my most precious treasures and holds an honored place in our attic after both of our sons, Art and Cliff, took it to Baylor as well.

In the fall of 1953, I was packing that trunk for college. It was a miracle to be accepted to that Baptist school of higher education, as most who knew me doubted I would ever get out of high school. In fact, I barely met the requirements to graduate from Denison High School, Class of 1953, and I was entering Baylor University on academic probation.

Another miracle was my parents found enough money to pay my first-quarter tuition, along with living expenses. I was eighteen years old and knew it would take all my effort and theirs to keep me there. I had a paying job from the first day of college until the last, sometimes more than one, and studied when I could.

When anyone asked why I did not ever make the Dean's List while in my four years at Baylor University, I have a good excuse. It was because at one time I had six paying jobs to help keep me in school financially. I had three on the campus: as a dorm director, which gave me my room; freshman girls' dining room server, which gave me my meals; and student laundry manager, which provided me with clean and pressed clothing. But, that was not all.

I had three off-campus jobs: brick masons' helper on the Law School construction job, football program salesman on Saturday afternoons, and A-1 Ambulance Company medical attendant on Saturday nights. I did not last long as an ambulance medical attendant, and besides it did not pay very well.

All of the paying jobs, plus being involved in campus life as a yell leader and class president, and a social life that included dating Ann, left little time for my academic life.

My faith life as a Christian at Baylor continued to grow under much encouragement, for which I was grateful. Daily chapel services, Baptist Student Union gatherings on Wednesday nights, missions on Friday nights, and church on Sunday deepened my spiritual roots and gave me a Christian world view. Even though the academics were almost impossible for a country boy like me, I found university life exciting. It was a time of personal growth and development, despite the difficulties.

Because I didn't know any other fellow male students from my high school graduation class going to Baylor, I took pot luck for my roommates. When my parents drove me up in front of Kokernot Hall, the men's freshman dorm, I had no idea who I would live with my first year. I only knew they were freshman students at Baylor, just like me.

When I carried my first load of clothes and personal effects into Room 201, my roommate was already there. Ralph Meyers from Arkansas was my roomie. The room was not large enough for one person, and with three, it made for real cozy living. Hal C. Wingo from San Antonio was moved in with us because of room shortages.

We didn't fight each other for space in the restroom or showers; they were down the hall, and there you had to tussle with seventy-five other freshmen.

Right off, I realized Meyers was the studious one, books only, and A's, lots of A's, but not much play. He had planned a career in the military, and ROTC was a course requirement for him as well. We each had an Air Force silver tan dress uniform hanging in our small closet. He would wind up retiring as a lieutenant colonel from the Air Force after more than two decades of service to our country on active duty.

When Wingo introduced himself, he was "Sonny Wingo." I could not get away from that name. But he spelled it wrong; it should have been "Sunny." Now, he was more my kind of guy. He was smart, real smart, so we weren't alike in every way. But he liked to have fun, and so did I. He laughed a lot, had an eye for girls, always planned a good time, and was friendly beyond words. His second language would be French, and later, he and his girlfriend and future wife, Paula Brown, both would speak French, which they learned at Baylor. His father was Rev. Hal C. Wingo Sr., a Baptist pastor in San Antonio. This roommate came from strong Christian roots, and we had similar belief systems.

He and I would room together all four years at Baylor, except in the summer semesters. You see, Wingo passed all his courses with flying colors and wasn't required to make up any failures in the summer. As a journalism major he would usually return home to seek out experience writing for a newspaper or some other media outlet. I can honestly say "Hal C.," as I called him, was one of the best roommates I ever had, except for the one I have today (my wife).

Wingo was in Air Force ROTC too, so all three of us would roll out at 0530 every Wednesday for ROTC formation, marching, and battalion briefings. We even went to Air Force summer camp together at Davis-Monthan Air Force Base in Arizona between our junior and senior years. A deer crashed into our car in West Texas, on the way to camp, slowed us down a bit as we had to pull the grill out of the engine.

Hal C. was a gifted writer, a wordsmith. He is probably the only person ever to walk off the street into the Time-Life Building in New York with no appointment and get a major starting editorial job. He would spend the next three decades plus, after his Air Force stint, working around the world for *Life* magazine.

After covering the Vietnam War and living in Hong Kong for years, he was called back to New York City to fill a management position. When *Life* suspended weekly publication in December 1972, Wingo joined the editorial group that led to the creation of *People* magazine, also published by Time Incorporated. Today it is still a favorite component and cash cow of the Time empire.

By the way, that French-speaking beauty, Paula Brown of Texarkana, Texas, has been his wife for more than a half century. He owes me a big favor, because I introduced them at Baylor.

Hal C. and I have been friends for six decades. There is nothing in life like a friend of long, long standing. Hal C. is special.

During my freshman year, I quickly decided that books, study, and tests had to be balanced with girls, football, fun, and work. So in the second quarter of my first year, after being chosen president of the freshman class, I ran for and was elected Baylor yell leader. Now this was in the days before cheerleaders. Like the Texas A&M Aggies at College Station, Baylor had four men lead the yells, and we did it in a manly fashion. Cheerleaders and dancing girls would come much later, with an emphasis on sight instead of sound.

My first assignment in the fall of 1954 as a Baylor yell leader was to attend Welcome Week at Latham Springs Baptist Encampment. Along with Don and Dick Berry, brothers from South Carolina, and Dwaine Green of Fort Worth, my duty was to teach the new freshman class all the Bear spirit yells. Of course, while the boys in the class did pretty well, the lovely, young girls needed special attention.

There was this one black-haired, brown-eyed beauty from Fort Worth who stood out in a very special way. Ann March really needed some help, and I volunteered to coach her, which required my full time and attention. Any Bear would do that!

We met in September 1954, her first week at Baylor. She was special then, in 1954, and she is special today, years later. "We're the Greatest of the Great. We're the Class of '58," was her class slogan. I found out quickly that at least one member of that class was great, and her greatness increased with me day after day, month after month, and year after year. It still is increasing.

She was elected a Baylor Beauty and was featured in the 1954-55 *Baylor University Round Up*, the university yearbook, as I knew she would. Anyone with even one good eye could see that. However, it was her inner beauty, because of her love for the Lord, that always shown through and still does even to this day. I was always close by and was never really serious about anyone except her.

I knew I had the inside track in my race for her affections when she asked me to keep her 1950 Studebaker convertible, because freshman girls could not have a car on campus. That gave me the chance to drive her around when she needed a chauffeur. She was my Miss Daisy!

After completing two years and two summer school semesters at Baylor, I was offered a job as assistant vice president of safety with Dad's railroad, the KATY. I was seriously considering it because I had already had three jobs with the Missouri, Kansas, and Texas Railroad, and Dad had been an assistant super-intendent of safety at one time. Also, my family was in hard times and money had run out, so it was the right time to leave school and go to work at a real job with a great railroad.

Ann was against my dropping out of Baylor and begged me to pray more about it. God could provide for me and if it was His will for me to stay in school, she argued, He would make that possible. I had worked so hard, some-times having at least three campus or city jobs while trying to make my grades.

I went home during the time I was thinking about the job offer, as the quarter would end in only a few weeks. However, I had to give the railroad my decision soon. A high school friend and fellow Baylor Bear, Myrna Brown, the oldest daughter of the S. J. Brown family of Denison, had heard I was not go-ing to be able to continue my education at Baylor because of the lack of funds.

Her daddy, a city farmer, was a deacon at First Baptist Church in Denison. I worked for him during the wheat harvest, combining, plowing, and planting in Colorado in the summer. While I was still in high school, I would spend

Saturdays working on his big farm outside of Pottsboro. During my college years, any time I would go home on the weekend, I would pick up a little pocket money working twelve or thirteen hours on a Saturday for Mr. Brown. He would pick me up at zero dark 30 and bring me home at dark 60. It was a long day, but hard work was just pure fun to me. I enjoyed it.

I could drive anything with a motor, or ride any animal that was broke, or nearly broke. At heart, I was a country boy who lived in the city, just like Mr. Brown.

I had even helped a mother cow give birth to a baby calf by pulling the legs of that little critter out of the back part of its mother. It was a cold, cold morning, and that little newborn smoked like it was on fire as it came into the world.

When we came in that evening, Mr. Brown pulled an envelope out of his denim jacket pocket. I don't remember his exact words, but it was something like this: "Sunny, I hear you need a little financial help to stay down at Baylor. I want to help you get your education, and I want you to stay in school until you graduate. This will help you do that." He handed me the white envelope with Brown Farms in the upper left corner, and with my name, Sunny Stricklin, typed on it in the middle.

I tried not to cry in front of him, as I began to thank him for his kindness. As I got out of the old Chevrolet truck, I heard him add, "Now, Sunny, this is not a loan. It is a gift, so don't you ever worry about paying me back," as he drove off.

I walked into our house to eat a late supper Mother had kept warm for me in the oven. I was still crying when I entered the house, and my mother asked what was wrong. There was nothing wrong; all was right.

The check for fifteen hundred dollars dollars would pay my entire next quarter at Baylor—books, tuition, and all. I thanked Mr. Brown a thousand times over for his help and even tried to pay him back after I graduated and entered the military. No, it wasn't a loan, he would always say; it was a gift.

S. J. Brown, along with his wife, and daughter Myrna, are in heaven today. I look forward to seeing them again when I get home. I want to thank him one more time.

Needless to say, I turned down the railroad job offer, and Ann was pleased.

As I look back over my years at Baylor and life since, I have been richly blessed and helped by many friends I first met on the campus. Friends who have served on the board of directors of multiple ministries have prayed much for us and given their financial and friendship resources to encourage and motivate us to "stay at the task and keep charging." You may have never met them or even heard of them; however, they are some of God's best followers.

Ann finally got serious about spending our lives together her junior year, which was my senior year; I was serious much earlier than she was. Normally, boys give the girl a ring; however, she gave me one! Yes, it was my class ring for 1957. To this day, I do not know how she afforded it; I knew about her finances, and they were not much better than mine. I wore it for fifty-three years before it was stolen out of my locker at a country club. So, guess what? Ann went back to the original company that made Baylor class rings and got me the 1957 version, only this time she put a diamond in it instead of green glass. Her finances, and mine, have improved over the years.

Then it was my turn. In her senior year, on the eve of Baylor Homecoming in 1957, I gave her an engagement ring. The night I slipped it on her finger, it was totally paid for with money earned working for the Burlington, Rock Island, and Chicago Railroad. The next morning, she represented her senior class of 1958 by riding on their float in the homecoming parade. On her finger was the ring that committed our lives to be married. I thought fifteen hundred dollars was a huge amount of money, and I shook when I wrote the check. I saved enough, however, to pay for our honeymoon at the Broadmoor, a five-star hotel in Colorado Springs, as well as expenses for my first year in grad school.

Nearly fifteen hundred dollars was a large amount of money in 1957. It is still pretty big today. I would drive down to Waco from Fort Worth every time I could. It was a three-hour round trip; I would drive it even for a two-hour visit with her, as she was well worth it. I did it in a borrowed car, because I did not own one.

As I shared previously, I was working in Fort Worth as a brakeman on a train crew after graduation from Baylor, while taking courses as a layman at Southwestern Baptist Theological Seminary, before marriage and entering active duty in the Air Force.

I was making more than a thousand dollars a month working for the railroad and going to grad school. That was big money to me. I would make more than a hundred dollars a day as the front-end brakeman on freight trains running north and south out of Fort Worth. I was probably the only theological student ever to study homiletics on a GE engine running sixty-five miles an hour pulling 110 freight cars and a caboose.

Even though I surmised it was illegal, against railroad rules, the most fun I ever had working for the Rock Island, or any other railroad for that matter, was shooting jackrabbits off the front end of the road switcher on the spur track going over to Gainesville. Now, it wasn't me who had the .22-caliber pistol in my hand grip; it was another brakeman with whom I was working. However, I have to admit I took my turns shooting as rabbits would jump up and run across the tracks in front of us. It was a hard shot to make, and most often those floppy-eared critters would be safe as if they were in the briar patch.

My own dad would have fired me if I had been working for his KATY, just as if I had been gambling on railroad property. That was taboo, also, and I admit I did that a time or two until one night he almost caught me and other gang members playing cards for cash. He scared me so badly, I never played cards again.

The Rock Island work was good for a man who was going soon to be married. Money does pay bills. I had learned long ago: always spend less than you make, give first to God's work, save some, and spend some as God's money manager.

We promised Ann's parents that we would not get married until after she graduated, because I was one year ahead of her. It was a bad promise as far as I was concerned; however, we kept our word. She graduated at 11 a.m. on May 23, 1958, and we were married at 6 p.m. that evening at First Baptist Church in Waco. All of our friends were there for graduation, so why not?

As I stood at the altar with light rays shining through the chapel's stained glass windows, I thought, I have only known this beautiful girl four years, and now I am going to live with her the rest of my life. My mind drifted back to all the meaningful and fun times we had together, and most of them just a few blocks down the street on the campus of Baylor.

I almost laughed out loud as I recalled sitting with her on the banks of Waco Creek that ran through the campus. It was a cool, early spring night and she did not have to be in the dorm until 11 o'clock. I will let you imagine the conversation and events of the evening. However, I was not thinking about the final exam I had at 8 o'clock the next morning in advanced European history, under the hardest and best history professor at Baylor, Robert Reid.

We rushed to get her in the dorm before the door closed and punishment followed. I went back to Brooks Hall and studied all night, as much as I could. Needless to say, I failed the exam and the course. However, I made an A in wife selection and relationship development that has lasted a lifetime. I always wondered how I would use European history anyway. I knew how I would use a wife, and I must tell you, I made the right choice.

That night at the creek, we were right beside the USAF Reserve Officers Training Course parade ground. I had signed up with ROTC my freshman year and planned to enter Air Force active duty upon graduation. Every Wednesday morning at 0630 hours, in my proper silver tan dress attire, I would stand at attention as the flag bearer for my company. What made it pleasant was Ann in her issued dress white uniform as an ROTC sponsor. She was worth getting up early for. Just to see her was thrilling.

As the wedding music was playing and I was standing at the front of the chapel looking back for her to enter, I thanked God that He allowed me to be there for this thrilling event of our wedding. The fact is I nearly missed it, and some other lucky fellow could have stood in my place.

It was April 16, 1957, a Sunday morning that was partly cloudy with a light wind out of the south. I hooked up my safety harnesses and called "Clear" before I pushed the start button. The PA12 Super Cub aircraft roared to life.

I taxied out from the hanger toward the active runway and prepared to take off for my final cross-country flight to finish my basic flying course as a part of my Air Force ROTC training. I covered the check list and got a green light from the tower, because this small craft did not have a radio.

I cleared the airport fence and began my climb. I had a full tank of fuel and was two hours away from Brownwood, my halfway point. However, I would stop at Mineral Wells for coffee because I was in no hurry. I was to meet Ann for church that night, so time was not a factor. I did not realize then how close I would come to not keeping our date.

After taking off from Mineral Wells Airport, with the coffee still smoking in the cockpit, I turned southeast and checked my map. I climbed and leveled off at ten thousand feet. The weather forecast looked good: partly cloudy, ceiling broken at eight thousand feet, visibility five miles, wind ten miles an hour from the south, no major clouds, and no rain.

As I looked out across the nose of the plane, a long way out in front of me, I noticed clouds building up, higher and higher. The plane was rocking now, and it became more difficult to keep the wings level. I powered back and then suddenly was gripped with fear. I could not see the ground.

Clouds had swept under me, and now all I could see was clouds in all four directions, even though I was not in them yet. It was evident I would be soon, because the cloud formation I had been watching was now up to probably fifty thousand feet, and the base layer kept me from seeing the ground.

Even a non-experienced pilot, with only a learner's permit and fewer than thirty-five hours of flying time, recognizes when he is in trouble, real trouble. Without a radio, I could not communicate with anyone. However, it did not take a radio to pray, to communicate with the Lord God. So I began praying: "God, what should I do? Should I go on and hope the forecast was correct and the weather would improve?"

My gas gauge was well below half full, as I was to refuel in Brownwood. I had been flying for more than two hours and if I was still on course, I should be getting close to my destination. In only a few minutes I would be in those big, black clouds, ones I could see streaks of lighting flashing out from, and surely rain, and maybe hail.

"God, help me to think. Tell me what I should do. How do I get out of this mess? Lord, spare my life. Protect me from myself and my inexperience. God help me!"

I recalled an instructor telling our class in ground school: "If you ever get trapped on top of a cloud layer and you cannot see the ground, trim up the plane, reduce your power and set up a glide going down at two hundred feet a minute. No matter what you feel, keep your wings level, and only keep the stick between the palms of your hands; do not correct anything as long as your wings are level." That is what I did.

I started down. In only a minute or two I was in the clouds. I could barely see the big rubber wheels below me, and the red and green lights on the wing were invisible. The plane was rolling and pitching, and I fought to keep the wings as level as I could. I was dropping at two hundred feet a minute and my speed was about ninety knots, sometimes more.

I descended to eight thousand feet, then seven thousand. The gas gauge was bouncing on empty, and I knew I did not have much fuel left. Six thousand, five thousand, four thousand, three thousand; still, I could not see anything except clouds and water condensation on my windshield. At two thousand feet the engine continued to idle; at one thousand, I still could not see the ground. I did not know where I was or what was below me. I hoped the altimeter was correct, as I did not have any sea level settings or pressure.

At five hundred feet there was still no ground visible, only clouds and the hum of the engine. Now the fuel showed empty, and it was not bouncing. Somewhere, as I went through one hundred feet, I caught a quick glimpse off the left wing of a row of power lines running down the side of a road in the country.

I pulled back on the stick, because it looked like they were crossing in front of my path, and went back into the dark clouds, blinding me again. At such a slow speed, I could easily have stalled and crashed nose down.

The next thing I knew I was plowing into a field, and mud and water were covering the cockpit. The prop was mangled and bent completely back into the airframe. The little gas I had left was running down the wings and dripping into the cockpit. I reached over with a bloody hand and turned off the switches that could have sparked a fire fed by gasoline that would have burned me to death. I could smell gasoline as I watched it drip into the cockpit from the tanks in the wings. In an emergency landing, you always cut off the switches before touching down. I did a lot things wrong that day!

My right hand had banged into the instrument panel where a metal bolt had stabbed me. Every time my heart beat, blood squirted out of the hole in my hand. As I sat in my seat, somewhat dazed and still shaking, I took my handkerchief out and wrapped it around the gushing wound.

I unsnapped my safety belts and crawled out of the plane, which was up on its nose. I stepped into mud and water up to my knees, leaned on the plane, and thanked God for sparing my life. I knew I had come really close to death, and yet it was not my time. God had something for me to do, even though on that Sunday morning I did not know what it was. I did know I had an assignment from Him. If not, I would now be dead, my body mangled in the remains of that metal and yellow canvas plane that had hit the ground without me ever really seeing it.

What I thought were clouds had been fog that went all the way to the ground. I could see nothing more than fifty feet away in that farmer's plowed field somewhere in southwest Texas.

I did not know where I was. I did not know where a road was. I did not know where a house was. I could not hear any sound. All was quiet and still like death, so I started walking. I didn't know what direction I was headed; it made no difference.

Before long I found a road, climbed a barbed wire fence and found a farm house. There was an old pickup in the side drive, so I banged on the door.

An old man, a farmer I presumed, opened the door and just stared at me, blood, mud, and all.

"Sir, can I use your phone? I had an aircraft accident down the road and I need to call my flight instructor and tell him where I am. By the way, where am I?" I asked.

The old man continued to stare at me and finally responded, "Are you that darn fool who almost tore the roof off my barn and scared my cows half to death?" I had to admit I probably was. There weren't too many pilots flying that foggy morning, so I couldn't blame anyone else.

The day ended up better than it began because this farmer and his wife were Baptists, and I went to church with them. In fact, I taught the Sunday school class with my hand bandaged and my boots still muddy. I even got a home-cooked meal while I waited with dread for my flight instructor to fly out and pick me up.

When he arrived and we went to examine my plane, the fog had burned off and the sun was shining. On either side of the approach I had made without sight, rock and sand hills rose abruptly two or three hundred feet high. They would not have made a soft or safe landing.

I flew only two more hours after that, final rides with the FAA and the

ROTC flying school. I passed both. However, it would be seventeen years before I would fly again, for fear had made an imperishable imprint on my mind and my spirit.

"You're a lucky young man to be alive today," the FAA accident investigator told me afterward. "Why, you did something Braniff Airlines wouldn't do with its one hundred million dollars' worth of landing equipment at Love Field in Dallas, land with zero visibility." I knew luck had nothing to do with it, and neither did my piloting skills.

Today, I hold a commercial license, with twin engine and instrument ratings. I have logged several hundred hours of flying time and learned one important lesson. If you get trapped on top of the clouds, do a 180-degree turn and fly out of them.

But now flying was not on my mind. Ann was coming down the aisle.

As husband and wife, we began a life together in a covenant relationship with each other and Almighty God. Our marriage has lasted since 1958 and continues. Our love for each other and our Lord has deepened with the warmth of devotion and commitment. The love we had in the beginning was only a spark, for today it is a blazing inferno that is indescribable in human terms.

In the military and Christian service, we have traveled the world together, living in London, then near the Berlin Wall before it came down. We experienced unspeakable joy in the birth of two sons (Art in 1961 and Cliff in 1964), witnessed two Baylor graduations, marriages to two wonderful and godly ladies, Belinda (Art) and Robin (Cliff), and the birth of four grandchildren: Allison and Ashley to Belinda and Art, and Cal and Colton to Robin and Cliff.

Our oldest son, Art, actually Gilford A. Stricklin Jr., was born in Greenville, South Carolina, with the military paying the expenses, while Clifford Benjamin (Cliff) Stricklin was born in Fort Worth, Texas, with his father paying for medical services. These two boys have become godly Christian men.

In my military and ministry assignments, I estimate I have been away from home for about five years. I missed my Ann and our boys every minute of every day, especially in the evenings. Ann was both father and mother for our sons during my absences, and she did a superb job rearing them, teaching them, and grounding them in faith in Christ.

All of this was done while I was on assignments for God and man somewhere in the world. She kept a map of the world on the boys' bedroom wall with a pin marking the spot where Daddy was. They would pray for that red dot on the map in some foreign country, for that was Daddy. Because I have been in ninety foreign countries and traveled nearly two million miles, there were many countries from which to choose.

We have had the sadness of all families, burying our parents, dealing with the problems of rearing children, handling sickness that threatened to end life here, plus the disagreements in life that come to everyone.

However, with the foundation of faith and the bedrock of true love, life together has been most pleasant, enjoyable, and meaningful. Here on this earth, it does not get much better than that. Life is not perfect, and you always have good days and bad; however, in this relationship of long standing there have been many more joyful, contented, and pleasant days than any other kind.

After Baylor and our wedding, we launched into the Air Force, spending three years in South Carolina, nearly twelve hundred miles from her parents and mine, which proved to be a great start for married life. She was a school teacher in a rural setting, and I was a second lieutenant.

My life has been so blessed by our Lord, so protected from the evil one, so cared for in every way and every day, that I sometimes weep trying to express my gratitude to the Almighty. Every good thing that has ever happened to me, any good deeds I have ever done, have all been because of God's grace and mercy.

I have done nothing; He has done it all. I rejoice and praise Him as I have desired to follow His leading, experiencing His counsel with His eye on me. I wonder what is next. Surely He will show me, lead me, and provide for me the way He has done all these years.

My life's motto, from 1 Corinthians 15:10a, is, "But by the grace of God I am what I am..." Our life's Scripture verse is Matthew 6:33, "But seek first the kingdom of God and His righteousness, and all these things shall be added to you." I live each day by these powerful words of promise.

5

THE ARMY, YES;
CORPORATE AMERICA, I DON'T KNOW

When I signed up for Air Force Reserve Officer Training Corps (ROTC) at Baylor University in Waco, Texas, in the fall of 1953, I never imagined I would wear a military uniform off and on for the next forty-one years. I would earn the title "veteran" by serving on active duty and in the Reserve for both the Air Force and the US Army.

Those years of military duty would broaden my ideas of life and living. They would allow me to meet and work with all types of people, with all types of personalities. My experiences also would give me a great love for America with its many freedoms of liberty and the pursuit of happiness for all.

For a country boy from far North Texas who barely went out of his county until he left for college, I had to learn quickly.

In my first day in the Air Force, I promptly learned I was out of uniform. A full colonel had the joy of "squaring me away" and pointing out my failures. He never had to do it again, for which I was grateful.

A big master sergeant looked over my records and checked my active duty orders. As he worked, he chewed on a wet, unlit cigar, rolling it with precision from one side of his mouth to the other. With a critical tone in his voice, he said something like this: "Lieutenant Stricklin, I see you are a ROTC graduate. You are an English and business major from Baylor. Well, we are going to make an information officer out of you. You report to Colonel Stefansson in building 3604. He will direct your duties."

That was the extent of the scientific methods used to assess my skill set and choose my job. However, that choice was a disguised blessing from God. As the Assistant Wing Information Officer, I was selected to be the aide of Brigadier

General Andrew B. Cannon, Commander of the 63rd Troop Carrier Wing at Donaldson Air Force Base, South Carolina. In that role, I would fly around the world, sometimes with General Cannon and sometimes alone. I logged more flying hours as an additional crew member on a C-124 Globemaster than most pilots. I spent many hours on "old Shaky."

That four-engine bird was not the fastest plane in the Air Force fleet, but it was dependable. The nose of the plane would open up wide and high enough to drive three two-and-a-half-ton trucks inside, and after the doors were closed, that plane could deliver those trucks halfway around the world.

It took more than a week to fly from South Carolina to McMurdo Sound, Antarctica, which was nearly fifteen thousand miles the way we went. We took off on a cement runway ten thousand feet long and landed on a frozen Ross Sea at the edge of the Antarctic continent.

There is no telling how many hours I sat listening to the loud roar of those four engines as I flew above many countries of the world, from North America to the South Pacific and Antarctica and from North Africa to Europe. Years later I would cover Asia, Southeast Asia, and most of the countries of the Pacific Rim. No wonder I am almost deaf. It was caused by the noise of those engines.

While in Greenville, South Carolina, for three years of military duty, Ann and I became good friends with Billie and Cliff Barrows. Cliff was Billy Graham's music director for his evangelistic crusades around the world. Even though I went several times with Cliff up to Black Mountain, North Carolina, to Billy Graham's home to record the *Hour of Decision* radio program, I never dreamed I would one day be Dr. Graham's special assistant. At the time I was an Air Force general's personal assistant, and that's all I could think about.

I remember that early Saturday morning departure with Cliff, as we drove north out of Greenville, heading toward Black Mountain, about 140 miles away. Evangelist Billy Graham was a world-renowned figure, always one of the top ten most respected people in the world, and I was going to his home. My heart pounded and excitement increased with each passing mile.

We drove through the Montreat entrance and turned off the main road onto a winding smaller road up the mountain until we passed through a high-security fence. On up the road until we came to a home that looked like a mountain cabin. As we parked the Pontiac station wagon and got out, Cliff began gathering up his reel-to-reel recorder that would tape Mr. Graham's sermon for the *Hour of Decision*. We started walking up a winding rock path toward the front door, and suddenly the door opened. There stood a rather tall, thin man with disheveled hair, casual blue denim pants, and a sport shirt hanging loosely out over his trousers. He didn't look much like a preacher to me, not at all.

Shaking hands, I met Mr. Graham for the first time as we stood in the door of his welcoming mountain home. He was gracious, and I felt important just being in his presence, as I looked into his piercing blue eyes. He ushered us into the library. I noticed a chair in the corner where I immediately sat down. In the library there were many books and a simple desk with a lamp on it. Cliff was preparing the recorder, stretching the cord and microphone to the desk.

When all was ready, Cliff pointed to Mr. Graham to begin his message. For the next twenty-two or twenty-three minutes, I sat spellbound listening and watching this mighty man of God deliver his sermon. He stood behind his desk, and with his casual clothes on and a well-worn Bible in hand, he preached "the stars down." Sweat rolled down his face, and his shirt was dampened with perspiration, as he quoted Scriptures and gave illustrations building his biblical case for salvation through trust in Jesus Christ. He moved and dodged and dipped like a prize fighter as he jabbed the air with his right index finger to emphasize a major point he was making.

Cliff began the countdown for the last five minutes of the recording, four, three, two, and one to the end. Mr. Graham closed the sermon the way he began: with power and persuasion. There we were in this small library room of maybe ten by fifteen feet with only three people present. He preached as if there were a million people listening, and there would be on Mutual Radio when broadcast the next day, Sunday afternoon, on the *Hour of Decision* with Billy Graham. That was the first time I heard Mr. Graham deliver a sermon in person; however, I would hear him live 213 times in stadiums and arenas around the world as I served on the Billy Graham team from 1965 to 1970.

In 1961, three days before President John F. Kennedy froze all military personnel on active duty in the wake of the Cuban missile crisis, I mustered out of the Air Force, completing my three-year active-duty assignment, and was moved to the Reserve. For the next twelve years, I had the distinction of possibly being the oldest captain in the Air Force Reserve.

Ann and I, with our infant son, Art, moved back to Fort Worth, Texas, in 1961, driving a 1959 Ford Fairlane 500, baby blue and white. The 1947 maroon Packard we had bought for $150, our first automobile when I began my Air Force career, had died.

Soon I entered Texas Christian University's School of Journalism, as well as Southwestern Baptist Theological Seminary, simultaneously.

I was going to three schools at the same time, one undergraduate and two graduate schools. You remember I had been a young man who could neither read nor spell, and math was beyond me. Now I was a graduate from Baylor University with a bachelor's degree in business, and before long I would have a second bachelor's degree, this one in journalism from Texas Christian University, also in Fort Worth.

Not only that, but Dr. John Earl Seelig, vice president for communications and public relations at Southwestern Baptist Theological Seminary, had hired me as his news director with responsibilities for the seminary magazine, news releases, and all public communications. I was working twenty hours a week, plus being a husband, a dad, a graduate student, and still active in the Air Force Reserve.

Our second son, Cliff, was born on April 20, 1964, while I was the grader for Dr. Cal Guy, director of the missions department at Southwestern. While Ann was in labor, she checked the answers on a test I was grading between labor pains. It was truly a team effort. That night after Cliff was born, I liberated some yellow roses from a neighbor's rose bush, placed them in a styrofoam cup, and presented them to her in the hospital. Finances were tight at that time, but those roses were some of the most memorable flowers I have ever given her.

I loved to preach, and still do. After more than sixty years, I preached my first sermon in the spring of 1954 to the small rural congregation in First Baptist Church, Pottsboro, Texas. This was just down the KATY Railroad from Sadler, where I had started life in 1934.

At the close of each spring semester, the seminary held Student Preaching Week. The four best preachers were chosen from the student body and preached one day during the week in chapel. When Dr. Brown, who headed the homiletics department, told me I was one of those selected as a student preacher, I thought he was joking. Not me, a man who wasn't even ordained or licensed, and was known on campus as the Layman. He was not joking, and from that minute until I closed my message in chapel I was scared to death. However, God anointed me for the occasion. He received the glory, and I spoke His words, the right combination for any spiritual effort.

My first and second stint at Southwestern took five years, and I would come back for the third stint in 1983 and 1984. My first degree was a bachelor of divinity, non-language, meaning no Hebrew or Greek. I already had two bachelor's degrees, with well over two hundred hours, and now anther bachelor's. I came back with studies in both biblical languages, plus some other specialized theological courses, to qualify for the master of divinity degree.

As I think back on those days of full-time work, multi-campuses, and multi-studies, plus family responsibilities and church assignments, I don't know how it all was achieved, except by God's divine empowerment, one day at a time.

My heart is still with Southwestern, and so is our money. We began an endowed scholarship fund there many years ago, and we have consistently added to it over the years. It is now quite significant and is helping several students financially to reach their degree goal.

I learned how to be a student, how to study, and how to achieve in the classroom. I had a very slow start; however, that changed over the years and I really wasn't brain damaged.

Ann was teaching English at Tech High School to help support our family. I made more A's the first semester at TCU in 1961 than I made at Baylor University in the four years I was there, including summer school.

I had joined the staff of the *Fort Worth Star-Telegram* in 1963 as a cub reporter. When it was discovered I was a seminary student, my tag name by my fellow journalists was Deacon.

I was not the best reporter on the city beat, not even close. There were others who had been there for years, a lifetime almost. Mr. Mac was the city editor and was a salty old man with a round, wrinkled face, broad shoulders, and big stomach. He didn't talk, just growled. I was scared to death of him and had to face him every day of the work week. I am not sure how I got Saturday and Sunday off, but for some reason they seemed to think I worked on Sunday and probably needed to get ready on Saturday, because deacons and preachers really only work one day a week anyway, Sunday.

I had been working on the paper only since April 1963, at the beginning salary of fifty dollars per week. I worked from 2 p.m. to 11 p.m., with time off for dinner. My reporting was general assignments on the city side with a special assignment to write a religion column of the highlights of Sunday sermons that ran on Monday. The paper wanted to provide something for those readers who did not go to church, so I was their Sunday worship communicator.

Now and again, I would get a prize assignment to fill in for the police reporter who was the up-and-coming star reporter. Bob Schieffer, a fellow graduate from TCU, was a gifted journalist. He always wore a dark business suit with a dark-colored dress hat, turned down in the front. He looked just like a detective. In fact, many of the policemen and detectives in Fort Worth thought he was on the force. He would show up at murder scenes, bank robberies, street fights, fires, anywhere police were on the scene. He looked official, talked official, acted official, and was official.

My wife, Ann, was from Fort Worth and was a student and fellow cheerleader from North Side High School with Bob Schieffer, who would go on to be the senior CBS-TV journalist and host of *Face the Nation*. Bob discovered his life's role early on and stayed with it for more than fifty years, covering many national political conventions, more than four and a half decades at CBS in Washington, D.C.

I guess my only real claim to fame is I worked on the same newspaper with Bob, typed on the same Underwood upright typewriter with carbon paper that he did, and occasionally got my byline in the same edition of the *Telegram* as he did. We have remained friends over the years, and Ann and I enjoy seeing him and his wife, Pat, when we have visited the nation's capital.

Bob always seemed to have a nose for news and was always at the right place at the right time to get the big story; it would prove to be true again on the biggest story we would ever cover.

Prior to 9/11, I am sure one of the greatest days of sorrow for our country during my lifetime was the tragedy in Dallas on November 22, 1963.

I was driving down Interstate 35E in Fort Worth, heading for work on that Friday afternoon, when the radio music was interrupted by a news bulletin: "President Kennedy has been shot in his motorcade in Dealey Plaza, downtown Dallas."

I could hardly believe what I heard, for President Kennedy had just left Fort Worth, so I only pressed harder on the accelerator knowing our newsroom would be in urgent activity. When I arrived, there were people on the phones, pounding on typewriters, shouting instructions across the room. Chaos was everywhere, with one of our reporters on the scene in Dallas, already calling in copy. Others were on the way.

The editor made a quick decision we would print an extra edition that afternoon and have it on the street before the sun went down. No one could remember the last extra edition the paper had put out, but it was thought to be Pearl Harbor in 1941. Newspapers don't run many extras. For that to happen, the news must be catastrophic in nature, with worldwide implications.

The assassination of the thirty-ninth president of the United States of American fell in that category. I knew right away this would not be a normal eight-hour day, not in the least. The newsroom and presses were active twenty-four hours, along with the staff. I worked all night and most of the following morning as we continued to report the developing story, with a new president, Lyndon Baines Johnson, the former vice president, from Texas.

Lee Harvey Oswald, who was working at the Texas Book Depositary, killed Dallas police officer J. D. Tippit in Oak Cliff before Oswald was taken into custody and charged with murdering the president. However, the story did not end there, not at all.

Before another twenty-four hours went by, the accused assassin of the president would be dead. As Oswald was being transferred to another jail, he was shot while in the basement of the downtown Dallas police station by Jack Ruby, a local nightclub owner who hung out with police.

The *Star-Telegram*'s presses rolled again for the second extra in less than forty-eight hours. That had never happened before. It has been approximately fifty years since those three busy days; it has never happened since, and I doubt it ever will.

Most of our reporters worked thirty-six hours straight or more in those hectic historic days. Some staff worked seventy-two hours without sleep or leaving the newsroom, with coffee and food being delivered to them. Here and there you would see a person with head on the desk catching a few minutes of shut-eye.

Schieffer, as he often did, got a break to produce one of the biggest stories printed in either extra. He obtained a personal interview with Oswald's mother, who was living in Fort Worth at that time. It was well done, and he won many accolades for this story and many of his others, too.

After two years at the *Star-Telegram* under Mr. Mac and Jack Butler, the paper's editor, I moved on to edit the Texas Alcohol and Narcotics Education (TANE) magazine and coordinate the Speakers Bureau, as well as speaking for the organization. This was my work assignment while I finished my seminary degree. There, I met Vera Bolin, and she, along with her husband, Carl, and their family, would become lifelong friends with Ann and me and our sons.

During those years in my part-time military career, I was assigned to the Office of the Secretary of the Air Force, Office of Information, at the Pentagon in Washington, D.C. Finally, as I was completing my seminary degree in 1965, I was assigned to the Information Office of the 12th Bomb Group at Carswell Air Force Base, Texas, on the outskirts of Fort Worth.

Working with the Billy Graham Association

Because Ann and I had met and become close friends with Cliff Barrows and his wife, Billie, in 1958, through them also meeting Dr. Graham, I was invited to join the Billy Graham team after I graduated from TCU in 1963 and Southwestern in 1965. I would work under Dr. Stan Mooneyham, who was responsible for all of the association's advertising and information services. After less than a year, he was selected to head up the 1967 World Congress on Evangelism in Berlin, West Germany.

Then, Dr. Graham asked me to become his special assistant as press secretary for him and the association. I was no longer just the country boy from Grayson County, Texas; I was an Air Force officer, a veteran, a graduate of Baylor, TCU, and Southwestern Seminary. And yet, at thirty, I was still, in most of my ministry colleagues' eyes, wet behind the ears. I was neither licensed nor ordained as a clergyman, with my title still "layman."

Most of the other members of Dr. Graham's team, and in his close-knit circle of ministry leaders, were men who had been with him since he started in 1949 in Los Angeles. Here I walked in as the youngest man in the group, a kid who just finished seminary as a layman. I had never been a pastor or held any top ministry position.

I had been a newspaper reporter, helped put out two extras of the Fort Worth *Star-Telegram* within forty-eight hours when President Kennedy was assassinated in Dallas and Lee Harvey Oswald was murdered a few hours later. However, how did that compare with the other Graham team leaders? Not very well, as I recall. It was not because of my accomplishments that I was with Dr. Graham almost every day when we were traveling. No, it was only because of my job.

When the *New York Times* wanted a quote from Dr. Graham, I was the man to get it. I have seen the world's best-known evangelist and one of the greatest Christian servants since the apostle Paul in almost every circumstance possible, in the middle of the day and the middle of the night, in church, and out of church, asleep and awake.

I had been with the team for only a few months when I was told Dr. Graham wanted to talk to me. It was in 1966, before an evening service at the Upper Piedmont Billy Graham Crusade in Greenville, South Carolina, where I had entered active duty in the Air Force years earlier.

Well, right off I was nervous. The boss wanted to see me! Why, I wondered as I made my way down a back hall in the coliseum, with the crowd gathering for the evening service.

When I walked in, I am sure he could detect I was rather nervous, even though I hoped I was hiding the butterflies in my stomach and my desert-dry throat. In his personal way, he motioned for me to sit down across from him.

Then he got up and began walking back and forth across the room as he talked. No one else was in the room.

"Gil, I have an assignment for you, and I believe you can do it," Dr. Graham said. Then he asked me to head his press department and move to London for the Greater London Billy Graham Crusade, working with all the UK press, nearly a dozen daily newspapers.

He went into some detail about how tough the British press was and how ungodly the reporters could be. It was his opinion I could really mess up if I said or did the wrong thing, and this was the most important responsibility I had ever had.

At that point, he abruptly stopped his pacing, wheeled around pointing his long index finger at me, and almost shouted, "And you had better be on your knees every day, because you need God to help you do this job."

I got up and walked out of his private area, literally shaking. I was sick at my stomach, and all I could hear was, "You had better be on your knees every day, because you need God to help you do this job."

A few days later, Ann and I, along with two sons Art, and Cliff, ages four and one, were on our way to the United Kingdom, with London our new home.

I never saw or heard anything Dr. Graham ever said or did that made me cynical or made me question his sincerity. He is a great man, a marvelous man of God, and one I love and admire to this day. He was a man without gall, truly a spiritual giant.

For five years I had the privilege of walking in his shadow, observing, learning, noting how he dealt with people, led by example, served as a servant, and gave generously. His character was impeccable and his skills rather normal, yet highly blessed of God. That's what I saw in the nearly two thousand days I hung out with Dr. Billy Graham, listening to him preach in person night after night. I traveled nearly 1.5 million miles and visited scores of countries around the world on assignment for Mr. Graham.

Of course, Billy Graham wasn't a perfect man. There was only one perfect man, and it wasn't Mr. Graham, you, or me. Mr. Graham was a man like all of us are, prone to funny and stressful moments. I remember when we were in Portland, Oregon, for a crusade. We had scheduled a press conference, before the Youth Night Service began, to greet the media and meet Miss Portland Rose Queen, a lovely young lady who was to give her Christian testimony during the service. Mr. Graham would join us as it was the first night to record for nationwide television production. On those nights he was always nervous, and I did not like to bother him with anything. I just wanted to stay out of the way.

Dr. Graham was in his private quarters at the coliseum looking over his sermon for the evening. I told two of his top aides, Walter Smyth and Dan Piatt, I was going to check on the press and if Mr. Graham came out before I got back to bring him to the press room.

It was time for the press conference, and Mr. Graham came out of his room and asked these men to show him to the press room. They faithfully led him away, stopping in a row and standing at attention as they opened the door. When Mr. Graham walked past them and then realized where he was, he quickly wheeled around and shouted, "I said the press room, not the rest room!" We all laughed later, but not then!

Another time, I had a glamorous assignment of lassoing a stray dog during the 1970 Billy Graham East Tennessee Crusade in Knoxville. Somehow this big old mangy dog got onto the football field at the University of Tennessee, where we were holding our meeting. I had to capture him. Of course the crowd was cheering the dog and booed me when I went after him. With seventy-five thousand people filling most of the stands, I walked to the fifty-yard line, approaching the dog. I called him with my best "dog voice" and took off my belt for a halter. The dog came to me, as I put my belt around his neck, leading him to the closest exit as the crowd booed with all their voices. As we walked, with me leading and pulling the dog, there were more boos. Finally the dog pulled away as my belt came over his head and set him free as he dashed away from me. The crowd went crazy with applause, for the dog had "scored."

Finally I got him the second time, and this time I carried him in my arms outside the stadium. Somehow the dog knocked off my special security pin from my suit coat, causing it to fall on the ground somewhere. That turned out to be a big problem for me, as President Richard Nixon was a special guest that Sunday afternoon and security was tightened for the president's visit. I tried to explain to the security officer who I was, a trusted member of Dr. Graham's personal staff. I told my dog story and I had somehow lost my security pin. It made no difference. You cannot enter here. We had one hundred press people with the president, as well as local media, and all of them looking for me. I pleaded, but to no avail.

As I turned away from the guards at the gate, I prayed, "Lord, I need your help. You see my security badge so show it to me. Let me see it. Please, Lord," and as I looked down there it was right at my feet. I grabbed it and put it back in my lapel; then I turned around and walked past the security personnel showing my badge. God helped me that day and on many others as well.

I did not know it then, but I would go on to implement many of the practices Mr. Graham used in his ministry and building the Billy Graham Evangelistic Association. I would apply them in my personal life, as well Marketplace Ministries, the organization I never dreamed of back then.

As I look back over my life, those five years were the most enjoyable, as well as the most difficult I ever experienced. They were hard years, traveling all those miles and away from Ann and our little boys, Art and Cliff, 75 percent of the time. I was always packing or unpacking, never just home. My wife was both father and mother to our sons, and she did an outstanding job of rearing them during their formative years. I can never thank God enough for my helpmate and sweetest friend and lover.

When someone asked me how often I was with Dr. Graham, I replied, "Too often," because when I was with him, I was always away from my family, and that was difficult. However, he paid the same price for more than fifty years that I paid for only five. I guess I should not complain.

Of course, we flew many of our lengthy and international flights on Pan

Am airlines, which is now out of business. If airline loyalty miles had been created back then, I would probably still be spending them!

When I was away from home, I was away for long, long periods of time. You just can't commute home on the weekend from Sydney, Australia, or Tokyo, Japan. No, you just lived in those foreign ports of call, usually working seven days a week. Preaching in churches on Sunday was a regular assignment.

I did not tell many of my team friends that I was not a preacher, not licensed or ordained to the gospel ministry. When assignments were handed out, this junior minister was given a pulpit supply just like the old veterans.

How else could I be the Sunday vicar at the Melbourne Cathedral in Melbourne, Australia? I climbed up those winding stairs to the high and lofty preacher's podium to address several hundred Anglican members of that congregation. It was one of the largest Anglican churches in Australia, and that country boy from Texas was to open God's Word on Sunday morning.

If they only knew how inexperienced I really was, and how scared, too. That morning I preached on the subject "New Hearts for Old" from a passage out of the Old Testament, Ezekiel 36:26. I had recently gone to Methodist Hospital to be with my friend and fellow teammate, Stan Mooneyham, when the world-famous heart surgeon Dr. Michael DeBakey operated on him. I stood with heart surgeon interns on a high platform grandstand overlooking the operating table to see every move by the surgery team. That experience was moving and emotional.

The introduction of my sermon was about Stan's surgery. I got very graphic and very detailed, including the heart and lung machines, the blood rushing through the tubes, and how I saw DeBakey cut the sternum with a power saw.

As I described how the blood flowed freely after the fourteen-inch chest incision, there was a gasp on about the fifth row back in the center section, and an elderly white-haired Aussie collapsed in his seat and slid on to the floor between the rows.

Ushers rushed in. They cleared the aisles around the fallen congregant, and six strong men picked up his body and carried him all the way to the back door like he was dead. There was a silent hush in that massive Gothic house of worship. I had paused to catch my breath and observe the action toward the front on my left.

When you can do nothing else, you can always pray. That is what I did! After a brief prayer for this unknown victim, I launched back into my sermon. I found out later he lived through his heart attack. I thanked God for that, because I would never have gotten over it if he had died because of my sermon. Needless to say, I was known from then on as the man whose sermons were so bad people will do anything to get out of hearing them.

A Career Change: The Baptist General Convention of Texas

In late 1969, I began praying about a new ministry assignment from my Lord. It was not long until an invitation came from Dr. C. Wade Freeman of Dallas to join the evangelism staff of the Baptist General Convention of Texas, Southern Baptists in Texas.

In January 1970, we moved from Atlanta to Dallas to begin a new ministry, one where I was at work eight to five and home almost every night. The Lord answered our prayers, and my family and I were grateful. I would spend the next fourteen years there in ministry, with an emphasis on evangelism. Personal evangelism, youth evangelism, and chaplain evangelism were my specialty areas of leadership.

Super Summer and the Youth Evangelism Conference were an opportunity to train fifteen thousand to seventeen thousand high school young people in the skill of sharing their faith. This was an exciting ministry and an opportunity to continue to develop my leadership skills by recruiting and mentoring a staff and overseeing an expanding a budget of six figures.

At the height of the Vietnam War, and before the draft went out in 1974, there were about 125 Southern Baptist chaplains serving in Texas, with most of them in the military. Fort Hood, Fort Sam Houston, Carswell, Randolph, and Lackland Air Force bases were in Texas, as well as a huge Navy facility in Corpus Christi, and all of them had chaplains. Add to that other institutions such as prisons and hospitals, and the number of Southern Baptist commissioned chaplains was large.

I organized and launched a ministry to support, encourage, and help fund programs for chaplains, as well as undergird their personal and family lives. It was a much appreciated ministry, and I got to know and see the effective ministry that chaplains achieved both for military and civilian personnel.

It was out of that relationship with scores of military chaplains that I gained an increasing desire to swap my Air Force blue uniform for an Army green uniform, and to change from being a writer of Air Force stories to becoming a verbal proclaimer of the gospel as a chaplain.

On March 23, 1973, I resigned my commission as a USAF officer and immediately was commissioned an Army officer, pinning on the cross and captain's railroad tracks on my new Army uniform. I was now a chaplain, and for the next twenty-two years I would serve in the Army Chaplains' Corps, both on active duty in Desert Storm as well as in the Reserve.

My personal goal was to serve as a general officer in the Chaplains' Corps, one of only three general chaplain slots in the entire Army, active, reserve, and guard. My chances of making it were slim; however, I would do everything possible to achieve a star rank and serve at the highest level of leadership. To that end, I completed every chaplain's training program and was graduated from the Army War College and National Defense University, the highest military education you can attain.

But those efforts proved to be not enough.

My being a general officer was not God's divine purpose. Instead, He gave me another assignment—this time in the civilian world, as a marketplace chaplain. I had been in the military marketplace, and now I was about to launch forth into the civilian marketplace, an assignment that would last for decades, far after retirement from the Army.

If I had been promoted to a brigadier general, I may never have fulfilled my last and greatest assignment from my heavenly Commander. Again, I learned you cannot humanly achieve what God does not desire for your life, no matter how hard you try, and I tried really hard!

Still, I had some inspiring assignments as a senior Army chaplain with the rank of colonel. The most meaningful, in fact, the greatest assignment I had in thirty-seven years of military service was my two Reserve tours at America's most sacred soil, Arlington National Cemetery in Arlington, Virginia, across the Potomac River from the Washington Monument.

While living in Dallas and serving with the Baptist General Convention of Texas, I was active in the Army Reserve. I would be on duty anywhere from 50 to 125 days a year. This would include my regular weekend training duties on Friday night and all day Saturday and Sunday. Then, during the year, I would attend chaplain conferences, special forums, and Army training, including schools for field grade officers. I spent a lot of time dressed in my Army green uniform.

Of course, I would spend fifteen to seventeen days in summer training each year. For most of the years, between 1973 and 1994, I was in Dallas. Before I retired from the Army, I was with the Reserve as the Senior Hospital Chaplain, 807th Medical Brigade in Seagoville, Texas, and the 94th General Hospital in Mesquite, Texas. Also, I was assigned for duty as a Senior Reserve Chaplain with the US Army Medical Command, Fort Sam Houston, Texas, where I took the retirement review as the ranking retiring officer on my last day of Army duty, September 11, 1994.

I had served approximately four thousand days in the military when I took off my uniform for the last time as an active member. I still don my Army dress blues for military funerals and other patriotic events. I retired at Fort Sam Houston in San Antonio, Texas, with a moving ceremony where I was the senior officer and reviewed the troops. It was the closing act of an important aspect of my life, serving in the United States Air Force and Army.

While fulfilling my extensive military responsibilities, I still had a full-time ministry with a heavy workload. It was almost like working two full-time jobs with multiple bosses, and a balancing act between family and work, civilian ministry, and military ministry.

It seems those two obligations crossed each other constantly. While being a civilian clergyman with statewide responsibilities, and in between regular Army military ministry duties, I would be called by a member of my Army unit with a need or crisis that could not wait.

A sergeant called one day and asked if I did funerals for civilians. Then he told me his eighty-six-year-old mother was in the hospital, and the family did not think she would make it through the week. They were planning her funeral.

"Sure, I perform funerals," I said in answering his query. "What hospital is your mother in?"

"No, you do not need to go to the hospital," he replied. "We are just doing some advance planning."

"Where is your mother?" I persisted. "And when are you and your family going to be there?"

That night I made my first visit to Methodist Hospital in Oak Cliff to visit a soldier's mother. It was the first of many visits, until one day a few weeks later I stood with her family and my friends to say the last words of memory about this dear lady at her life celebration service.

I got another call from a young private in the 94th General Hospital. He said he had a friend who was living with this girl, and they had been talking about getting married. Then he asked, "Why should someone get married, if they already love one another, are happy and living together?"

Well, I began my message on covenant marriage, a marriage between a man and a woman, with God the third part of their relationship. I spoke about a covenant instead of a contract. A contract can be broken; however, a covenant can never be broken or done away with.

I went on and on, and it was probably far more than he wanted to hear. When I paused to catch my breath before starting on another point, he said, "Chaplain, will you come meet with my friend and his live-in girlfriend and tell them all you said to me?

"Sure, I would be glad to do that," I said, and we set a time at a McDonald's for lunch.

When I got there on the appointed date, there sat the young private with a pretty little girl by his side. They looked so young, so bright, and so fresh.

He quickly told me he was "the friend," and this was Mary, his girlfriend whom he loved.

Well, I married that young couple one Saturday afternoon not long after our McDonald's luncheon date. I had previously introduced them to Jesus, and now the covenant was completed: a young man, his lover, and Almighty God!

These are only two illustrations of dozens of requests for pastoral care I was asked to provide for military-civilians I was with on drill weekends. I was doing most things my pastor was doing, including preaching on Sunday.

6

CHAPLAINS IN THE WORKPLACE?
YOU CAN'T DO IT, NEVER WILL HAPPEN

God gave me this thought: If the need for a minister, and in my case a military chaplain, was so evident in the lives of all those people in my military unit who did not attend any church except the military chapel, what about all the other people out there in the workplaces of America? Who is the minister who takes care of them, who answers their calls, who reaches out to support them? The sad answer: No one.

Even if people do not go to church and do not have a minister, they still are going to die and need to be buried; they still become ill, go to the hospital, and need to be visited; they still fall in love and want to be married; they still break the law, are sent to prison, and need a visit; they still have problems and need to be encouraged and supported; they still suffer sorrow and loss and need to be given hope. They need to be shown God's love through acts of kindness by someone who genuinely cares with a heart of compassion.

That was the thought, from God I am certain, and that lodged in my heart one day and would never go away. Never! That was the seed planted by the heavenly Father in the soil of my soul that would one day, three years later, bring to fruition an organization called Marketplace Ministries, an employee care service provided by business chaplains in the workplaces of the world.

Ann and I begin to talk and pray in 1981 and 1982 about this "crazy idea" I had of doing for civilians what I did for Army personnel. I tried my best to explain how many people called me out of our unit about needing pastoral care of some type. They call in the morning and at night, too. I could hardly keep up with the requests for help.

She asked penetrating questions like, "Who do you know who is doing this? Who do you know who is successful in providing this type of service?"

Of course, I did not know anyone. In fact as I tried to achieve my due diligence, I could find only about a half dozen big corporations who had their own in-house chaplains, with a North Carolina tobacco company being one of them.

However, there was a historical precedent. Local clergymen would visit burlap bag factories in Charleston, South Carolina, in the 1800s to help young children who labored long, hot, dirty hours in smelly facilities when there were no child labor laws.

This was the closest thing I could find to chaplains in the workplace. The clergymen were motivated by the same thing that moved my heart, to help people, to care for them, to encourage them, to uplift them, meeting their needs physically, materially, and spiritually, to tell them God loves them, and they have never done anything to lower their value in His sight.

Ann and I prayed and talked with each other and with God. We did not talk about me being a marketplace chaplain every day; however, we did talk about it often. This went on for three years, and I kept telling God I could not quit my ministry job and go try to be a civilian chaplain to the marketplace because my wife had questions. I blamed it all on her.

One day Ann suggested I go talk with our Pastor, Dr. W. A. Criswell of First Baptist Church of Dallas, one of the earliest megachurches in the country. He had already been the pastor for nearly forty years at that time. He had written fifty books and would write twenty-five more before he finished his clergy career. Good idea, I thought; Pastor Criswell was a spiritually brilliant follower of Christ and he, if anyone, would have the answer for me. Should I try to form this new ministry, even if my wife did not want me to? He would tell me.

When the day came for my appointment with my pastor, I was there bright and early, standing tall and ready for the answer to my dilemma. I was presented by his executive assistant (in those days she was called a secretary), and as I walked into his office, he got up from behind a mahogany desk that seemed to stretch a block long. To me, it took him five minutes to briskly walk from behind this beautiful desk where he did much of his writing.

It was his custom to address anyone younger than he was, and now he was in his upper sixties, by the title "Lad." I was a lad at forty-nine, nearly fifty.

As he put his arm around my shoulder, he said, "Lad, how can I help you? How can the pastor help you?"

I told my story how I felt God wanted me to quit my position with Texas Baptists and go out by myself to begin a new ministry as a chaplain in the marketplace. I added as genteelly as I could that my wife did not think we should do it. I had a God-blessed ministry where I was, and I should just stay there for now. I closed my story by saying, "Pastor, I don't know what to do."

For a minute, all was silent as he just looked at me as tears formed in the corners of my eyes. His face was kind and gentle, and he said nothing; then came his reply.

"Why, Lad," he said, "That is easy; just wait on God. Wait on God. If God is in this, as you wait on Him, you cannot get away from His call for you to do this new ministry. You will have to go and do it. If God is not in this for you and Ann, then this idea will pass away and you will know you are to continue to serve where you are. So I say again, just wait on God."

The meeting was brief and easy. I was expecting a deep theological treatise from a man with two earned doctorates. However, all I got was, "Wait on God."

As I turned and walked toward his office door and he walked back around his huge desk, he called to me again.

"Now, Lad," he said, "If you do this new ministry as a chaplain, I will give you five thousand dollars as your first contributor."

I could hardly speak. I thought I was hearing things. I remember saying some kind of a weak thank you because I was stunned. I got what I came for, spiritual insight into my dilemma, and went away with much more than I asked or expected, a promise of five thousand dollars.

Walking across Ervay Street to my office in the Baptist Building, I could hardly wait to tell Ann what the pastor said. Wait on God, with money in hand if we went forward with this crazy idea about being a civilian chaplain, a minister in the marketplace.

The Army, yes; corporate America, I still don't know. I will just wait on God.

Ann and I were talking again about this crazy idea that now had become more of a possible idea of me being a civilian chaplain in the marketplace. That was a tough financial year for us with one son in Baylor University and Ann not working outside the home.

I remember one time Ann's godly mother, Hattie Mae March, and I were sharing a car ride together. She brought up the crazy idea I had and said Ann was very concerned about it, our family, and how it would all work out. She didn't try to talk me out of it but only expressed Ann's concern. I was concerned as well, but was still waiting on God.

However, I was working three jobs and staying extremely busy as an evangelism minister with Texas Baptists, a chaplain with the Army Reserve, and a motivational speaker with Zig Ziglar. Of course, I never had just one work assignment; it was always two jobs or more.

Zig, who was a world-famous author and motivational speaker living in Dallas, became my friend in 1975 when we met on a Braniff Airlines flight to Kansas City. I was on active duty as a major at the Command and General Staff College at Fort Leavenworth, Kansas. Even though Zig and I both belonged to First Baptist Church of Dallas, where he taught a large business leaders' Sunday school class, we had never met. However, from then on we would be co-laborers together in the kingdom's work, as well as fellow speakers and friends like family for the rest of our lives.

Not long after that, Zig called me one day and asked if I was still doing motivational speaking. I assured him I was and had spoken in August to twenty school teachers' groups for in-service training. I thought he remembered I had told him I wanted to be as good as he was someday. He invited me to speak at his "Born to Win Seminar" which he put on regularly in Dallas.

He knew I was an aerobics follower of Dr. Kenneth H. Cooper of the Cooper Clinic, where I have had a physical examination every year since 1982, and was a dedicated exercise and conditioning practitioner. Zig wanted me to speak on "Physical Conditioning for Successful Living."

The morning I spoke, as soon as I began, Zig slipped in the back door over on the side and quietly sat down. Here I was making my first presentation for Zig, and in the audience was the number one motivational speaker in North America and possibly the whole world. I was nervous, shaking somewhat, and sharing to the best of my professional ability. I tried not to look at him, and on occasion when I did, he would smile and give me a thumbs up with total approval.

That was the first of scores of times that Zig would recommend me to speak in his place. When they could not book him, because of a date conflict or a budget restraint, Zig would suggest me, or his executive assistant would quote Mr. Ziglar in how outstanding I was as a motivational speaker. I was the second best, according to Zig, and I would do "an excellent job" for them.

How else could God have opened the doors to some of America's largest corporations than for me to stand before a large audience and give a humorous motivational speech? I never dreamed I would speak to the entire executive sales force of General Motors-Pontiac Motor Division in Detroit or at McDonald's University at Elm Brook, Illinois, for Golden Arches executives.

All over the country, I would fly in to speak once or twice and fly back to Dallas missing only one day out of my office on my regular job. I would make more money in one day speaking as a Zig Ziglar motivational speaker than I would make working for Texas Baptists in a month.

One year I mailed out fifteen thousand to twenty thousand speaking brochures to school districts in six states surrounding Texas. Sometimes in August alone I would earn enough to pay an entire semester for one of our sons at Baylor; occasionally I could come close to paying for the entire year for tuition and books.

Now you know what I mean when I say Zig Ziglar sent my boys to college. Also, even though I sincerely tried to pay him a speaker's fee for booking me in these high-paying speaking gigs, he never took a penny, not one. He recommended me for seven years, 1979 to 1986. I probably earned upwards of a half million dollars or more because of his generosity and friendship. I will never forget that either; I loved and respected him deeply. My friendship with Zig and Jean Ziglar ran deep, really deep, for they were like family.

On or about July 3, 1983, Ann and I were enjoying a late morning cup of coffee, just talking. Of course, the subject turned to what was I going to do in my ministry, stay where I was or go in a new direction, moving from the military to the marketplace, still being a chaplain for both.

It wasn't really that Ann was not supportive or was against what I was considering; she was just much more practical about life and living it. She wondered how we would eat, and would I just stay around the house all day with no job and nothing to do. How would we pay Baylor if Zig stopped using me or if I just was not good enough to speak for those giant corporations? She knew I did not make much money with Texas Baptists; however, they did pay every month and that was something.

It was not just Ann who had reservations about this change in my work and ministry life. I had a lot of questions too, and God knew all about them. Even though I inclined to hide behind Ann's reluctance, my faith was not super strong either, and my doubts were many.

Our life's biblical verse, which we had carved in our fireplace's wooden mantel many years later in the house we built, was Matthew 6:33, "Seek ye first the kingdom of God, and His righteousness, and all these things shall be added unto you." (KJV) When you read the six or eight verses before verse 33, it tells us God will provide food, clothing, and victory over worry when we put Him first above all else. We both believed that was the answer…with God first, everything else would be OK.

As we continued to talk, I reached over in a chair at the breakfast table and picked up one of those legal-size yellow lined pads.

I told Ann I too had many reasons why we should not launch out to form a new ministry, one that no one else was doing, at least no one else I knew. I paused and looked down at the first page. On it were items 1 through 14, items I had written.

1. I was too old at forty-nine, and soon to be fifty, to start a new ministry.

2. I did not want to work in a para-church organization, for I knew what my denominational colleagues thought about organizations that were in "competition with the church." Besides, I had already worked for the most prestigious para-church ministry in the world—The Billy Graham Evangelistic Association.

3. I was not in a strong financial position, and if things "went south" I could not continue paying my sons' college tuition.

4. No one I told about my idea gave me overwhelming support; in fact, many offered no support.

5. I did not know for certain if I had waited on God long enough, the way Dr. Criswell told me to.

The reasons went on and on. And then, this should have been #1 because it was the most important one of all: I didn't think Ann wanted me to quit my present ministry job that God was blessing. I didn't either.

However, I turned up the page and there were fifteen words for the one reason we should do it. I had written out these words which I began reading to Ann: "The best I can interpret, this is God's will for our lives at this time."

"If you can look me in the eye and tell me you believe this new ministry is God's will for us, then I think we should do it," I heard Ann say.

Then she added we could sell our house, she would go back to work teaching school, and we should start this new ministry as soon as possible.

When she said that, with me being the spiritual leader in my family, I responded by saying, "Now, let's not rush into this. Maybe we need to pray a little more. It has only been three years of considering what God wants us to do."

Now I did not have the excuse that Ann was hesitant about me leaving my job and beginning a total new ministry that no one else was doing. However, we settled it that morning. Unless God totally blocked us from our plan, I would resign from my position, giving sixty days' notice, and begin this new ministry on January 1, 1984.

That day, not one person had asked me to be their chaplain and support their workers and family members, and I wondered if anyone would. I surely hoped so because I could not go back on our agreed word to follow God in a new adventure of a new ministry.

The die was cast! That day, and many more thereafter, I wondered if civilian chaplaincy in the workplace would be accepted, if it would be as effective as in the military. And yet, I was going to begin, and as Dwight L. Moody said, "With God as your partner, make your plans big."

Leaving the Baptist General Convention of Texas

I wrote my letter of resignation from the Baptist General Convention of Texas, Evangelism Division, on November 1, 1983, and gave it to my director, Dr. Carlos McLeod. Now I had officially quit a position I had held for two months shy of fourteen years.

After Dr. McLeod read my letter, his first words were that he would pray for me. Then he asked, "What are you going to do?"

I replied, "I don't know; I've just got an idea."

"Well, then I am really going to pray for you because if you don't know what you are going to do, and you just quit your job, you will need all of my prayers, that's for certain," McLeod said.

Then I began to tell Carlos about how I hoped to do in the civilian sector what I done in the Army.

When he asked me who I was going to work for as I chaplain, I was a little embarrassed. I had to confess I did not have anyone yet.

Carlos looked at me with the expression of a man who has just watched someone who can't swim go off the deep end.

His knowledge that I did not have a job may have influenced his generosity to me. In mid-December, he called me into his office and, to my total surprise, asked me if I would serve as a consultant to him and the division to help find the person who would take my place.

"I will pay you your full salary for six months, and health insurance, too," he said. "You can do your chaplain's work, if you get any, come meet with me occasionally, and help me interview prospective staff members until we find someone. I guarantee you six months of consultation fees."

Wow, God had done it again, and Ann would sleep better now that we had a guaranteed salary until July 1, 1984. It was an answer to a prayer I never prayed; however, I guessed Ann may have.

December of 1983, I formed a Board of Directors composed of men who I admired and were my friends. The first board was composed of

Louis Cole – Chairman	Max Legg
Dr. BO Baker	Mark Lovvorn
Dr. Pat Beckham	Ben March
Os Chrisman	Ken Stohner Jr.
Aaron Colvin	Phil Swatzell
Dr. C. Wade Freeman	Gil Stricklin, founder and president
James Jeffrey	

Director Os Chrisman, an attorney, worked pro bono to get our 501(c)(3) status.

I had already begun talking with every Christian business owner I knew in my church. I told them what I was going to do, a chaplain in businesses caring for workers and their families.

I was rather naïve, to say the least, because I thought I would have business owners standing in line wanting me to be their company chaplain. The first ten business leaders I stood before to tell my story, my call from God, all quickly slammed the door of possible opportunity.

"You cannot do that, Gil," the first client company prospect said emphatically. He went on to explain you cannot be that religious in the secular arena with the separation of church and state.

"You know what you are going to do?" the next one asked, adding, "You are going to get owners sued, that's what you are going to do. You are going to make people mad…you being a Baptist and all."

"Good idea, Gil, and for the Army it is OK," said another successful business owner. "However, it will never work in corporate America. The workplace is too diverse for a chaplain to minister at work."

"I wouldn't do that for anything," were the first words out of another businessman's mouth. "I would bet money you will be sued during the first six months doing something like this."

"If I hired you as my chaplain, I would have to hire Muslims, Buddhists, and Jews, and everything else to satisfy my workers. No, I couldn't do something like that," still another said.

I kept talking with many business leaders in our congregation. I just knew I would find at least one who would hire me, just one.

Finally, I was talking with a friend. He was a godly man and owned his own company. Yes, I should have talked with him first. I knew he would hire me. Surely, as a deacon at the church and a good and godly man, he would want a chaplain for his people.

I gave my best sales pitch, even though I knew God would have to do the real selling. This had to be something from the Spirit. I was hopeful this would be my first client company and my first civilian chaplain's job.

"Who are you serving as a chaplain at present?" he asked, waiting for my answer.

"Well," I said, followed by a long pause as I tried to think how to say it best. "I want you to be the first company to hire me and Marketplace Ministries as your chaplain."

He quickly replied, "Gil, go get some experience for a couple of years with this idea and come back and see me. Maybe we could do it then."

Even after nearly thirty years of providing this service, not one of those men I talked with early on ever hired me or our ministry. Today, not one of them is still in business, as they have grown old, died, sold their companies, or lost them in bad times.

There are things in life, when you only have one chance, and if you miss that one chance you have missed it forever. It is kind of sad if you think about it.

That was one of those times when I asked God again if He really meant for me to launch a new ministry to provide chaplains who care for workers and their families. At the same time, I was wondering if I could get my old job back because they had not hired anyone yet.

What is that verse about putting your hand to the plough and then looking back (Luke 9:62)? No, I will not look back, not now, not ever?

What was that businessman's name I met in Zig Ziglar's Born to Win seminar? He invited me to speak at his company prayer breakfast. That was years ago. What was his name?

Ed Bonneau. I found it. He owned The Bonneau Companies of Farmers Branch, Texas. As well as I remember he was an elder in the Church of Christ, and his father was one of those old-time West Texas Church of Christ evangelists. I would call Ed.

A few days later, December 17 as I recall, I was in a Mexican restaurant sitting across the table from the man I met through Zig, and who I had not seen for two or three years. I got him to come have lunch with me by telling him he had never had a clergyman buy his lunch, or anything else, and I wanted us to make history together. I think he came just to see if I really meant it, and I did.

I began to share with this good and godly businessman about my idea for business chaplains in the workplace. By now I had my pitch down pat, hewn, smooth and word perfect.

Even before I got halfway through, Ed interrupted me and said, "Sounds like a great idea to me. Come be my company chaplain. I have tried for years to be the company chaplain. However, I hire and fire people as the boss and sign all the checks. No one has walked in my office asking for help with a bad marriage or how to rear children. I think they may come to you."

I could hardly believe my ears. Did he just tell me he wanted me to be his company chaplain?

"You come out to our company the first Monday of the new year, and I will introduce you as our new company chaplain, a new employee benefit, without any costs to the employees," he continued. "What do you charge, Gil?"

It was all happening so fast I couldn't keep up. What do I charge? I hadn't even considered that aspect of being a chaplain. He is a member of the Church of Christ, and he just hired a Southern Baptist to be his chaplain. Can you believe that? None of my Baptists buddies at the church would hire me as their chaplain. Now this new acquaintance had just hired me, his first chaplain and my first client. I could not believe it; yet, it was true. I knew it was. He told me for certain.

"What do you charge for your services, Gil?" I heard Bonneau ask the second time.

"Well, Ed, just whatever you think it is worth," I mumbled. "I will come out to your company every Monday and spend all day, be on call 24/7/365 for all your employees and their family members. You can pay me what you think it is worth."

"I will pay you fifteen hundred dollars a month," he said without even stuttering. "Is that OK?"

Well, it was not OK; that was far too much money for me for one day a week, so I told him so.

"Ed, that is far too much money to pay for what I can do," I retorted back to him. "I will settle for much less."

No, he would have nothing to do with it, and it was settled: fifteen hundred dollars a month, eighteen thousand dollars annually.

God, Ed, and Carlos had overwhelmed me with financial stability, at least for six months. The house would not have to be sold, Ann would not have to go back to school teaching, and our son would not have to drop out of Baylor University, at least not now.

Ann could hardly believe it when I told her we got our first client, a Church of Christ elder at that. In her mind the best thing was I would not be hanging around the house every day, at least not on Mondays. Monday was The Bonneau Company's day, for I was its chaplain.

My parish had 150 working members, and now those employees and their 417 family members had a minister, a Marketplace minister to care for them, to help them, to marry and bury them, as well as visit them in the hospital or in prison. Yes, I was their chaplain.

About two weeks later, after that historic lunch with Ed Bonneau, me paying and him hiring, I stood before five different groups of The Bonneau Company's employees. Ed introduced me as the new company chaplain. I was the go-to person for any employee or family needs or for any help. This was a confidential service, and Ed would never ask and I would never tell about any employee problems I was dealing with. Now America's largest distributor of sunglasses had a company chaplain, and so did their employees and family members.

Later that morning, after the introductions were complete, I stood alone, the company chaplain. Everyone else had a "real" job, and I had an office. I went there and put up a few books and got some office supplies. By then it was lunch time, so I went to the kitchen and broke out my sack lunch.

I waited until almost all the employees had found their seats, then walked over and sat with them. There wasn't a whole lot of conversation, so I talked about the Cowboys and their season, along with basketball and who might win it all.

Before long, the lunch hour was over and everyone went back to work, real work.

I began that ministry just wandering around and learning the company. It took all afternoon, and I still did not get to meet everyone or learn what they did in the company. The next Tuesday, I didn't have anything else to do, so I was drinking coffee at 0700 hours in The Bonneau Company kitchen greeting every person who came to work. Someone said he thought I was only there on Mondays.

"No, I'll come out here every day for a while," I responded. "I want to learn every job, what everyone does here for Bonneau."

The second day was just about like the first. No chaplain duties, no prospects of need, and no crises that I could see. It was just people working, eating, drinking coffee at break time, and going home at the end of the day.

Once I had an employee call and ask when I could come for a visit. Since I wasn't doing anything, I told him I would be there soon.

Finally, after standing around and talking with folks, I went to see Ed. I told him I wanted him to give me a real job so l could just work like everyone else.

He said they needed a man in the warehouse to pack orders of sunglasses, and it was the hottest place in the building. For the next two months, the chaplain was an order puller and packer. This Marketplace chaplain didn't marry or bury anyone. He was not asked to help in any situation, and he began to wonder if being a chaplain in the secular workplace was a good idea after all.

As I was packing glasses one day, a dear lady from the tagging room came up and asked, "Are you that preacher man?"

I told her I was the company chaplain. How could I help?

She told me her mother had a stroke the previous night and she was in Baylor Hospital in downtown Dallas. The lady wondered if I had time to go down and check on her because she could not get there until after work.

I told her I would go right away. After grabbing my suit out of the car and changing out of my jeans and tee shirt, I drove to Baylor Hospital and found the lady's dear mother. I spent quite some time with her, met the nurses, and was even there when the doctor came by. After putting together a major report on her condition and prospects for the future, which was not all good, I went back to the company.

The lady was deeply appreciative. I had prayed for her mom, and her mom was also grateful. That was the first official duty I ever did as a civilian chaplain, The Bonneau Company chaplain.

It would be far from my last. I began my day for many days thereafter by going to Baylor Hospital to visit the mother of the nice lady in the tagging room. I gave a daily medical report to the daughter after she had been there the night before.

A few months later when mom went home to heaven, her daughter asked me to do her funeral, because she did not have a local clergyman. I was pleased to assist the family with mom's life celebration service, for now she was just like my mom, too. She was a close and special friend. I guess you always remember your first funeral as a civilian chaplain, and I certainly did.

Since I was working for The Bonneau Company and didn't have any other clients, I continued to go there every day. I got out of the house, which pleased Ann, and I gave Ed forty hours a week. Now I was building friendships with almost everyone at the company, real trust among workers, and a confidence level that if they had a problem I would do everything possible to help them.

More and more individuals or their family members came to me for some kind of support, some kind of help. The chaplain idea was new to everyone, so it took some time to bridge the information gap of exactly what I could do to help them—and whether I would really do it.

Every evening when I went home, Ann would ask for an activity report of ministry for the day. She kept a ministry log of what I did and who I met with, what the problem was, and how I helped. That daily journal would become the standard Ministry Activities Report that is given back to every client. Sometimes as many as one hundred in one month; however, then it was only one report after six months.

I had been up and going as a business chaplain for about three months when I got a telephone call from a fellow church member, David E. Wicker III, president and CEO of Sysco Food Systems, Dallas Division. He asked me to come out to his office and visit with him.

Wicker, a good man who was a deacon in our church, wasn't one of those business men I talked to in November or December 1983 when I was trying to talk anyone into hiring me as their chaplain. I don't know why I did not go see David. I guess it was because he did not own his company; he had sold his business, Wicker, Inc., a fresh and frozen fish and vegetable distributing company, to Sysco previously.

However, now he wanted to talk with me. What about? He didn't say.

When I walked into his office, David, my friend for nearly fifteen years, asked me to tell him how my new ministry as a business chaplain was going. I gave him my report on how it had developed with The Bonneau Company, the hospital visits I had made, the funeral I performed, and the many other confidential pastoral discussions I had with employees and family members.

I was not certain if he had called Ed Bonneau or not. However, I was confident Ed would give me a strong and favorable recommendation. He might even tell Wicker I was one of his best order packers.

I was surprised, yet thrilled, when I left his office that afternoon in late March of 1984, as Marketplace had its second client company, one with five hundred employees and more than thirteen hundred family members. Now my congregation, as their chaplain, totaled more than twenty-five hundred people.

How could one chaplain care for that large number of people? I wondered about that even though I did not voice my concern to anyone except Ann. I guess I would have to work harder and sleep less.

My office, that 1974 blue Datsun station wagon with my briefcase and now two file folders with everything in them for Bonneau and Sysco, would be seen shuttling back and forth between my two clients. Also, almost any day it would be seen parked at one of the twenty-two Dallas area hospitals, or one of the local prisons, nursing homes, or someone's home.

The 1974 Datsun was in pretty bad shape when it hit its eleventh birthday, and nearly one hundred thousand miles of transportation duty. In fact, it dripped and burned more oil that some old West Texas oil wells produce in a day. Ed Bonneau often complained I was leaving large, and deep, oil spots on his parking lot, and he was afraid they were a fire hazard to his buildings.

I knew he was joking, until one day I examined the place where I parked; sure enough he was right, truly a fire hazard to his buildings and to my car. Well, it was less expensive to buy a case of cheap oil than to get the engine repaired so I just keep pouring in oil and leaving behind a trail of billowing white smoke.

Ed Bonneau and Barbara, his sweet and kind wife, invited Ann and me to have dinner with them. We met at a lovely restaurant, in a Dallas hotel, for an enjoyable evening of fellowship with special friends. Toward the end of the meal, and after finishing desserts, Ed reached into his side coat pocket and slid a set of car keys over to my plate and said, "Ann and Gil, Barbara and I want you to have a little better car so we are giving you a used Ford product." We were stunned, sitting in silence, as no one had ever given us a car.

After trying to say words of appreciation, we got up and walked out into the parking lot. There sat a slightly used brown Lincoln Continental. We drove it until it died with nearly 150,000 miles on it, all Marketplace miles, and with no oil spots on the company parking lot.

A lot of people have done good things for us over the years, and we have made it with a little help from friends, like Ed and Barbara. However, no couple has done more than these special friends, because they were the first to hire us in 1984.

Before April was over, Hank Dickerson, owner of Hank Dickerson & Company of Dallas, a large and successful commercial real estate corporation, hired me. I was not only the company chaplain; however, I had additional duties of writing and editing the company in-house magazine, as well as helping train beginning real estate sales agents every Wednesday morning at 0700 hours. I guess you could say I did a variety of jobs for Hank.

He was a good friend and fellow Baylor University alumni. Hank was star athlete for the Baylor football team and had taken his sports skills and military experience to build a most successful commercial venture in Dallas. This highly respected individual made millions of dollars in his business and had the wisdom to hire a company chaplain.

Now after only four months of operation under the first name of Tri-Dimensional Consulting Service, the organization's name was changed to Marketplace Ministries Foundation and then to the permanent name of Marketplace Ministries Inc. We now had three clients, and one lone chaplain was to care for and help all those people day and night, 24/7/365.

You know a company is very successful when you walk into their huge office reception area and see an enormous vase of fresh-cut flowers, delivered every weekday morning from a high-class florist. I often wondered what Dickerson's fresh flower budget was for a year; I knew it had to be massive, and thought it was probably larger than the entire budget of our whole organization.

I was working extremely hard, trying to visit every employee every week, answering scores of telephone calls, planning weddings, performing funerals. I could not keep up and was struggling to provide A+ chaplain service. I didn't know what to do, so I continued to work harder, often seven days a week.

Even though I was still doing weekend training and ministry for the Army Reserve, my job with the Texas Southern Baptists had run out, and we had hired my replacement. Now I only had two jobs, and the civilian chaplaincy was now the greatest in ministry opportunities.

The summer rocked along, and September came around for the beginning of fall 1984. It was still very hot late that month in Dallas, and I had buried two-year-old Jana Worm, the little angel. Her dad, David, had become one of my best friends, and I tried to see him every week when I went to Sysco Food Systems.

Before that month ended, we would sign our fourth client company and our first banking enterprise. Darrell Lafitte was chairman, president, and CEO of North Dallas Bank and Trust Company, a very strong bank with personal service and much appreciation for their employees. I knew Darrell slightly through mutual friends; however, I could not claim him as a close friend. He was not one of the business owners I talked with last December and January. I didn't even think about him or his bank.

When a company hires your service, you never know how long they will keep you, how long they will support the service you provide. Lafitte hired me that September, and even though he left the bank a few months later to begin Cornerstone Bank, North Dallas Bank would contract our service for three decades and counting. Lafitte eventually hired our services for his new bank as well.

Our chaplains have gone through three changes at the top of North Dallas Bank's leadership chain, and each time the choice has been made to keep the ministry in place. To this date, North Dallas Bank, now under the leadership of Mike Shipman, is the longest ongoing client the ministry has ever had.

With the addition of the bank, the number of parishioners totaled 3,288 individuals, with 870 of them workers in the four companies. I realized I could no longer do it alone; I desperately needed another chaplain.

Before the end of the first year, Bobby Waite became that second chaplain. We divided the workload and made a schedule for our worksite visits. I was no longer alone.

In those days of working with Chaplain Bobby, I never dreamed that one day we would cross twenty-eight hundred chaplains reaching toward three thousand. If fact, then I would have said you were crazy even to think in those large numbers.

There were many moving stories of two chaplains helping more people than you could count. Here is one I remember, one I will never forget.

With many years in the Army Chaplain Corps, and being with troops in the United States and on foreign soil, I knew individuals who really did not like the chaplain and those who thought he was lazy, unproductive, and unnecessary. There were those individuals who cussed the loudest when the chaplain was standing close, and he had to hear dirty jokes along with the rest of his group of fellow soldiers.

That was true for civilian workers, too. However, those guys did not bother me. My ears were not "virgins," and I had heard it all before anyway. Besides, I was going to love them, speak to them, and share with them just like everyone else. They could not stop me.

He was a giant of a man and a delivery truck driver for Sysco. Since I had the early shift for that company, I was there many mornings by 5 or 5:30 a.m., long before the sun came up over Dallas. I would get there to drink coffee and speak to every driver before he climbed into his truck for a full day of deliveries to restaurants, school cafeterias, and other food serving facilities.

This big fellow, an African-American, was kind of a ringleader of the drivers, a senior driver with long tenure at Sysco. He could cuss worse than any man I had ever heard. Remember, I had heard a lot of them! He was a bad dude, and it was evident he did not like me, or any chaplain or clergyman for that matter.

However, he did like the two or three dozen donuts I brought many mornings for the drivers to have with their coffee. That had won a friendship with most of those guys.

Even while reaching out to get a fresh, warm donut, this man, who weighed close to three hundred pounds and stood at least 6' 6", would begin a dirty joke. When he finished his story the rest of the drivers in the room didn't know whether to laugh or not. I didn't laugh; however, there were always a few who did.

One early morning when I walked in for my donut distribution, I noticed that the big man was not there. After passing out my donut stash, I asked about my special giant friend. I was told his wife had cancer and she was being operated on that morning.

After asking several men in the room, as well as the driver foreman, I found out she was being treated at Baylor Hospital downtown. I didn't even think about it; I just rushed back to my car and started driving to Baylor.

I parked and walked inside. After finding out his wife's room number, I made my way to the third floor. I paused and knocked on the door. I heard that low, deep voice say, "Come in."

After praying fervently, I pushed open the door and walked in. I am sure he was totally surprised to see me there in this dark hour just before surgery. He stammered and stuttered a little as he told his wife I was the company chaplain, who brought donuts to the drivers.

I introduced myself by name because I knew he did not know it. I told them that I had gone to the Sysco drivers' coffee meeting and found out his wife was having surgery, so I wanted to come down and be with them.

About that time the door opened and the gurney pushed by a surgery attendant had come for her. I asked the attendant to give me two or three more minutes. He closed the door.

I looked at the big man and said, "Do you mind if I pray for your wife, and the surgeon who will operate on her today, asking God to be with them that they may free her from cancer?"

He reached over to hold his wife's hand and said, "Yes, that would be fine, Chaplain." I could not help but notice tear puddles in his eyes.

I prayed earnestly for his wife, the surgeon, those standing around the operating table, and those on the operating team. I prayed for her safety throughout the procedure, that the surgery would be successful and soon she would have her health again.

When I closed my prayer, she was crying, too, and she thanked me over and over for coming down and praying for her.

I told her husband I would meet him in the surgery waiting room. I walked out of the room and down the hall.

This big fellow came into the waiting room a little later as he went with his wife to the prep area, and then she went to surgery. It was to be a long surgery, eight to ten hours. I stayed with him all day.

We had lunch together and drank enough coffee to float a battleship. We talked about everything, about how he grew up, where and how he met his wife, how many kids they had, and almost every detail about his life. We even talked about his mother, who was a marvelous Christian lady and how he once had gone to church.

Something strange happened that day, really strange. I didn't hear him say one curse word all day. In fact, I never heard him say a curse word ever again, and no dirty jokes, either.

From then on, when I met with the drivers to deliver my donuts, he would say in his deep, booming voice, "The Donut Chaplain is here, no more dirty talk. Clean it up, clean it up."

Every time I would see him thereafter, he would say, "My wife really did appreciate you coming down to the hospital to pray for her. That meant a whole lot to her."

Then he would add, "To me, too."

7

NEW OPPORTUNITIES AND PEOPLE

We closed the financial books of 1984, our first year, in the black, the beginning of a record of closing on the positive side of the ledger every year, with no red ink for more than three decades. It was close a few of those years, and the economic picture was sometimes difficult. However, God's sufficiency was always there and the needs of the ministry were always met. We had enough finances to meet every budget requirement, with a "little bit" to spare. This first year saw the ministry gain four new clients, with a total income of $86,102, $18,297 of that coming from general contributions. The breakdown was 79 percent client service fees and 21 percent support gifts.

The end of 1985, was coming to a close, and we were preparing to celebrate our second anniversary of Marketplace Ministries in Dallas. The second year's total income was up about 11.4 percent, or $96,014, with the number of clients doubling to eight. We now had four chaplains in Dallas.

As December 1985 came to a close, we had celebrated "Two Incredible Years" of ministry with a banquet at the newly opened Crescent Court Hotel, owned by Caroline Rose Hunt, in the heart of downtown Dallas. Two hundred fifty of our friends came to the complimentary dinner, and no one enjoyed it more than I did, except maybe my pastor, the esteemed Dr. W. A. Criswell of First Baptist Church of Dallas. This white-haired gentleman and theological scholar would be the church's pastor for more than a half century, and he was our pastor from 1970 until his passing in January 2002. You may recall, he was the one who gave me biblical wisdom to "wait on God" and then followed that up with a five-thousand-dollar check as our first financial donor.

With eight client companies and many file folders for each one, the office situation became more difficult, as my briefcases were still stacked in the back of the 1974 blue Datsun station wagon. Maybe we needed a real office, I thought, so I began to look around for something small and inexpensive for our limited budget.

Our client, North Dallas Bank and Trust Company, had the North Dallas Bank Tower connected to the bank with twelve stories of office space. It just so happened there was a tiny space of about five hundred square feet we could rent. Our first office, outside of the mobile Datsun office, was not much larger than a broom closet; however, it was a real office with a secretary four hours a day, three days a week.

In the North Dallas Bank Tower, we graduated to larger and larger office space, and finally to a suite on the twelfth floor. After eighteen years of having our office in the North Dallas Bank Tower, in 2010 we were invited to move to the new Hope Center Building in Plano, Texas, by June Hunt of Hope for the Heart. The building houses forty-five Christian ministries, and our office is on the top floor in approximately fifteen thousand square feet of beautiful space.

As we closed our second year with the budget met and all bills paid, we began to think about other cities that needed chaplains. I had gone to Waco, Texas, as a freshman at Baylor University in the fall of 1953. Earlier that spring, much of downtown Waco had been wiped out by a powerful tornado, killing more than one hundred city residents. Death and destruction were still evident as we drove into the city toward the campus to begin my four years as a Baylor Bear.

Waco was like my second hometown, for I had spent four of the best years of my life there, work, studies, football games, dating a beautiful girl, attending church, and making friends. Yes, Waco was a special place to me, since I graduated from Baylor, fell in love with a Baylor Beauty, married her at the First Baptist Church of Waco, and entered the military there.

As Ann and I prayed about Waco as our first expansion city outside Dallas for Marketplace Ministries, I remembered by good friend, Earl Patrick, who was the president of Jim Stewart Realtors, the largest real estate company in the city. I called Earl and told him what we had been doing in Dallas for two years caring for workers through chaplains. Earl said, "Gil, come do that for my hundred employees in Waco." The short version of the story is that in December 1985, Earl Patrick, along with Jim Stewart, both Baylor alums and godly businessmen, agreed to begin our chaplain service for their company as soon as a chaplain could be recruited and hired. Jim Stewart Realtors in Waco became our first client company outside of Dallas.

We have now passed our twenty-fifth year of providing chaplain service to this company. There have been many changes in the company, as in most others; however, Earl Patrick as president still has a love for his employees and family members.

What comes first, the chicken or the egg? It is the same as asking whether chaplains or client companies come first with Marketplace Ministries. I am not certain about chickens. With Marketplace Ministries, the answer is clients. With a new client committed in Waco, we now desperately needed a chaplain. Patrick and Stewart were waiting for us to begin, and workers and their families were in need of help.

In January 1986, Dan P. Truitt was moving toward completing his PhD at Baylor University, with a focus on New Testament and ethics. He had been wondering how God was going to use him to serve others in his post-graduate career and into the future. Truitt had already earned a bachelor's degree from Texas A&M University and had been in the construction business before earning a master's degree in theology from Mid-America Baptist Theological Seminary in Memphis, Tennessee.

Along with his PhD studies, he had a steady part-time job as an education coordinator with the American Heart Association in Waco, and one day when he returned from lunch he found a note on his desk: "Call Gil Stricklin in Dallas" and the phone number.

When Truitt called me, a man he didn't know and had never met, I told him about this exciting, new opportunity with Marketplace Ministries as a chaplain sharing God's love through acts of kindness toward employees and their family members.

This Aggie liked the idea that while people do not have to go to church, they do have to get out of bed and go to work somewhere. If he could be the chaplain at their company to reach out to them with care and concern, that would open the door to tell them how to have purpose in life, with joy and peace, through Jesus Christ.

Not only would Truitt be approved to go into companies and support people with compassion and love, he would be paid to do that. It was a calling and a ministry job with a salary, which was about all there was back then in the benefits package.

We have come a long way since hiring the first five employees, not contract laborers but employees. Still today, we cannot match huge corporations of America with salary and benefits. However, we now have health insurance, matching 403(b) retirement funding, twenty paid days off a year and thirty days for some long-time employees. It is much better than it once was.

With close to three decades of tenure since joining Marketplace Ministries in 1986, Dr. Dan P. Truitt has the longest ministry seniority in the organization, other than me, the first chaplain. Truitt has his spot in the history of this ministry as the first chaplain ever hired outside of Dallas and is senior to some twenty-eight hundred other staff personnel.

Truitt did not sign on with us for the benefits package; no, he came aboard because God called him to this special duty outside the stained glass windows and four white walls of the sanitized environment called the church, to a place where religious songs and sermons are silent.

Over nearly thirty years, Truitt has filled several key leadership positions in this chaplains' service to secular corporations and religious ministries. Front-line chaplain, team leader, area coach, division director, vice president of national training, and vice president of international ministry are some of the vital spots he has filled in the more than ten thousand days he has served in this ministry.

Dr. Truitt and his family moved to Dallas in 1993 to begin a new assignment in our headquarters after establishing an office in Waco, enlarging the base of client companies, and recruiting, training, assigning, and supervising highly qualified chaplains.

"The simplicity of being able to bring the gospel of Christ to those people who are interested and inquire through the vehicle of workplace chaplaincy" is the most important aspect of this ministry, according to Truitt.

"Even in the international ministry, whether Mexico, Canada, or somewhere in Europe or Asia, Christ-honoring ministry happens with godly chaplains caring for workers and their families," he continued. "Chaplains' ministry is effective not only in the Bible Belt; it is effective every place we have begun since 1984. Chaplains showing God's love through compassion and care is not a religious thing or a cultural thing, because people are the same in their hearts, and the gospel is the same, too, wherever it is shared."

Truitt, along with me and the more than twenty-eight hundred chaplains spread across the United States, foreign countries, and the Commonwealth of Puerto Rico, believes the true test of Marketplace Ministries, Marketplace Chaplains USA and International, is to provide "authentic ministry" by "authentic followers of Jesus Christ" under all circumstances and in all locations, foreign or domestic.

In 2014, only three chaplains wear a gold double M longevity pin designed by James Avery, enhanced by a diamond, for twenty-five years or more of service with the ministry. Truitt is one of those, along with Berl Pedigo, who began our work in Fort Worth in 1988, and I am the other.

Today, we have chaplains and staff who wear the fifteen-, ten-, and five-year pins, as the ministry has less than a 2 percent turnover rate among chaplains and executive leaders. Many times a chaplain who is also a local church pastor accepts a new church call. As they take on duties with a new congregation, they often take up a new chaplain's assignment, too, doing the same ministry with client companies in a new geographical location. They may be assigned under a new division director and even a new region vice president; however, their ministry is the same in the church and outside of it.

When we started, there were no cell phones; only doctors had car phones. We used pagers, hundreds of pagers. We developed a system so our chaplains would know the urgency of the alerts they received on their pagers. You would page the number you wanted the chaplain to call, then add a "1" if the need was urgent and required an immediate response; a "2" if the response could wait ten minutes; or a "3" if it could wait one hour. When the page was received, the chaplains would look for the 1, 2, or 3 and locate a pay phone if they were traveling. Though our technology today is upgraded from pagers to cell phones, our commitment to timely response to employee needs remains the same.

Another significant staff addition came out of those early years in Waco, Susanne Walters, our first female chaplain, who joined our staff in Waco in 1988. It took nearly four years; however, I finally learned this ministry in the workplace required ladies to work with ladies. They could do and say things men cannot do or say, and should not. We made this decision for several good reasons. One of them was the potential moral problem posed by discussion of family and marriage issues with someone of the opposite sex. This may be one reason no chaplain has ever been charged with a moral collapse or a sexual situation. Every day we pray for holiness in our lives, all of our chaplains and staff, that there be purity in our hearts, minds, and actions.

God also blessed us greatly with client growth in those early years of Marketplace Ministries in Waco, and it was through an acquaintance I made years earlier as a Baylor student.

When I enlisted in the Air Force Reserve Officer Training Corps at Baylor, a young Air Force captain named Herb Reynolds was my enlistment officer. I did not know it then and neither did he; however, thirty-three years later he would be Dr. Herbert H. Reynolds, president of Baylor University, and a close friend for more than three decades. Dr. Reynolds would play a key role in our client expansion in Waco. Because Baylor was the heart of the city and the life blood of the community and because of Dr. Reynolds's integrity and leadership, he had great influence among business leaders, and he used it to help us grow our client base there.

By the end of 1988 we had a two-year solid track record of service to Jim Stewart Realtors and a few other smaller clients. Dr. Reynolds invited several Waco business owners to have lunch with him in the Student Union Building

Drawing Room on the campus of Baylor. On that day, a dozen business owners showed up to have lunch with Reynolds and to hear about "an exciting new chaplain's ministry in Waco." Earl Patrick came and gave a positive testimony for the chaplain service at his company.

After a delicious lunch I also spoke to the group. This explanation was a brief, pointed one about the services for employees at work. There was no way these company owners would have ever come to have lunch with me or to hear me speak. However, they came when my friend, the president, invited them. Our Waco clientele doubled within a few weeks after that event.

It was not long after that luncheon when a man who was one of the ministry's board members and my dearest mentor, James N. Jeffrey, introduced me to a business executive who later would join our stable of clients in Waco. Paul J. Meyer, possibly the most successful business magnate in Waco history, brought us aboard for thirteen of his companies headquartered in the city. Even though Paul heard that great voice saying "Come up hither" in 2010, and is now waiting for us to join him in heaven, we still serve his organizations with chaplains. Also, his generous financial support has been a strong underpinning for God's work.

To close out 1986, the Marketplace Ministries' chaplain team numbered twelve who were caring for 2,435 employees and 6,574 family members. Our city count was two, and our chaplain team was composed of men and women speaking both English and Spanish. Even though chaplains were serving in only two cities after three years, God had much bigger plans for His ministry, with divine providence ruling over human inability.

Before we had a first city, Dallas, and even when the chaplains' service was only a dream on my heart, I made a list of five hundred cities in which I would ask God to allow us to minister. Of course, I put on the list the big metropolitan centers like Los Angeles, New York City, Atlanta, Orlando, Kansas City, St. Louis, Albuquerque, Phoenix, Las Vegas, Long Beach, San Francisco, and others.

However, I don't recall putting Greencastle, Pennsylvania, on my list. I am sure I did not even think of Leavenworth, Kansas, or Broken Arrow, Oklahoma, plus dozens of other small towns. However, we have chaplains in all of them today. In fact, God had done more than we could "ask or think" in seeking His blessings on His ministry. In 2014, we are in nearly a thousand cities in our nation, plus several foreign cities as well, where we care for workers, with compassion and love.

How do you explain all of this, except using the words "miracle" and "God"? Someone said we are a thirty-year overnight success, and only God could have done all that has been achieved and is still being achieved. Human efforts have not caused the ministry to expand every year since 1984. It was our

Lord who did all of this, and we had the privilege of being there when He did it, achieving outstanding success in sharing God's love through acts of kindness by people called chaplains.

When a news writer asked me if I had planned all of these results, I laughed. I responded truthfully by saying, "No not at all. I am the most surprised person in all of this. The only thing we have done is not to mess up what God is doing, and I pray every day we won't."

Dan Truitt always says the most evident blessing of God on this ministry is the dedicated and qualified people He sends to serve with us. The service we offer is no better than our least qualified chaplain, for it is chaplains who perform our A+ class service.

We have great people who are good and godly chaplains. Our staff average age is approximately fifty-five years, with twenty years of ministry and work experience, along with thirty-five years of knowing Christ as Savior and walking in fellowship with Him as His disciple.

I liked **Don Smith** the first time I met him, an East Texas man who joined our team on January 1, 1990. Don had many years of business experience as an executive with Burlington Industries. For quite some time he led their manufacturing effort in Greensboro, North Carolina. With his strong faith and deep devotion to our Lord, Don provided much-needed leadership to our fast-growing effort. After serving in Dallas, he was later moved back to his native East Texas. Don coordinated the work at Pilgrim's Pride based in Pittsburgh, Texas, the ministry's largest client. He has been good and godly counsel to me, and he still serves God as National Accounts Manager of our largest clients across the nation.

Larry Ramsey was one of the most important hires we ever made. Someone in my church told me about a man who wanted to go into Christian ministry, even though he was a very successful advertising executive. I will never forget the first time Larry came to our office, wearing an expensive suit and Italian loafers. He had a pleasant, outgoing personality, a typical salesman. We had a nice visit, and I was moved by his sense of calling to do God's work. However, as an Army colonel, I was not keen on facial hair. He needed to shave his beard. One year to the day of our first meeting, September 1, 1995, we hired Ramsey as a region vice president. Nearly everyone who has come to work for us has taken a reduction in pay, not all but most. Larry took a pay and bonus cut of one hundred thousand dollars from his job with a New York advertising firm, selling advertising time to television stations, and he was clean-shaven on his first day of work.

His gift was sales, so very soon he was named our first director of marketing for the ministry, and Larry began selling the idea of chaplains to companies all over America. He had a true passion for the Lord's work and a remarkable sense of humor that kept us all laughing during some tough early days in the ministry. But, God needed a top salesman who could make everyone smile, so he called Larry A. Ramsey home to glory on February 2, 2007.

Larry hired **Jason Brown** in 2002 from Wrangler and CRT Computer Company as his first assistant, and today Jason has the title of vice president of marketing. He has been used of God to bring the concept of chaplains to companies in America and all over the world. He graduated from Texas Tech with a business degree, and in his spare time he became a world champion saddle bronc rider on the pro rodeo circuit. Five years later Larry would leave us for a better place with the Lord, and Jason Brown took over leadership of the marketing team.

Maceo Gray, who was born in Dallas, came to join us as a chaplain leader from an engineering firm in Kansas City on October 5, 1995. He was a Dallas Theological Seminary graduate, being the outstanding graduate of his class. He served as a chaplain, as well as a division director in Dallas, before moving back to Kansas City to oversee our work there with Bickford Senior Living Centers throughout the Midwest, along with several other client companies. Maceo still serves as a chaplain with Marketplace.

Today the executive leadership team is stronger under the umbrella of Marketplace Ministries, Inc. We have four subsidiaries: Marketplace Chaplains International, Marketplace Chaplains USA, and Railroad Chaplains, plus the Marketplace Ministries Foundation. Each of these is a major thrust within the ministry and is headed by an effective leader.

The largest responsibility for about 85 percent of the Ministry is **George Cotter**. Since joining Marketplace Ministries in 2002, Cotter has served as a front-line chaplain, the most important position in the ministry, a division director, a region vice president, and now president of Marketplace Chaplains USA. George is a businessman with a theological education, having earned a degree from Dallas Theological Seminary, with a biblical studies with languages degree.

In 2006, when we were searching for a president and chief operating officer for Marketplace Ministries, it was Ann who said, "Have you ever thought about **Dick De Witt**?"

I had known Dick for twenty-seven years at that time, and he was already serving part-time on the Marketplace marketing staff while he was building his new retirement home on a golf course in Florida. He had completed thirty years of running a large fresh-fish business that stretched from Buffalo, New York, all the way to Florida. However, he had recently sold his part of the business and was going to play golf, sail his big boat, and take life easier. A part of that new schedule meant he and his wife, Marvel, would spend much more time with their grandchildren, as well as their daughter and her husband.

When Ann posed her question that evening, I nearly laughed. "How ridiculous; do you think Dick would sell his home in Buffalo, and the new one in Florida, give up sailing, and move all the way down here to Texas; do you think a retired man would do that?"

"Don't you think he would do it, if it was God's will?" Ann calmly replied.

The next month I met Dick and Marvel at Disney World in Orlando, where I was speaking at a client company prayer breakfast. We met over dinner, and I told them we were looking for the new president and COO, and the board of directors and I wanted them to pray about moving to Dallas to accept that position.

They were silent for a long time, and then promised to pray about it.

A few weeks later, they had sold their Buffalo home and sailboat and were seeking a buyer for their Florida dream home, while packing to move to Dallas. Dick began leading our team in the fall of 2006. He was God's man for the job, no question about it.

Dick and I have laughed together, prayed together, and worked together. He is a good and godly man, a superb leader who builds consensus. I like to say he has extended my life and ministry by ten years. It was a big red-letter day on the ministry calendar when Dick De Witt accepted his retirement position with Marketplace Ministries. He has broadened and deepened the ministry in many ways. The ministry is far better, stronger, and larger now than before he came, and he gives God all the credit, glory, and honor.

One thing is certain. God is the best ministry "head hunter" there is, and He found many wonderful people to serve with over the years. Every time we needed new leaders in specific positions, it was the Lord who recruited and brought them to us. It might have seemed it happened just by chance. But, hiring good people was divine providence.

8

CARING FOR TODAY'S EMPLOYEES IN AMERICA AND AROUND THE WORLD

America has expanded its population and built its superstructure on immigration, with people coming to "the land of the free and home of the brave" from all over the world. We have literally hundreds of subcultures made up of people who have come to this country with a desire to fulfill the American dream. They have brought their experience, education, language, social practices, culture, and religion to their new home. Those practicing scores of different religions come here to freely exercise their faith. Their religious choices are protected, just as are the faiths of Christians or Jews. These new legal Americans, and eleven million illegal immigrants, may eat differently, think differently, speak differently, rear children differently, and worship differently, and yet they are in America's work force.

As we moved from the infant days of this ministry in the 1980s into the early to mid-1990s, it was becoming increasingly obvious that the growing cultural diversity in the United States was being manifested in workplaces throughout the country, including most of companies we were serving as chaplains.

The questions that faced us as we were completing our first decade of ministry were, Could we continue doing what we were accomplishing as evangelical Christians in the workplace? Could we be authentically Christian and yet, at the same time through acts of kindness, show God's love for people of many cultures and of all faiths—or none?

How do you serve such a vast array of people from all over the world? How do you show God's love through acts of kindness and do it without "religious harassment"? How do you build relationships with people who are different from you in so many ways?

Over the past decades of doing just that, we have discovered that while people look and sound different, they're really the same on the inside, in their hearts, spirits, emotions, and minds. We have found the average persons in the workplace do not really care which faith is represented; they just want to know I am sincere, genuine, and real. Will I help them?

Chaplains have had some of their best and closest relationships with people from distant countries. One chaplain even helped lead a funeral with a Buddhist priest. I would almost bet money that was the first time in my city, and maybe my entire state, that a Buddhist and a Baptist performed a funeral together.

People all over the world are searching for happiness, trying to get their basic needs met on a daily basis. They want the warmth of a relationship with family and friends, as well as a purpose for life.

Because our chaplains are committed to associate with all employees in the businesses they serve, it is easy to care for them, reach out to them, uplift and love them. These employees respond in positive ways, and many of their lives are changed for all eternity by entering into a relationship with Jesus Christ.

We are seeing daily confirmation that a culturally diverse Chaplain Care Team can really help a culturally diverse workforce. Early on we had African-American, Hispanic, and Caucasian chaplains interfacing with those same ethnicities. Today we have developed the ability to reach seven language groups, including Vietnamese and Bosnian. Of course, both men and women would serve the workforce of our contracted clients.

Cultural diversity was not the only change affecting America and its workforce. No one would debate the fact that our society has experienced other drastic changes in the last fifty to seventy-five years. Nothing and no one escapes change over time. Much of the change is evident in moral and ethical collapse, with out-of-wedlock births at high levels, fewer fathers in the home, couples living together without being married, the greed of insider trading, the rise in sexually transmitted diseases, with AIDS and HIV threatening the world.

The question facing us as a young but rapidly growing ministry was, Can we be "all things to all men," as the apostle Paul inspired us to be (1 Corinthians 9:19-23), and minister effectively to a workforce that is both culturally and morally diverse? I knew we were not out there in the work arena to judge people's character, evaluate their lifestyle, or condemn their activities. We were not there to proselytize or preach; however, we are chaplains, and that has everything to do with caring for people and, at their initiative, sharing biblical truths that change eternal destinies.

The answer to this question, from every day of our history, is a resounding YES! When we enter partnerships of employee care with business leaders who make their employees their highest priority, the results are nothing less than amazing. Let me explain.

I have come to realize there are two lines in any business, both vitally important, but one more important than the other. The first line that all successful businesses are concerned about is the bottom line. This line has to do with profit, money, and dividends for stockholders. It is all about finances. You realize if you do not have black numbers at the bottom of your financial statement, that business will not remain operational for long. That is true because every company has to pay salaries and bills and purchase supplies to be made into products. It is called overhead, and overhead must never be larger than income.

The bottom line is vital; it is the life blood of any company. However, I am confident there is another line even more important than the bottom line.

The top line is the first line of any successful and lasting economic enterprise. What is the top line? The employee, the associate, the partner, or the worker is the top line. These people are truly the most important aspect of business, any business.

Some businesses have come to realize the truth of that statement. These company leaders certainly include the hundreds of companies served by Marketplace Chaplains USA or Marketplace Chaplains International. These corporations, and many others, have come to the conclusion that if the company takes care of the top line, all of those who work together in seeking to achieve the mission of the company, performing their job with excellence, then they will take care of the bottom line. You take care of people; they will take care of profit.

Now, allow me to attempt to explain the approach of Marketplace chaplains in our partnership with these business leaders in caring for their top line. This approach is the same, both in the United States and in other countries, as well as the Commonwealth of Puerto Rico.

Our approach is called an Employee Care Service (ECS). Marketplace Ministries is thought to be the first and largest service to business employees of its kind in both this country and others. I never claim to be the founder of this service, because I believe the Founder was Almighty God, and by divine providence I was the first employee. I never dreamed of this job, nor did I ask for it. I laugh and admit the good Lord was pretty hard up to assign me to this marketplace task, to see a marketplace miracle.

Let me state three concepts that clarify the emphasis of Marketplace Ministries' Employee Care Service.

First, this ECS provided by chaplains is personalized. That means chaplains visit the worksite every week, sometimes every day of the week. They seek to know every employee on a personal, first-name basis. From the beginning of this service with a new client company, the purpose of workplace visits is to build a relationship with workers, a trust level, and a genuine and deep friendship. When you have a true friend, a friend of confidence, you will turn to that person for help and support when you have a problem.

It is the chaplain who comes by to drink coffee with you, asks about your family, your life, and how he or she can help. Every week across America and in foreign ports of call, our chaplains will make more than three thousand worksite visits and have contact with tens of thousands of workers.

Worksite visits are one of the two major bookends of the twenty-one services chaplains offer. The second is 24/7/365 availability. Anytime, all the time, your chaplain is ready to help.

Third, a chaplain's ECS is proactive. Chaplains do not merely react to problem issues; in fact, they are present and involved before the problem happens and grows beyond control. Whenever a negative or crisis situation begins, chaplains are already onsite and ready to help.

If an individual senses there is something going wrong in his or her marriage, something it seems their spouse is struggling with, they can visit with the company chaplain. Either partner in the marriage can get help before the divorce papers are delivered. If chaplains can intervene early on, before the death of a relationship, a marriage might be saved.

When problems start, chaplains are with people at work to help them navigate the rough waters of a crisis, usually accompanied by loss and sorrow. Not only do chaplains get involved personally with workers and their families, but also they serve as coordinator for referral services for the client company. Chaplains help people get the primary help they need, whatever it is, and wherever it is.

You probably have already presumed this: the Marketplace Ministries ECS uses a Bible-based strategy. We do not bill ourselves as psychotherapists, psychologists, psychiatrists, or counselors; we are chaplains who provide compassionate and loving pastoral care for the human spirit. We are first a humanitarian service provider that every person needs at some point in his or her life. As chaplains, we care for the spiritual dimension of individuals who want it. Every individual is composed of mind, body, and spirit. Chaplains are in the practice of encouraging and enhancing the human spirit of all employees.

Because the marketplace model of chaplaincy is designed after the military model, many of the duties and responsibilities follow the military pattern. Everything from standards of conduct, which must be lived up to by all chaplains, to giving equal care and concern for all people, regardless of whether they have a formal faith or not, regardless of lifestyle, regardless of conduct or character. Everyone gets equal, loving support from the chaplain.

Twenty-four hours a day, seven days a week, 365 days a year, any time and all the time, a chaplain's duty is to help others if they need it and if they request it. A chaplain, whether military or civilian, responds to a person in need whether it's 3 p.m. or 3 a.m. If a company has a chaplain service, never again will an employee have to go it alone, if he or she does not want to.

Marketplace Ministries is a faith-based strategic initiative, providing an Employee Care Service to contracted client companies by assigning chaplains to those companies. Is the service strictly religious in nature? The answer is no. Then what is it? It is a humanitarian approach with a traditional Christian foundation.

The staff is composed of chaplains, and all are people of sincere Christian faith. Each one has a personal commitment to Jesus Christ, and we do not feel we need to apologize for that fact. However, as chaplains in the workplace, we do not push religion. That is not the agenda. The only time a chaplain will discuss spiritual and faith issues is at the initiative of the employee, when the worker asks for information or requests to discuss a religious question or subject. That is the rule of engagement.

Let me tell you some other things chaplains will NOT do. Chaplains will not turn a business into a church. They do not come into a company carrying Bibles, large or small, wearing religious garb, singing religious songs, preaching, or proselytizing, seeking to change beliefs or church affiliation. No, chaplains are experienced in how to live and be genuine examples of faith at work, yet without religiously harassing or offending anyone.

Chaplains do not spy on anyone's lifestyle, condemning people or divulging private information to others. These caring individuals will not become company detectives to search out who is stealing from the company and report to management.

Chaplains are not there to evaluate workers, whether good or bad, and report on them. Confidential information is kept between the chaplain and the worker. Exceptions to that general practice include if the employee breaks a felony law such as abusing a child, threatening to incur injury or death to a fellow employee or anyone else, or causing major damage to the company's wellbeing (e.g., smoking pot while driving a company vehicle).

Chaplains will not represent employees to management or management to employees. Their role is not to be an arbitrator. A report in *Bloomberg Businessweek*, "The Rise of the Corporate Chaplain" by Mark Oppenheimer (August 23, 2012), describes the services of Marketplace Ministries: "We raise an umbrella of compassion over both labor and management." The presence and helping spirit of chaplains can ultimately create a safer, happier, and better workplace. Hundreds of company owners would make that their own evaluation, too.

Now that you understand what chaplains will not do in the workplace, it is time to share many of the service practices they will often accomplish. Chaplains are available to employees at work, home, at times of leisure, or anywhere and anytime they are needed.

Caring and servant-minded company leaders are most often unique. Not every company would consider adding an Employee Care Service like ours; however, many open their business doors and caring hearts to bring chaplains aboard. These types of successful companies value their employees, help them, encourage them, and express appreciation for them and their families. Chaplains bring a human dimension that sustains people at work.

Workers who choose to involve a company chaplain do so voluntarily. No one has to meet with a chaplain, and no worker would ever be ordered to see a chaplain. Companies provide health insurance but do not require employees to go to the doctor. It is up to you to decide. It is the same with chaplains; no one requires you to talk to a chaplain.

It is a fact that approximately 70 percent of the nation's workforce does not have a formal relationship with a priest, rabbi, or clergyman to help them in times of need. That is a huge number of people who do not have a faith figure to support them in this life.

These non-attached people are generally not atheists, agnostics, or skeptics, and they are not mad at God. They are good people who are married, have children, and work hard. Typically, Sunday is a day of rest and leisure without any consideration for church worship or organized religion. Yet, these same people experience problems with no one to turn to unless the company has a chaplain.

When they become ill, they need someone to visit them in the hospital, and pray for them if they desire; when they die, the family needs to bury them. Some ask the company chaplain to officiate at a funeral or a wedding, while others need someone to visit a prisoner or rejoice with over a new baby; some even want the little one dedicated to God. All of these, plus many more, are things chaplains do, and employees turn to chaplains because there is no one else. The chaplain is their friend who cares about them. Our records show that up to 75 percent of company employees or their family members will turn to the company chaplain in any twelve-month period of service.

We have two groups of chaplains in Marketplace Ministries, Marketplace Chaplains USA and Marketplace Chaplains International. We have employed chaplains and a second group called the resource staff. Nearly three thousand men and women compose our employed chaplains, while an additional two hundred to three hundred fit in the resource staff category.

Our employed personnel are individuals who have met all of the chaplain requirements for Marketplace Ministries to serve as paid, front-line chaplains serving employees of client companies. Our chaplains have signed our statement of faith and understand and comply with our standards of conduct, as well as other obligations and requirements. These individuals are employees of Marketplace Ministries, and we pay their salaries and withhold IRS taxes like any other company.

The resource staff is composed of representatives of other religious or faith groups who, because of their religious beliefs, could not qualify to be hired as an employee of the ministry; however, they are called upon for "resource assignments to assist a family of their religion or faith group." Jews, Buddhists, Muslims, Baha'i, and others could be in this category.

Occasionally, for example, an employee dies and the family asks the company chaplain to secure the assistance of a representative of that family's faith. In this way, funerals of employees who belong to one of another religious group could be served by a representative of that person's faith.

Mr. Lee was an employee of a client company in Fort Worth. This elderly man, who worked for a large printing company, had suffered with cancer for quite some time. His company chaplain had been a source of encouragement to Mr. Lee and his family. When Mr. Lee died, his wife asked the chaplain if he could get a Buddhist priest to help with the funeral, as the Lees were Vietnamese Buddhists.

Of course, the chaplain quickly agreed to help. At that moment, we didn't know if we would have to fly in a Buddhist priest from Los Angeles or elsewhere. However, a priest was secured from the Dallas Buddhist Temple in northeast Dallas.

There was another twist in this funeral event. Mrs. Lee told the chaplain her husband always liked him and spoke often of the kind and caring spirit the chaplain showed as he made his rounds at the company. Then she asked him to participate in the funeral service, where he was able to share Christian truth with those who attended.

In another case, a seventeen-year-old Muslim youth committed suicide. Within hours of the tragedy, the chaplain was at his family's home. Soon, the chaplain and the grieving father were sharing in the sorrow that was in both of their hearts.

When God gave me the idea for chaplains in the marketplace, I knew there was a vital need in the lives of those 70 percent of workers who had no practical faith, no church relationship. However, I have to admit I was naïve about the other 30 percent of the working population who did go to church and who did have a pastor or priest. Could we help them without taking the place of their minister? That was not a part of our mission, for we are sincere supporters of the local church and the relationship between members and their ministers.

We discovered that church people did not ask us to marry their young adult children, baptize babies, or perform family funerals. We were not normally involved with family in these times of joy and sorrow. No, their minister was there with them, and that is the way it should be.

However, we did make another discovery. If a Christian churchman or woman had a moral collapse, sometimes the last person they would turn to for help was their own minister, someone they had to face at worship on Sunday. If a man is in an extramarital affair, the pain of confessing that to anyone was horrible, and many cannot do it. A wife who is hiding an alcohol problem often will not go to her pastor for help. There are many other problems that never get to the minister at the church. He is willing to help; however, sometimes he does not get the opportunity until it is too late.

What we have discovered in our three decades of workplace ministry is that church people who have personal problems, situations that are embarrassing and emotional, many times do not go to their minister. However, they do turn to the company chaplain for help and support. It happens every day.

Pastoral care statistics accomplished in this ministry since 1984 are staggering, almost beyond comprehension. These are some of these approximate numbers we have tracked: 100,000 hospital visits; 2,500 prison and jail visits; 10,000 funerals; 8 million confidential pastoral discussions, both formal and informal; 3,000 weddings; upward to 128,000 professions of faith; 250,000 people joining or rejoining a local church; more than 2 million worksite visits by chaplains around the world. All of this, plus much more, was accomplished in 3,735,000 service hours for employees and families in our client companies.

Chaplains are almost always members of their client company's Death and Critical Incident Notification Team. If someone is killed in an accident or dies on the job of natural causes, chaplains are part of the loving team of company leaders who take the sad news to loved ones. The chaplains usually lead the way in making this difficult notification.

A company that loves is a company that cares. Love is translated C-A-R-E! Care is shown in helpful, practical ways that lift people up to higher ground.

Chaplains assist management and employees in dealing with workplace sexual harassment, in support of company policy guidelines. Post-termination care and support in looking for another job for laid-off or terminated workers is a key ingredient of chaplain service. The desired result is a smooth transition to another work environment. Also, it possibly prevents potential retaliation, including workplace homicide, thought to be the fastest growing form of murder in America today. Company management and employees are often targets of a fellow employee's hate and anger. Chaplains also draft letters of concern, sympathy, appreciation, and congratulations for the CEO and/or president that go to employees or family members.

They write articles of interest for company publications, as requested by management. When asked, chaplains advise the company on matters of religion, morals, ethics, and morale. In this way we can hold up an ethical mirror to both labor and management. These special servant leaders are available to speak for in-house or outside events when an inspirational speaker is desired by management. They provide personal improvement books, pamphlets, booklets, tracts, and DVDs to employees and family members to teach principles for successful and joyful living. These are distributed at no additional expense to the company or any expense to employees or families.

Chaplains can also represent the company to their clients, customers, and suppliers where it would be appropriate (e.g., death, serious illness, accidents, and funerals).

Our Employee Care Service is committed to genuine accountability for quality service to employees and their families, as well as to company leaders and owners. To support this commitment, Marketplace chaplains provides regular service reports to all client company leaders. These detailed reports, without names or any specific identification of employees or family members, give a comprehensive picture of what has transpired since the last report. These reports help quantify the services of Marketplace chaplains to employees and their families. Company leaders then can judge whether chaplains represent a wise expenditure that produces lasting, positive results.

This service helps make a safer and more pleasant work environment. When someone is available 24/7/365 to help workers deal with problems, both at work and at home, stress is greatly reduced. The spirit of concern lowers conflicts between employees as well as between labor and management.

This service, when implemented for three or more years, often positively changes the company culture and helps create an atmosphere that values people and sincerely cares for workers and their families. Chaplains help relieve managers from spending an average of nine weeks per year in resolving personality clashes between employees. Managers are left with more time to do their primary jobs of fulfilling the mission of the company, directly affecting the bottom line.

Morale has improved in every company that has hired this ECS, using chaplains as front-line care providers. Positive attitudes are evident in workers when chaplains are walking among them. Personnel tend to stay on the job longer, lowering turnover rates, when a caring spirit is exemplified by company leaders. Many companies have seen absenteeism and turnover rates drastically decline after implementing the ECS for one year or longer. Often, productivity increases when personal problems of employees are dealt with by an outside third party. For example, it has been shown that productivity can decrease 40 percent when a person experiences a divorce; however, some of that drop in production can be negated by proper and ongoing confidential pastoral care.

Having a strong and influential chaplain service helps undergird a more ethical tone for doing business. Helping individual employees make wise and ethical decisions positively affects the quality of service to customers, as well as the employees' personal lives.

Helping employees become connected people is one of the chaplain's most enjoyable challenges. It involves helping workers find a place of belonging, a place where they can experience friendship and be a part of community, inside and outside the workplace. America, as well as other nations, is full of disconnected people of all ages desperate to make connections with friends and others in a family atmosphere. Chaplains work hard in this effort of creating family at work.

Chaplains also provide care for the soul of each worker or family member. This is done without being overly religious and with no religious harassment. The search for spirituality is one of the deepest issues in most humanity today. Many people are simply empty at the core.

"Soul care" means paying attention to what is happening in people's lives, where they really live. This ECS provided by chaplains offers soul care and spiritual meaning in the most secular of businesses, without being offensive, problematic, or overly religious.

All of us at some time have experienced the title of a *Newsweek* cover story "Work Is Hell" (September 1996). Many people say that is true for their workplace today. But does work really have to be a hellish experience? Can't work be something meaningful and satisfying? There are many who say it can be and is. If you are going to spend 60 percent of your waking hours doing something related to your work and profession, then surely your workplace should be a friendly, kind, pleasant, safe place.

That is what the Marketplace Employee Care Service is all about. We help make the workplace enjoyable, a significant place in your life. Our chaplains stand in the corner of laborers and managers. When life knocks them down, bloodies them, hurts them, and brings them pain, chaplains are there to pick them up, bandage them, and get them back on the road of life again, living at their best, and happy doing it. Everyone is injured physically, emotionally, or spiritually at some point; they need support when they are.

Here in Texas, we say chaplains are a whole lot like a pickup truck. They have much in common. You might not think you want a pickup truck; however, there will come a time when you need one. You might not think you want a chaplain in your life, but there will come a time when you need one. It could be today, or it might be tomorrow. However, you will need a chaplain one day; we all will. That much is certain.

9

ARLINGTON NATIONAL CEMETERY

A Prelude at America's Most Sacred Soil

With Marketplace Ministries in its fifth year of service, I was still serving as a chaplain with the Army Reserve Chaplains' Corps. Marketplace Ministries was expanding into new cities and building a dedicated staff, spreading further across Texas and creeping into other states as well.

As a senior chaplain colonel, I was serving with the 807th Medical Brigade, headquartered in Seagoville, Texas, known for being the home of a federal prison. I was the brigade chaplain, working alongside two other chaplains and chaplain assistants.

On occasion, the brigade would break up into various sections and fulfill its summer training in different posts. For my summer training in 1989, and again in 1991, I was asked to backfill the senior Army chaplain's position at Fort Myer, Virginia. This post claimed to house more Army generals than any post in the military.

For seventeen days while the regular chaplain was on leave, I served as the Protestant chaplain at Fort Myer Chapel. Additionally, I was the senior Army chaplain at Arlington National Cemetery in Virginia, adjacent to Fort Myer, where some fifteen Army funerals are conducted each day. I performed an average of four funerals per day, Monday through Friday.

My Army assignment at Arlington National Cemetery was the most meaningful and moving experience I had during my thirty-seven years as a military officer serving my country in the Air Force and Army. I will never forget those incredible days of ministry.

During my lifetime, I have known nearly three dozen wars, conflicts, and police actions on our land and foreign lands as well. Each took the lives of

America's finest citizens. These men and women loved their country and were patriots who gave their blood for our freedoms.

I have seen the price of military devotion, from an NCO in our Army hospital in Frankfurt, Germany, dying from injuries sustained during Desert Storm, to telling a military mom her one-year-old baby just died from Sudden Infant Death Syndrome (SIDS). World War II, Korea, Vietnam, Kosovo, Panama, Kuwait, Afghanistan, Iraq, on and on goes the list of military conflicts of our country over the past seven and a half decades. They taught me freedom is never free. It is paid for with the high cost of blood and death.

A hushed and holy atmosphere surrounds the white crosses and Stars of David that mark the landscape as far as you can see at Arlington National Cemetery. They are precise, in perfect alignment, with the grass manicured to perfection.

It was on these sacred grounds that I performed nearly one hundred funerals in the approximately twenty-five weekdays I walked those hills and valleys.

"Let us here highly resolve that these honored dead shall not have died in vain," said President Abraham Lincoln, closing his Gettysburg Address on November 19, 1863, at the dedication of the national cemetery on the Civil War battleground at Gettysburg, Pennsylvania.

In 1920, his sentiment was reaffirmed when his words were permanently engraved in the new Memorial Amphitheatre at Arlington National Cemetery. President Lincoln's words remind all who visit that for more than two hundred years, more than 1.4 million American men and women have given their lives in defense of this great nation, and their contributions to our liberty must never be forgotten.

Arlington National Cemetery is more than just a military burial ground; it is our most important sacred national shrine.

Most visitors do not know the cemetery was born out of tragic necessity. During the Civil War, thousands of soldiers and civilians died in the unrelenting battles in and around Washington, D.C., and across the North and South. As a grim testament to the human cost of that war, there was a shortage of appropriate space in which to bury the dead. It was in the afternoon of a June day in 1864 that US Secretary of War, Edwin N. Stanton, signed a document that designated Confederate General Robert E. Lee's wife's estate of 250 acres as a military burial ground.

Forty-seven Union soldiers were buried in the back yard of the Lee mansion, with the assurance that General Lee would never live there again. Years before the war, Lee had been a cadet at West Point, along with nearly two hundred other officer candidates and military professors who would choose to fight for their homeland in the south with Confederate forces, in what many called the War of Northern Aggression. You may hear that description even today, especially in the South.

Now more than 400,000 people are buried in Arlington's more than six hundred acres. Nearly 4,000 more are added every year.

A large portion of the hilly grounds and paths is shaded by huge oak, poplar, pecan, cherry, and maple trees, some standing at attention one hundred feet tall. In these grounds high above the Potomac lie the remains of presidents and privates, officers and enlisted soldiers, Supreme Court justices and unnamed slaves, each one with a story. There is the most decorated Army infantry soldier of World War II, Audie Murphy, a Texan and Medal of Honor winner. You will also find world heavyweight boxing champ Joe Lewis, and of course President John F. Kennedy, a World War II veteran.

I had the high honor of burying members of the military and civilian family members, from a nineteen-year-old private first class who was killed in a training accident at Fort Hood, Texas, to a highly decorated major general.

Because I was assigned at Arlington for such a brief number of days on two different occasions, I was able to prepare personal information about the deceased for every funeral I officiated. I usually had three or four days of lead time before a funeral, and I worked many nights calling family members of the deceased to learn their life story. The more I knew about the individual, the better.

One of my most appreciated compliments while serving at Arlington came after Louise's funeral. I had escorted the family to the curb closest to the burial site and stood at attention with a salute when the family got in their cars and departed.

After the family drove away, I turned around and discovered a little lady standing behind me. She said, "Chaplain, Louise must have been your dearest friend, for you knew her so well."

I did not say it then, but I had never met the dear lady I buried that morning, except through the love and lives of those who did know her as mother, sister, cousin, aunt, and friend. Everyone is special, and everyone has a life story. It was my obligation and opportunity to tell part of each of their life stories.

The changing of the guard at The Tomb of the Unknown Soldier is the most moving event you could ever hope to see, and to observe it is never to forget it.

The Tomb of the Unknown Soldier, also known as the Tombs of the Unknowns, represents every major war in American history, except the American Revolution. The first Unknown who did not come home from war was placed in Arlington on November 11, 1921, after the First World War. More than sixteen hundred American doughboys were buried in France, where they died, with one of them being selected in the most secret of procedures as the soldier to represent all US military personnel who died in that war and who were unidentifiable.

Soldiers from World War II and the Korean War were buried in Arlington on Memorial Day in 1958, with President Dwight D. Eisenhower, the former general, leading the ceremony.

The Vietnam Unknowns were secretly selected from those who died in the 1960s or 1970s. On the west side of the monument are these words: "Here rests in honored glory an American soldier known but to God."

The tomb is guarded by members of the crack 3rd US Infantry Regiment, part of the oldest continuous infantry division in the Army. Known as The Old Guard, the Presidents' Own, this elite troop unit is the Army Honor Guard and escort of the president. Its soldiers participate in upwards of thirty-five hundred ceremonies annually at the White House, the Pentagon, and many other national memorials. They are headquartered at Fort Myer Army installation, adjacent to the cemetery. They also participate in Army military funeral rites, as well as being a part of state funerals. These special individuals have been involved in every president's funeral since 1948, and you always remember the riderless black horse with military boots turned backward, to indicate the death of the rider.

It is my wish to be buried at Arlington, and I have already received qualified approval for my burial there. My wife, Ann, says with a smile that she will probably have to go there first and save me a place. She has always saved me a place at many events, over the years of our marriage.

At every military funeral, in recognition of the sacrifices the individual has given for his country, "Taps" is played.

Let me describe for you one of the last funerals I performed at Arlington in the summer of 1991, shortly after I was called to active duty as a part of Operation Desert Storm. This is a funeral I will never forget, thanks to a young boy who touched my heart and moved my soul.

The solemn, muffled drums were beating clearly above the cadence of the troops' marching feet and the clip-clop of the horses pulling the black-draped caisson and its flag-covered coffin. We wound our way through the most hallowed soil of our nation, directly across from the Washington Monument.

The trees, reaching for the blue sky, occasionally cast a welcome shadow across the route to the burial site, giving some relief from the humidity and 100-degree temperature.

This full honors military funeral for a chief warrant officer and former senior helicopter test pilot was my fifteenth ceremony honoring the dead that week. Each funeral is different, yet the same, for each one is a pocket of sorrow in the heart of our nation's capital.

"How do you think I look, Chaplain Stricklin?" the fourteen-year-old boy asked as we marched military style in the funeral procession.

"Why, you look sharper than any young man I've ever seen. You look just great," I replied, trying to keep in step with the drumbeat.

He was dressed in a solid white suit and dark brown shoes shined to a high gloss. Those shoes would have met the standards of Army basic training. His wide tie of gold and brown on beige had a stick pin in it, up high and centered perfectly.

"Well, this suit I'm wearing," responded the boy, "is the suit my daddy wore when he married my mother nearly twenty years ago. And this is his stick pin. I thought he'd be pleased if I wore them today."

Tears again came to my eyes as I glanced over my left shoulder to see the flag-covered casket which held his father's body.

"I'm sure he'd be pleased. He'd be proud of the way you look today, with your shoes shined and all. Yes sir, I'm certain he would tell you how nice you look, too," is all I could say. The words came hard, sticking in my dry throat.

The boy looked so young to be without a father, a father who encouraged him in church attendance, scouting, school, and family outings. Then, I thought about my own two sons.

We rounded another bend in the road, down the hill, crossed Roosevelt Drive, and turned right onto Eisenhower Drive, as the Army band, "Pershing's Own," began playing "The Battle Hymn of the Republic."

For a moment my mind wandered into history, and I could hear the sounds of battle with shells bursting and shouts of war. I could see the Union blue and Confederate gray with flags flying. It was the song, I guess, that took me back.

The music stopped, but the drumbeat continued as the procession moved on to the burial site. As we came to a halt, I took my place to the side where the shined and polished soldiers carefully and meticulously removed the coffin. The son of the man we were burying turned with me as we led the troops to the freshly dug grave. Then the young lad took his place beside his mother and sat down. Other family members and friends closed ranks around the few chairs with green covers.

I spoke carefully the final words and led in a prayer. My portion of the interment was quickly concluded, but the military part of the ceremony continued. I slowly raised my white-gloved hand to the edge of my dress blue hat as the gunshots echoed across the valley to the east. Then, the trumpeter blew "Taps."

In perfect precision, each of the eight Old Guard soldiers performed his duty as streams of perspiration rolled down their faces like silent rivers. All their movements were smooth, lending themselves to military dignity, as they folded the flag that covered the coffin. The officer in charge, a captain whose handsome looks made him fit for a recruiting poster, presented me the flag and saluted.

I turned to the tearful widow, slowly bending down to place the perfectly folded flag, in the form of a triangle, into her outstretched hands. I softly spoke sincere words on behalf of the president of the United States, expressing the appreciation of a grateful nation for the dedicated and faithful service of her dear husband. I rose up, stepped back, and saluted.

A kind Arlington Lady, on special assignment from the Army's Chief of Staff, followed me to speak words of sympathy to the family. Her words were brief, and she left the family a beautifully inscribed card containing details of the service.

I hugged the young son, and he hugged me back. I couldn't say anything, but I hoped this communicated my deep feelings of love and sympathy in the loss of his father. I saluted one last time as the car carrying the widow and young son slowly pulled away from the curb and drove out of sight.

The Army driver was waiting to return me for the sixteenth funeral, my final one for Friday afternoon. I thought much about the preceding week of activities as we drove to meet the family.

What an honor it was to have met some of our nation's finest families, to stand with them in their time of sorrow, to give hope and encouragement, and to be a representative of the president, the US Army, and our grateful nation.

There was more sorrow than joy during my weeks serving at Arlington. The Word of God reminds us to "weep with those who weep," but I can imagine after a few weeks or months of funeral duty at Arlington, tears would run out, although the compassion of your heart would not. Even though the chaplains participate in more than three hundred funerals a month at Arlington, they guard carefully the reality there are no cookie-cutter funeral services. They seek diligently and prayerfully to insure the family of the loved one will experience comfort, hope, and spiritual renewal, and that each individual service reflects grandeur, beauty, and dignity, providing fond memories forever at Arlington, America's sacred soil.

As I spoke at the funeral of the wife of a World War I veteran buried at Arlington Cemetery in 1952, I was touched by her sense of humor. Her daughter shared with me that her mother had written her own obituary because she "wanted to make sure it was correct." As I recounted this to those attending the funeral, there was a chorus of laughter. In my hand, I held her obituary from a Florida newspaper which began by stating she was active in a Presbyterian church, because to her that was the most important part of her life.

The most military family I ministered to included several sons and sons-in-law who were Army or Navy full colonels, as well as an Air Force general. This family had roots in the military back to a great-grandfather who was a former Army Chief of Staff. I felt comfortable with them, because I had served in both the Air Force and Army, plus being attached to the Navy for duty in Antarctica decades earlier.

There were other families, and each one made an imperishable imprint on my life: the mother of a twenty-one-year-old private killed in a car wreck; the wife and two daughters of a thirty-two-year-old chief warrant officer who died jogging; the first sergeant whose forty-one-year-old wife died in his arms after suffering a myocardial infarction; the family of a saintly ninety-three-year-old lady who came home to Arlington where her second lieutenant husband had been buried in 1944, and another lady who, two days before she buried her husband, had learned of her own diagnosis of terminal pancreatic cancer, the same disease that claimed her spouse.

But the one person I'll always remember is the sweet, elderly woman who, when I presented her the flag, said, "Oh, Chaplain, I love the Army."

Because, you see, I love the Army, too!

My love recalls the experiences I had in the Army as a chaplain, where God began to birth Marketplace Ministries. It is unusual the way divine providence brings to pass events and experiences that mold your life to be what God has planned for you. At the same time, one life can touch hundreds of thousands of other lives who need support, help, compassion, provision, care. God wants us all to have eternal fellowship with Him in heaven. No man has done anything or been anything to lessen his value in the sight of this loving and forgiving Father.

The reflections of Arlington will remain with me the rest of my life. Those thirty-four days of legacy touched my heart and soul, helping prepare me for what God was doing in another Army, the workforce of the world. That army needs chaplains, too.

10

IRON SHARPENING IRON

Godly Men as My Mentors

Over the last forty years as a chaplain in the US Army and civilian marketplace, and serving fifteen years in the US Air Force, I have had some good and godly men who have mentored, inspired, motivated, and discipled me to be all God wanted me to be. These men are a combination of father figures, brother figures, and co-laborers who make up spiritual friends, my spiritual heroes. They have been the "human fertilizer" for the growth of Marketplace Ministries.

I am not saying these are the only people who have influenced me for God and His work, or the only ones who have helped me grow in grace. However, I am saying these men have greatly influenced, inspired, helped, and blessed me as I went about the King's ministry.

These are meaningful mentors who are on the top of my long list, yet who stand with many others: Reverend W. Glyn Evans of Hingham, Massachusetts; Dr. Tom Brandon of Sherman, Texas; Reverend Canon Ralph McCune of Dallas, Texas; Dr. Neil Ashcraft of Dallas, Texas; Dr. H. D. McCarty of Fayetteville, Arkansas; and Jim McManus of Grover Beach, California. They covered me with prayer and friendship, being an encouragement when things were difficult and times were hard.

When I needed special prayers by special men, I contacted my mentors, my six iron sharpeners, with a desire for their prayers before the throne of God. I have known, no matter how busy they were, as soon as they heard my request, they would drop what they were doing and pray. As these were all righteous men, I was assured their prayers would avail much. I have seen it happen many times over the years, and I am grateful for this special band of brothers I have had in the faith, even though some are now in heaven.

W. Glyn Evans

In the late 1980s, early one morning long before the sun came up over Dallas, I was in the Marketplace Ministries' prayer room. As I was having my morning devotions, meeting with the Lord God, I picked up a small paperback devotional book someone had given me. *Daily with the King* was the title, and I read the brief devotional for that morning.

It was powerful and moving, touching my heart as well as my mind, and I was blessed. I looked at the cover and noted the name Glyn Evans. Reading that book became a regular practice each morning. *Daily with the King* quickly was a close companion as I met with the King each day. The devotionals in the book were such a blessing, and one day I thought, *I wonder who this Glyn Evans is? What kind of man is he who can write such meaningful messages that move hearts closer to God?* I continued to think, *I wonder where he lives and what he does?*

On a morning in the spring of that year, I said to myself, "Today, I am going to call Glyn Evans." However, with the day's activities and many work responsibilities, I forgot about my early morning words of promise as I went about my tasks.

As I was leaving the office late that evening, I paused, as I always do, to thank God for the day, and asked Him if it is His will and not mine that He will allow me to come back just one more day to serve Him, seeking to witness in His name.

After saying a silent "Amen," I started for the door when I sensed the voice of God: "You didn't call Glyn Evans." I was stopped in my tracks and quickly thought of all the reasons why I could not make that telephone call. I didn't even have a number to call or know exactly where he lived. I took another step toward the door, and again the voice in my mind and heart, "You didn't call Glyn Evans."

So I wheeled around and walked into the prayer room nearby and picked up the phone. I recalled seeing on the book cover that Reverend Evans was the pastor of the South Shore Baptist Church in Hingham, Massachusetts, so I started with that area code looking for a Glyn Evans. Sure enough, the operator gave me a number and I called it.

"Hello," a warm voice answered.

"Sir," I said rather reluctantly, "I am calling a Glyn Evans who wrote the book *Daily with the King*. Do I have author of that book?"

"Yes, you do," said the stranger, yet friend on the other end of the line. I began to tell him how much his book had blessed, helped, and inspired my spiritual life.

That phone call began a close Christian friendship that lasted twenty-seven years, and was the first of hundreds of telephone calls to Brother Glyn over the years. In fact, we fellowshipped and prayed almost every Monday morning during those years.

Glyn and his wife, Henrietta, lived in Hingham, Massachusetts, and were married for sixty-nine years before his death in 2012. They have two sons and a daughter, with two of them nearby. He grew up in Wales, UK, and came to the United States to attend college. Glyn would have celebrated his ninety-fifth birthday on May 5, 2013. For years, he served the Lord through prayer for kingdom work and mentoring "younger" men like me. He was a pastor for more than thirty years and served as a minister at large for the Conservative Baptist Association of New England for many more. He was a faithful warrior in the army of the Lord for more than seven decades.

He wrote *Daily with the King* for Moody Press many years ago now, with a hundred thousand copies in print. What began as a personal journal of God's insight to him from Scripture has become one of the most inspiring devotional books Moody has ever produced. It has been translated into many foreign languages.

Glyn Evans had another claim to fame; he was a fellow student with William Franklin Graham (known to the world as evangelist Billy Graham) at Wheaton College. Those fellow students remained friends until Glyn's death. From my evaluation of knowing both these men well for many years, it is evident they had an abundance of similar character traits and a dynamic faith approach to life and living it.

Glyn and Henrietta were some of Marketplace Ministries' strongest and most enthusiastic supporters. He called the chaplains' service to care for workers and their family members "the remarkable work of God."

My sweet friend and prayer partner since 1987 is home now in heaven. The thing I will miss most is hearing him say, "Now let me pray for you and the ministry," followed by a bold, powerful, and God-honoring prayer I knew was in the process of being answered as soon as he said, "Amen."

Dr. Tom Brandon

Dr. Tom Brandon served as senior pastor of First Baptist Church of Sherman, Texas, for nearly three decades. He and his wife, Dolly, have partnered together in God's work for well more than half a century.

This minister first influenced the Stricklin family in the 1970s when I came to Dallas while working for the Baptist General Convention of Texas, to serve in the Texas Baptist Evangelism Division. Later he became pastor to our oldest son, Art, when he was working in the Sherman-Denison, Texas, area and was a member of First Baptist Church of Sherman.

Over the past few years, Dick De Witt, president and COO of Marketplace Ministries, and I have driven up US State Highway 75 many times to meet with Brother Tom, study a portion of God's Word, and pray together. Those times were spiritual high water marks for both of us.

Tom, along with Dolly, served as the national support center staff prayer warriors and visited our national headquarters' office in Plano, Texas, regularly to fellowship and minister to our employees. Tom Brandon is one of God's choicest servants and one of our best chaplains, as well as a ministry prayer warrior. He continues to affect my life and this ministry, more than words could ever express. Tom is eighty-six now and heading home to heaven; his health is failing and memory slipping. However, he is still a godly and good man, a man who influenced me greatly.

Reverend Canon Ralph McCune

Ralph McCune, or "Father Ralph" as he is affectionately known, has been my friend for sixty years. We were students together at Southwestern Baptist Theological Seminary in Fort Worth, Texas. The Episcopal canon and his lovely wife, Jan, have been married for forty years and have served the Lord as a team through all their married years, as well as their single years.

As former chairman of the spiritual resources committee for the Marketplace Ministries board of directors, Father Ralph propelled our thrust in prayer being the hallmark of everything the ministry does. This godly man, who has suffered various forms of ill health, has been a true example of the kingdom of God in man, exhibiting peace, joy, and righteousness of the Holy Spirit. As an Episcopal who is an evangelical, he fits well with me and the ninety-three denominations on our staff. Church denomination is not the emphasis in this ministry; Jesus Christ is.

When Father Ralph prays, you quickly know it is not the first time for him to go boldly to the throne of God. When I need a prayer, which is often, the call goes out to Father Ralph, for he is my example of godly praying.

Dr. Neil Ashcraft

For nearly three decades, Dr. Neil Ashcraft was the senior pastor of Scofield Church, a spiritual legacy in the city of Dallas, with close association to Dallas Theological Seminary.

Of all my mentors, this quiet, confident, and godly man is my example of patience with mercy, all from the Lord. If I could have patience, kindness, and love of anyone, outside of Christ, it would be like that of Neil Ashcraft.

The former Marketplace Ministries vice president of marketing, Larry

Ramsey, who is in heaven now waiting on us to arrive, was the person who introduced me to Brother Neil. He talked so much about this man and said so many godly things to describe him, I thought he was talking about Jesus; however, it was his pastor, Dr. Neil Ashcraft. Our second son, Cliff, and his family were members at Scofield Church, and Neil was their pastor.

Neil became and is very special to me. He joined our staff after retiring from Scofield Church. After serving as a chaplain for several years, he knows well how to pray for this work of God at work. In addition, he is well aware of the challenges and rewards of serving inside and outside the walls of a local church.

This dear brother and one of my spiritual heroes, along with his wife, Joanna, who is now in heaven, have encouraged me to stay in battle, as they did for years. He holds up this ministry with prayer, personal words of encouragement spoken to me in the office and on the golf course. I desire to be like him, for he is like Christ.

James McManus

This saint is one of the most articulate and brilliant theologians of our Lord and His teachings of any man I know. He has walked with God by faith for many years, and all of those years, he has experienced illness, pain, and physical limitations, including his speech. He has been in and out of more hospitals and doctors' offices than most medical responders who are there on a daily basis.

Even though he is slowed physically, his speed is high when it comes to the spiritual. You do not have to talk with him long, listening very carefully to understand his words, to know you are talking with a man of God, a very special apostle of our Lord.

I have known Jim and his wife, Joann, for many years, and their friendship has been an indescribable blessing from our Lord. When I think of saints who have suffered without complaining or getting angry with the Father and lived a victorious life for Jesus Christ, I think of Jim McManus. He is truly a man without gall, having a faith deep, sincere, and meaningful in his relationship with his Lord.

Jim serves God through prayer and writings. He is the western region prayer warrior with Marketplace Ministries, as well as senior contributor to the *Marketplace Magazine*. His specialty is writing on prayer.

This man is my hero, and if or when I face the pain of life he lives with, I just pay I can have some of the victory I see in him. What a suffering saint he is, and my spiritual mentor.

Dr. H. D. McCarty

This Arkansas pastor, who has served the Lord for decades in Fayetteville, Arkansas, and around the world, has been my friend since 1956. When we first met, he was Lieutenant McCarty, a US Air Force pilot stationed at James Connelly Air Force Base outside of Waco, Texas.

I was a junior at Baylor University, and all the fly boys would scout our campus for the beautiful girls, the Baylor Beauties. McCarty met and later married one, Shirley DeBerry, and so did I, Ann March. We met again, this time at Southwestern Baptist Theological Seminary in Fort Worth, Texas, in 1961. He gave up his wings for a cross and started down the road to become a brigadier general as deputy chief of chaplains in the Air Force Reserve.

Over the last nearly six decades we have visited in person and on the phone many times, and during every conversation, the Rabbi, as he is affectionately known, has shared with me some deep spiritual thoughts.

I laugh and say he is my most brilliant mentor, and he agrees, laughingly saying I don't have many smart friends. However, this earned doctorate degree holder, professor, senior pastor of University Baptist Church in Fayetteville, Arkansas, for thirty-nine years, Arkansas Razorback football team chaplain, general officer in the military, great American patriot, and a godly and deeply committed apostle of Christ, has uplifted my life along with thousands of others.

H. D. asked me to lead the ceremonial prayer at his general officer promotion ceremony at the Pentagon in Washington, D.C. Also, he has asked me to officiate at his funeral, the ultimate promotion ceremony.

This mentor has spoken at Marketplace Ministries' events dozens of times, helped market our chaplains' service, and was used of God to secure the largest client company we have in Mexico. His numberless prayers have bombarded the gates of heaven, and the results have been God's abundant blessings on me and this ministry of God's.

Every time we talk, we take up right where we left off the last time. We are brothers, and our faith in the living Lord binds us together closer than twins joined at birth. This man has helped me, encouraged me, inspired me, supported me, cared for me, and made me more like Christ. For, you see, that is what a mentor does.

These six godly men have blessed my life and this ministry, fulfilling Proverbs 27:17, "Iron sharpens iron, as one man sharpens another." We all need a spiritual hero to sharpen and inspire us to be more like Jesus. These men have done that for me, and I pray I have done that for someone else, another believer who is seeking to be more like our Lord.

11

BUSINESSMEN AS SHEPHERDS

If I live another thousand years, I will never forget that early Monday morning telephone call from the top executive of one of our client companies. I looked at my watch as I walked out of our staff prayer meeting, which showed 8:31, when I said, "Hello."

The words I heard shattered by heart. "My God, my son shot himself," were the words I heard between sobs of a father who had just found his son who had committed suicide. Within ten minutes, I was holding this friend in my arms, our tears mingling as they ran down our faces. The body was covered on the couch, detectives had picked up the weapon, and the coroner would arrive soon to take away the deceased.

A few days later, after performing the funeral service, I sat in that corporate leader's office. His hands were covering his face. Tears were streaming down between his fingers, and with sobs, I heard these words, "All I have ever done is make money. All I have ever done is make money. All I have ever done is make money."

He was a good man, a man of impeccable character, an honest man with virtue. At one time he had been active in a church and was a believer by his personal confession. His word was his bond, and his devotion to his business enterprise ran deep.

Yet, at that minute, he sensed his greatest achievement was the ability to make millions, and in the life crisis he faced, that was nothing. Money made no difference.

Neither this man, nor anyone else, will ever take any of this world's wealth with us when we are buried, not one penny. We realize the only money he took with him to heaven is what he sent on before him, nothing more and nothing less. The only money ever to take on an eternal dimension is money invested in the kingdom's enterprises, the Lord's work, money that is used to bring people into a dynamic and thrilling relationship with Christ or to teach from His word the wonder of who He really is and what He did on Calvary for every human being,

How many business leaders and corporate executives, who make millions of dollars, fly on private jets, eat at the finest and most expensive restaurants, live in million-dollar homes, and have a net worth in multimillions, would say when they came to the end of life, facing death and dying, their material wealth was worth nothing, not one thing? You cannot buy your way out of dying, and you can't take it with you. Then you have to ask, "What is money really worth, except as an opportunity to invest in others?"

Many business tycoons would say, like my friend, "All I have ever done is make money." In all honesty, if that is the only thing you or I have done, then we are total failures in fulfilling God's purpose for each of us. For His purpose for you and me is to glorify God, have fellowship with Him, and be more like His Son every day.

It does not give me any joy to have to tell you this; however, a large majority of powerful business executives who have reached financial success in the eyes of the world have failed to achieve God's purpose and plan for their lives. They have squandered their one and only opportunity in this life to glorify God, have fellowship with Him, and be more like His Son's image today than yesterday. Many business leaders in today's marketplace fail to exalt the higher truths of God and have intimate fellowship with Him as Savior and Lord. All of us are called to live with the fragrance and magnetism of Jesus.

Every businessperson who owns or leads a company, indeed all business-people who have subordinates answering to them and carrying out their orders, are considered from a biblical perspective to be shepherds. They are responsible for taking care of their sheep under their watchful eye, support, care, and love. That is what a biblical business leader does.

Because the workplace is the most dynamic and effective mission field in the world today, and because business leaders have the greatest opportunity to influence others for good and God, or for evil and the evil one, it is mandatory these men and women understand their role and pray they will fulfill it, as we pray for them.

All of us, every worker in the world, should have a vocation and an avocation in living life. For every true believer in our Lord and Savior Jesus Christ, the primary vocation is to do what we just stated: glorify God, have fellowship with Him, and live like Jesus lived. That is the number one priority for all who call themselves Christians. Then our avocation is the work we do, "as unto the Lord," to make a living, to make a livelihood, to put bread on the table and provide for our families and ourselves in meeting the material needs on this earth. Both are absolutely essential in this life and the one to come. We must always fulfill our vocation to glorify God over just gaining material wealth or financial assets. When we mingle these two, then the secular becomes sacred and the sacred affects the secular. God is glorified in our sweat, as well as in our sanctuary.

One of God's strongest signs of the last days of human history will be an economic one. In Revelation 13:17, we are told, "that no one may buy or sell except one who has the mark..." There are other Bible verses that bear out the same theme of economic ruin at end times.

Could what we are experiencing in our current society and business enterprises be the beginning of the end for this great nation called America, and other global economies as well? It well could be, because the wickedness of man's heart in greed, dishonesty, selfishness, gain without work, and passion for consumption all point in that direction.

Shepherds

The prophet Ezekiel lived, spoke, and wrote twenty-six hundred years ago; however, what he said for that day is just as current and contemporary for our day. In Ezekiel 34, the prophet is talking to political, religious, and business leaders of his day, as well as our day, the twenty-first century.

In these thirty-one verses of Ezekiel, the leaders of a society or culture are called shepherds, whether they are princes, economists, military and government leaders, or priests. Each position of leadership, each person in a responsible position, had a threefold obligation to be first, a prophet, a teller of truth; second, a priest, a helper of people; third, a potentate, a king, a leader, a ruler who rules himself first before ruling others.

Christians should pray for businesspersons, as they pray for themselves, that they function effectively in these three required areas of life and living. This is a must if our nation's economic system is to function effectively to the maximum benefits for all society and to all people. Businessperson, you must nail these down, for you must be as a true shepherd leader, a prophet, priest, and potentate.

The national financial crisis on Wall Street is playing havoc on Main Street and is due to ignorance of, or rejection of, these threefold duties. God declares today we have false shepherds leading us, false shepherds failing to fulfill their duties. Thus, we see corporate greed, CEOs doing insider trading for unearned financial gains, congressional passivity, and personal selfish gratification that dominates all other values and will not produce true shepherds. Millions of people have had their retirements stolen. These funds have been squandered by thieves or impotent individuals as would-be protectors betrayed the innocent lambs. Many have seen their small nest eggs of money and hope for some financial security in old age evaporate or be seriously depleted because of dishonesty.

In Ezekiel, the first litmus test for all businesspeople is to know the true shepherd leader, like the chief Shepherd Jesus Christ, denies himself for the people under or with him. In Ezekiel we see this warning: "Thus says the Lord GOD to the shepherds: "Woe to the shepherds of Israel who feed themselves!" (34:2). The life practice of false shepherds of that day and our day is the same: "Me now," and "Take care of me and neglect others."

Shepherds with this attitude toward others, especially those they are supposed to lead and care for, do not have a prophetic heart of love and compassion. The spirit of "Truth first" was no longer a priority in their lives. It may never have been, and if it had, that spirit has left them. Their personal practice as leaders was to take care of themselves, me and myself first and foremost, before anyone else or anything else.

They ate the curds, clothed themselves in the finest wool, slaughtered and ate the choice animals, and did not take care of the flock. These shepherds did not "strengthen the weak, or heal the sick, or bind up the injured" sheep. The wicked shepherds did not bring back the strays or search for the lost. No, these leaders "ruled them harshly and brutally."

In that day as in this day, sheep were scattered over the whole earth and were without a shepherd. The wild animals devoured them while no one searched for the wandering sheep. They were only pursued by those looking for their next meal.

The true Shepherd, the chief Shepherd, was a God who gave because He loved. He gave His only Son, sent from heaven, and did not keep Christ there to care for Himself, His fellowship, or His companionship. No, the whole world of sheep needed the Shepherd Savior, and each of them came before any of His personal needs. He looked and saw the needs of mankind and provided for them without any self-consideration.

Sir Winston Churchill is credited for saying, "We make a living by what we get. We make a life by what we give." Every shepherd-leader should always remember that little yet powerful quote and seek to practice it, knowing it is "more blessed to give than to receive."

The great English Bible scholar, Reverend Sidlow Baxter, made this beautiful statement: "The person who is full of himself can never represent the Christ who emptied Himself for others." That is the theme of Philippians 2:5-11, giving up self for others.

Shepherd Leaders

The true shepherd leader, like Jesus, learns to empower and lift up others. This is the second part of the text each of us must consider.

We are clearly warned the bad shepherds of Ezekiel's day did not "strengthen the weak, heal the sick, or bind up the injured" sheep. Most do not do it today, either.

Remember, the message of that day, like our day for most business shepherds, was "me best and me first." They had no genuine desire to help other people (sheep), to meet the needs of others, or reach out to others. These shepherds were far too busy taking care of themselves and forgetting others, or at best leaving them the scraps.

False shepherd leaders, whether in business, government, the church, or anywhere else, always see themselves as better, more deserving than anyone else. They love and magnify their role as exalted leader, CEO, owner, chairman, preacher, king, or potentate. They derive too much happiness from their own privileges and perks of their position to bring promise and prosperity to the common people.

Remember this definition of grace: "In Christ, God took the initiative on our behalf." A true shepherd leader with true grace is one who has been touched by God's grace and who is a person of spiritual nobility. That person is always looking for ways to take the initiative on behalf of others, helping people in every way possible, putting them first and self last.

In God's final judgment and personal accounting for all shepherds, as business leaders, you will never be asked by our Lord the size of your biggest salary or your net worth. There will be no inquiry into what style of automobile you drove or how big your home was or in what part of the city it was located. No, none of those questions will be asked.

However, the Judge of justice will ask, "How many of your employees, your fellow workers, did you influence for the kingdom and the family of faith? How many people will be in heaven because they worked for you or with you? How did you express my love for others by meeting their needs and helping comfort their hearts? How much of my financial assets, as God's money manager, did you give back to my kingdom's work, and how did you invest in eternity? What will last after your business, indeed your life, is over on this earth?" These are the questions of vital importance. What will be your answers to your Lord? Remember, silence is not an answer.

Now the third thing to remember about the true shepherd leader is that he, like Jesus, always displays and implements authentic love for all people. The shepherds of Ezekiel's day did just the opposite.

This is how Ezekiel 34:4-5 can be paraphrased, "You handle [lead] my people coldly and harshly [you bully and badger them] and don't care about their future, you throw them to the winds." How horrible compared with a loving Shepherd shown in God's Son Jesus Christ! This can be summed up in three errors: "Me now, me best, and me first."

Any shepherd, any leader, in any aspect of this life in business, politics, military, education, the church, or family who does not sincerely care about the people he or she is to serve and care for is unworthy of the name or position of shepherd leader. When workers, followers, or fellow employees discover their boss or fellow worker, their company, their leaders have no real heart for their lives, for them or for their families, their tendency is to scatter in desperate search for someone somewhere who does have a heart of evident compassion and genuine caring.

Without authentic love, care, help, and hope extended to them from their leaders, CEOs, boards of directors, and company owners, workers become prey to all the wolves of our society, thieves and con men who are ready to pounce and take advantage of the less fortunate. How can anyone call himself or herself a true shepherd, a godly leader, and have no real initiative to help show God's love and kindness to all those the Lord places under his or her influence and responsibility?

If you, or anyone you know, have any ambition to represent the chief Shepherd to others in the workplace, or anywhere else, then never forget this: "A God who cares can never be represented by people who don't."

Now the fourth and final part of these evaluations is that the true shepherd lives under the authority of the chief Shepherd. Also, the true shepherd leader, like Jesus, pays close attention to the Lord's warnings.

Ezekiel records, "Thus says the Lord GOD: "Behold, I *am* against the shepherds, and I will require My flock at their hand; I will cause them to cease feeding the sheep, and the shepherds shall feed themselves no more; for I will deliver My flock from their mouths, that they may no longer be food for them" (34:10).

The greatest sin here is the false shepherds saying, "Me alone."

No leader, no shepherd, no CEO, no president, no chairman, no vice president, no supervisor, no worker ever escapes the law of the truth from the One who said, "I am the way, the truth, and the life." Jesus did not come to be alone but to bring others to the Father. In doing so, he did not come to be served but to serve.

If you head an organization and are not serving others with passion to bring the truth to them, then the Lord tells us He could strip the truth from your life. For without Christ as our guide and empowerment, we are bound to fail in what matters most. If your first goal is not to search out how to help and support others, then why should the Lord search for you in your own personal dilemmas, crises, problems, and tragedies?

The true business shepherd is a potentate because he masters himself first before leading others. He is a priest because he is a master of caring for people, meeting their temporal and eternal needs here and now. He refuses to believe or say, me first, me best, me alone. Instead, the real shepherd leader believes and states: Christ now, Christ best, Christ first, and Christ alone!

Lonnie (Bo) Pilgrim was for many years the chairman and CEO of Pilgrim's Pride Corporation with an international headquarters in Pittsburg, Texas, 135 miles east of Dallas. It was one of the largest poultry producers in the world with fifty-six thousand employees at the height of its success. The man who founded the company and served there for more than six decades, before selling the company and retiring, is the most humble and godly businessmen I ever met or partnered with in the marketplace.

This businessman begins and ends every employee meeting, every stockholders' meeting, every board of directors' meeting with Scripture reading and prayer. This dedicated believer taught a men's Sunday school class at his church for more than fifty years.

Bo Pilgrim and his brother, Aubrey, began in the chicken business in 1946, shortly after military service during World War II. With God's help, they built Pilgrim's Pride into an 8.2-billion-dollar, world-class business. From two employees the company grew to employ fifty-six thousand partners spread across twenty states and one hundred cities, as well as Mexico, the Commonwealth of Puerto Rico, and other international operations.

This very successful businessman knows the only eternal aspect of any business, no matter how large, has to do with the hearts of his employees and the truth in the Word of God. Souls and the Bible are the only eternal lasting aspects of this life. That is why he placed his top priority on those things that bring workers and their family members into the family of faith.

Bo had four hundred Marketplace chaplains reaching out 24/7/365 to care and support his partners and their families. Chaplains were in the plants, distribution centers, marketing and administrative offices every day of the week, except Sunday, and sometimes then, too. They were in hospitals day and night when a partner or a family member was dying of cancer, in small country cemeteries or large city funeral homes conducting a funeral for a family who did not have a relationship with a minister. Chaplains could be found visiting a former partner or family member in a county jail or state or federal penitentiary, doing what Jesus did, seeing those in prison. These same chaplains often did what the Scriptures exhorted, "weep with those who weep." They were with people as God's representatives, showing His love through acts of beloved kindnesses. Bo Pilgrim proved over many decades that Pilgrim's Pride Corporation had a true shepherd leader with a true shepherd leader's heart to lead the company.

Pilgrim Cares, a team of those hundreds of chaplains, was always ready to speak a word of truth about Christ after showing God's love through acts of kindness. In the nineteen years of the partnership of caring between Pilgrim's Pride and Marketplace Chaplains USA, those four hundred care givers introduced more than nine thousand partners, or their family members, to Christ as Savior, with a great majority of them being baptized and joining a New Testament church as an expression of their newfound faith. And that is not all the story. An additional ten thousand-plus individuals, adults, young people, grandparents, and children, partners and family members who claimed to have once had a relationship with Christ and His church, but who had not been active in corporate worship or service for years, sometimes AWOL for decades, rejoined or joined for the first time a local congregation.

What are all those souls worth in the sight of the Father? According to Jesus, one person is worth all the money in the world, just one soul. What are eight thousand souls worth, and ten thousand more who rededicated their lives to the Lord? I am confident there is no other Fortune 100 company in the history of American business where the Holy Spirit brought more of God's love into individual workers' lives and families. Have you ever heard of anything like this?

The eternal legacy of Bo Pilgrim is not the millions of dollars he has made and millions more he has given to kingdom causes and human charities as God's money manager, as good as that is. His legacy is his vision of being a true shepherd leader to his people. Every true Christian business leader or worker must ask, "How many of my employees, or fellow workers, and family members will be in heaven because they worked for me, with me, and this company?"

When Bo gets to heaven, there will be many there with him, and many more coming, because they were employed in a chicken-processing plant of a company with chaplains who shared God's love with everyone possible.

This godly man and dedicated business executive went through difficult times with his company's stock falling in value from $37 a share to as low as $2.22 a share, losing company value and personal wealth in the hundreds of millions of dollars. But this man knows he brought nothing into this world and will take nothing out of it.

Also, Bo realizes no matter how this worldwide financial crisis ends, nothing can pluck the people he cared for out of God's loving hand; that is what's best to know for certain, and forever. True shepherd leaders like Lonnie Pilgrim put their primary interest in the spiritual corporation of the Lord from heaven. That stock is eternal and will never lose value.

As I pray, I plead to the Father to raise up anointed and true shepherd leaders in this nation and the world. We need more like this one.

12

SPECIAL EVENTS WITH INTEGRITY

A time to praise God for His divine providential blessing on His ministry, a time to have fun with friends on a golf course, and a time to inspire business leaders and friends has produced more than $2.1 million of financial support for Marketplace Ministries. Our first banquet, "Celebrating Two Incredible Years," was held in 1986. The Integrity Award banquet was initiated in 1994, and the Chaplain of the Year recognition began in 1995. The first Business Leaders and Friends Gathering at The Cove was held in 1997, while the first charity golf tournament teed off in the fall of 2000.

Since their beginning, each of these special events, emphasizing integrity, has continued to expand with a banquet held only once every five years, while the charity golf tournaments are held annually. The Business Leaders and Friends Gathering at The Cove, the Billy Graham Training Center, is planned about every three years. Thousands of friends of the ministry have participated in one or all of these.

For most ministries and charities, the major source of finances comes from contributions by donors. That is not true for this ministry because the client companies we serve give to our operational budget, which includes almost everything for which we need money.

However, there are always needs outside of the normal annual operations budget. For those special needs, which we cannot expect our clients to pay for, we ask our Marketplace partners for financial help. We give them an opportunity to be blessed by God for investing with us so we can reinvest their gifts that will bring souls into the kingdom and encourage Christians to be true apostles of our Lord.

The Integrity Award Banquets

Our first banquet was in 1986, designed to praise God for "Two Incredible Years." The banquet at the Crescent Hotel in Dallas was complimentary for the 250 people who attended. It was a wonderful evening honoring our Lord for His blessings on His fledgling ministry.

It was Ann who had the idea for the Integrity Award banquet, which I believe was an idea from the Lord. She thought we should celebrate what God had done in His ministry every five years on the anniversary of the ministry and honor people who had impeccable integrity in their lives. I liked the idea from the first time she mentioned it to me.

The first Integrity Award banquet was held September 13, 1994, at the Anatole Hotel in Dallas. The Integrity Award was presented to Edwin V. Bonneau and Barbara Bonneau for integrity in family, including their five children and twenty-six grandchildren. Prolific author Max Lucado was the featured speaker, and eleven hundred people attended.

The Integrity Award was designed by a renowned jewelry craftsman, James Avery of Kerrville, Texas. It is an eighteen-inch solid bronze cross on a walnut pedestal which is inscribed "Integrity, the Compass of the Heart" and the Scripture passage, "The integrity of the upright will guide them" (Proverbs 11:3).

Celebrating fifteen years of ministry, the next Integrity Award banquet was held in Dallas at the Anatole Hotel on September 11, 1999. Motivational speaker Zig Ziglar was the master of ceremonies, and George Beverly (Bev) Shea of the Billy Graham Evangelistic Association was presented the Integrity Award for integrity in ministry. The evening ended with all twelve hundred people in attendance singing along with Mr. Shea, accompanied by Kurt Kaiser, "How Great Thou Art."

On August 30, 2004, we celebrated twenty years of Ministry at Work, again at the Anatole Hotel with thirteen hundred people joining us for an inspirational evening. The Integrity Award was given Drs. James Dobson and Shirley Dobson and their children Danae and Ryan for integrity in ministry and Lonnie (Bo) Pilgrim and Patty Pilgrim for integrity in business.

The twenty-fifth anniversary celebration of Marketplace Ministries was held September 1, 2009, with thirteen hundred participants. The recipients of the Integrity Award that year were Dr. Gary Cook, president of Dallas Baptist University, for integrity in education, and Joni Eareckson Tada, of Joni and Friends, for integrity in ministry.

September 11, 2014, the Integrity Award banquet was held on Patriot Day (9/11), which also happened to be my 80th birthday. The Integrity Award was presented to LTG John Van Alstyne, for integrity in service to country, and Dr. Charles R. "Chuck" Swindoll, for integrity in ministry. It, too, was held in the Chantilly Ballroom of the Hilton Anatole Hotel in Dallas.

The finances produced by banquet participants have increased every year on a five-year cycle, with the last one raising $176,606. Total fund raising from the banquet effort totals $908,480.

Charity Golf Tournaments

The charity golf tournaments have been held since 2000 and have provided much more income for the ministry than the Integrity Award banquets. The banquets have cleared $526,650, while golf with an eternal purpose added to the ministry $1,041,022.

I must admit both these ideas to support the ministry financially came from the Stricklin family, wife Ann and son Art. I wish I could claim credit for these two successful practices; however, I was not even an encourager but somewhat of a road block. Well, not really a big road block, just a small one.

I had tried to hire Art to help me in the ministry when I could see we needed a person responsible for public relations, news media contacts, and producing *Marketplace Magazine*.

Art had been with the ministry only a short time when one day he walked in my office and announced, "Sir, I've got a great idea for a fund raiser. We need to have the Marketplace Ministries Golf Classic." I almost laughed.

I began my lecture why his "great idea" would not be successful in North Texas. I had many reasons why we should not try this. About 175 fund-raiser golf tournaments are held in the Dallas-Fort Worth area each year; we were too small a charity to sponsor a golf fund raiser; no one would play in our small golf outing; and there may have been two or three more reasons that I can't quite remember now. However, I made my point, and he left.

Art does not give up easily, however, and within the next few months he came back with the same arguments and golf logic of why we should have a golf fund raiser. I had my same reasons why it wouldn't work.

This went on for at least three or four years until I got tired of listening to him. So, one day I said, "OK, do it! This golf thing is all your responsibility."

The initial Marketplace Ministries Golf Classic was held in Dallas on Monday, October 28, 2002, at the prestigious Northwood Country Club with Dallas PGA tour superstar Justin Leonard in attendance as the honorary chairman, a role he faithfully carried out for twelve years. That year, we cleared nearly one hundred thousand dollars, and the tournament was a huge success from the first tee-off until the last. We have held a golf tournament at the Northwood Club, which is now a client company, every year since then and counting.

On Monday, April 18, 2011, the initial golf tournament was held at the Houston Oaks Country Club in Houston, Texas. In 2014, the Houston tournament was held at the beautiful Royal Oaks Country Club. We held the first tournament outside the state of Texas on Monday, October 1, 2012, at the Hawks Ridge Golf Club in Atlanta, Georgia. In 2013, we began an annual tournament at the Mira Vista Country Club in Fort Worth, Texas.

We have raised $2.1 million in Marketplace Ministries Golf Classics in four different cities from Dallas to Atlanta. We would like to have twenty golf tournaments a year and raise one million dollars annually. That would provide financial resources to do more ministry than ever. What I thought wouldn't be successful for us has proved to be a big success, thanks to my son Art. He organizes and directs all of our charity golf events.

Business Leaders' Gatherings at The Cove

In 1997, we inaugurated the business leaders' gathering at the Billy Graham Training Center, The Cove, located in the heart of the Blue Ridge Mountains outside of Asheville, North Carolina.

The business leaders' gathering was not begun as, and is not now, a true fundraising event for the ministry. We only charge what the venue costs the ministry, and we don't ask for money or even take up an offering. However, we have discovered the more people know how God is blessing an organization, the more money they want to invest in it.

That means that business executives who attend he gathering, who are richly blessed spiritually, are the same people who give to support Marketplace Ministries. Approximately a thousand men and women business owners and CEOs have spent four days at The Cove being inspired, uplifted, renewed, and spiritually motivated by God's Spirit.

The program presenters are some of the most effective conference speakers in America today. The music is equal to the speakers, and together they leave an imperishable imprint on the spiritual lives of those who participate.

Our first business leaders' gathering was held November 14-17, 1997. The theme was "God Is Able" (Ephesians 20:21) Cliff Barrows of the Billy Graham Team lead the music, accompanied by Kurt Kaiser. The Bible Study was taught by Dr. Neil Ashcraft, the recently retired pastor of the Scofield Memorial Church in Dallas, and was then employed by Marketplace Ministries as Director of Chaplain Care. Client presidents shared their spiritual testimonies. On Saturday night, George Beverly Shea presented a concert.

The second gathering was held December 1-4, 2000, and we called it Christmas at The Cove with the theme "O, Come Let Us Adore Him." "You are worthy, O Lord, to receive glory and honor and power" (Revelation 4:11a).

Cliff Barrows of the Billy Graham team lead the singing, and Kurt Kaiser played the piano. Larry Burkett, Christian financial leader, was the kick-off speaker; Chris Thomas of Torchbearers Ministries taught the Bible study, with his wife, Bonnie, speaking to the ladies' breakout sessions. The highlight of the event was the Saturday evening concert featuring George Beverly (Bev) Shea and Cliff Barrows. On Sunday morning, as we gathered in the chapel for our final session, large flakes of snow began to fall, and as we worshipped we truly adored our Lord. Snow covered everything.

On October 27-30, 2005, we gathered again at The Cove, with the theme "Seek God First" (Matthew 6:33). Speakers included Zig Ziglar, number one motivational speaker; Bo Pilgrim, businessman and client; Ken Blanchard, author of *The One Minute Manager*; and John Beckett, businessman and author. Chip Ingram, at the time president of Walk through the Bible, was the Bible teacher. Earnest Alexander was the soloist accompanied by Kurt Kaiser, and Bev Shea, America's beloved gospel singer, presented a concert on Saturday evening.

"The Joy of the Lord" ("for the joy of the Lord is your strength," Nehemiah 8:10b) was the theme of our third gathering of business leaders at The Cove, October 25-28, 2007. Chip Ingram was again the Bible teacher. Speakers included John K. Coors, president, chairman, and CEO of CoorsTek, Inc.; Neal Jeffrey, associate pastor of Prestonwood Baptist Church in Plano and a former professional football quarterback; and Drayton McLane, client, and at the time, chairman and CEO of the Houston Astros baseball club. Earnest Alexander, Kurt Kaiser, Cliff Barrows and, of course, Bev Shea rounded out the musical program.

"Where Your Treasure Is" ("For where your treasure is, there your heart will be also," Matthew 6:21) was the theme for the November 3-6, 2011, gathering at The Cove. Randy Alcorn, founder and director of Eternal Perspectives Ministries and author of thirty books, was the keynote speaker. Other speakers included Dr. Charles Lowery, president and CEO of Lowery Institute for Excellence; General John Van Alstyne; and Dr. O. S. Hawkins, president and CEO of GuideStone Financial Resources, who taught the Bible. Susie Hawkins spoke to the ladies' breakout sessions. Tenor Scot Cameron was the music leader and soloist for the event. The climax of the event was a presentation by almost 103-year-old Bev Shea, who shared his life stories and sang, to the delight of the 250 attendees.

Chaplains of the Year

In 1995 we decided to recognize a special chaplain annually as the Chaplain of the Year (COTY). This chaplain would be nominated by our client companies and selected for ministry above and beyond the call of duty. The executive committee of the board of directors would select the chaplain based on the written nominations from the clients. These chaplains would be representative of all the front-line chaplains who perform the ministry at work.

The COTY Award is the sculpture by Max Greiner Jr. of Jesus washing the feet of Peter, "The Divine Servant." It, along with a check, is presented annually to the COTY recipient at an Integrity banquet, a Cove gathering, or a Christmas dinner.

The first Chaplain of the Year was Mario Zamarron of Oklahoma (1995). Subsequent COTY recipients include:

1996 – Ann Forester	2005 – Berl Pedigo
1997 – Maceo Gray	2006 – Carroll (Hutch) Hutcheson
1998 – Geri Smith	2007 – Ari Morales
1999 – Lane Park	2008 – Janet Thimell
2000 – Dee Rucker	2009 – Cynthia Britain
2001 – John McDaniel	2010 – Elise Bissell
2002 – Gerald Rodgers	2011 – David Vernon
2003 – Clois Smith	2012 – Charlotte Turner
2004 – Andy Bunn	2013 – James Emery

Integrity Award banquets, golf, the Gatherings at the Cove, and Chaplains of the Year are four different ways to be blessed by God and strengthen His work in the business arenas of the world, from North America to Europe and from Asia to Central America. These are the things that have eternal value, time without end, and an investment that never loses value.

13

NATIONAL CRISES AND CHAPLAINS

9/11 and the First Gulf War

In my lifetime, the United States of America has faced police actions, limited conflicts, world war, the assassination of a president (along with several other attempted assassinations), attacks by Islamic terrorists, economic meltdowns, and riots.

World War II, the Korean War, the Cuban missile crisis, the Panama invasion, Iraq, and Afghanistan helped millions enjoy freedom. Never has this country used its military force to gain one foot of foreign soil or enslave one foreign citizen. We have gone to war or conflict only to set the captives free and restore the laws of the land.

Nothing prepared this nation for December 7, 1941, the day President Franklin D. Roosevelt said would "live in infamy." The Japanese Imperial Navy, with more than four hundred airplanes, delivered a surprise attack on the US fleet anchored at Pearl Harbor, Hawaii. More than two thousand sailors, marines, airmen, and soldiers died that day in a raid lasting less than two hours. A great portion of the US Navy's ships and planes were destroyed in the attack, left burning and sinking in Pacific waters. I remember as a seven-year-old boy seeing my mother crying, saying, "America is at war."

But a worse attack on American soil was yet to come.

The first sixty-five of my birthdays were happy ones, a time to celebrate another year of God's blessings and life's favors. However, that ended on September 11, 2001.

It was a beautiful early fall day in Dallas, Texas, just as it was in New York City. Our ministry gives each person the day off on their birthday so they can celebrate with family and friends, take it easy, consider the past year, and plan for the next one.

I was up early that morning and in my home office where I go to spend time in private worship.

Ann's voice cut through the air: "Come quick, our nation is under attack!" She had been watching a morning news program when it was interrupted with pictures of the North Tower of the World Trade Center burning in its upper floors. I dashed downstairs and rushed into the den where she stood facing the television.

I was watching another national crisis unfold before my eyes. People were running, first responders were arriving, and radio and television crews were setting up for worldwide broadcasts.

Panic and chaos enveloped lower Manhattan, and within a few more minutes the tragedy would double as a second airliner flew into the seventy-sixth floor of the South Tower. Flames shot hundreds of feet into the air, in all directions.

Ann and I stood in silence staring at the news being broadcast on the television to the world; I could not even hear the words of the reporters. Almost three thousand people would die that day in New York City, Washington, D.C., and a Pennsylvania field, where airliners had been made into missiles by Islamic terrorists. One of the hijacked aircraft never made it to its designated target in our nation's capital because passengers on the airplane fought back, resulting in it crashing before it could reach its destination of destruction.

"Let's roll" was the battle cry of a civilian American, Todd Beamer, who fought an early battle of the war on terrorism aboard hijacked United Airlines Flight 93, a battle still being fought today.

We watched as firemen, medical rescue teams, and policemen rushed into those burning towers as thousands of survivors rushed out. These heroes were heading up the emergency stairs as wounded, burned, frightened, and mentally injured people were heading down. Most were trying to get out, while first responders and rescue personnel were trying to get in to assist many people who were trapped in the upper floors.

Ann and I prayed that morning for the families suffering sorrow, loss, and destruction that touched so many lives. We prayed for our nation and the president. The remaining morning hours and much of the afternoon were spent in front of the television watching news footage from the various points of attack, as well as President Bush in Florida, then Louisiana, and finally back to Andrews Air Force Base, Maryland, and the White House.

Even though we were in no mood for celebration, Ann had fulfilled a tradition of more than fifty years by baking my favorite German chocolate birthday cake the night before. So, sometime that early evening of 9/11, we ate a piece of that delicious cake with a glass of cold milk. That was about all we ate all day; there were no candles, songs, or other forms of lightheartedness. This was the only sad birthday I had ever had. I will never forget that one, number sixty-six.

In the weeks following the 9/11 tragedy, I saw more news reports than I ever thought possible of fire and police chaplains assisting in more than four hundred funerals. The compassionate, dignified, professional service rendered by those special clergymen, priests, and rabbis brought chaplains to the forefront of public knowledge. Almost every day for weeks, the role chaplains played was shown in the lives of common people, working people blessed to have a pastoral care giver in their work arena. That is where they labored, men and women who were members of the team, friends who give special help in the times of special need.

The general public, which included business owners and executive leaders, heard and saw the stories of chaplains who "went above and beyond the normal call to duty" for their fellow man. Chaplaincy was a consistent topic of dialogue during those dark days.

Numerous stories came out about the ministry of chaplains to those first responders, as well as regular citizens who had begun another workday at the Twin Towers. One of those chaplains was a Catholic priest, Mychal Judge, who served a fire station down the street from a parish Catholic church, close to the Twin Towers.

When the alarm came for "all hands on deck" because of a major airplane crash, the priest, a chaplain, responded. With his protective fire gear and hard hat with the NYC Fire emblem on it, along with his identification badge proclaiming, "Chaplain—NYC Fire Department," he quickly made his way to his station in time to jump on the first truck out.

The red truck and crew pulled up close to a major entrance leading into the North Tower. Each man knew his duty, his equipment, and the task before him. So did the chaplain. Pieces of debris were falling from the building's top floors, which were burning. Many injured were being brought out of the building; it was like a war zone, very dangerous, and this was before anyone considered both towers might come down.

"Chaplain, chaplain," called a medic who was working on a man lying on the cement sidewalk in front of the North Tower. The chaplain dashed toward the injured individual to answer the call for help.

The injured man was dying. The chaplain knelt down beside him, unbuckled his helmet, and laid it aside as he bent over to begin offering the Catholic ritual called Last Rites. As he prayed, calling the name of Jesus, a piece of metal fell from above, hitting the chaplain in the head and killing him instantly.

The captain of the fire company asked some of his men to carry the covered body of their chaplain to the Catholic church, lay him on the altar, and make notification.

I have thought about that incident often. I have told many of our chaplains I would rather die in the line of duty, helping someone else who was suffering, than to gently pass away while lying on a bed of ease. As someone said, "I had rather wear out than rust out." I want to go out with my "harness on, pulling a load," helping someone in crisis. I want to be in the battle, on the front line, not in the rear. Our Lord has enough people taking it easy in the rear, a long way from the battle, when there are so many needing help and hope.

When I was commissioned an Air Force officer, receiving a second lieutenant's rank through Baylor University Air Force ROTC in May 1957, I was planning to enter active duty immediately. However, I took a one-year academic delay of entrance and went on active duty in August 1958. Ann would soon complete her senior year, and I did not want to wander very far from Waco and the Baylor campus.

After three years on Air Force active duty, I transferred to the active Air Force Reserve to serve another twelve years. With a theology degree and church experience, I moved from the Air Force to serve as a special staff officer to the Army Chaplains' Corps, where I spent another twenty-two years as a chaplain both on active duty and in the Reserve.

During one of the Reserve tours in 1989, I was assigned as the senior chaplain with the 94th General Hospital in Mesquite, Texas, a unit of the 807th Medical Brigade in Seagoville, Texas. I was a full colonel, equal rank with our commander, who was a doctor. We had fifty-five doctors, about two hundred nurses, and nearly four hundred other personnel who were everything from scrub techs to ambulance drivers.

Our unit was formed in 1949, just prior to the Korean War. The hospital had never been called to active duty, and it was rumored that was why most people joined it. That was not my reason. However, I have to admit it was a well-paying weekend job once a month, with no worry about being called up to serve on active duty.

No one knew Saddam Hussein would change all of that when he invaded Kuwait. That attack would change the military picture of this nation for decades.

The first Gulf War would be called Desert Storm. It was launched in January 1991 with the call-up of a massive number of reserve troops who were sent to Europe to replace active duty personnel being sent to the war zone. This was in preparation to launch a major effort to free Kuwait from Iraq's army, which had occupied much of Kuwait's territory.

As more and more reserve units were being activated, word was circulating the 94th might be called up as well. No one believed it, however, because it had never happened before; we were a huge unit with about seven hundred personnel. Think of the logistics of moving personnel and equipment of a thousand-bed hospital halfway around the world. One of our daughters-in-law even said confidently, "They won't call Gil up; he's too old!"

Still, the rumors persisted. The commanding officer was spending a great deal of time at the brigade headquarters, and the general who headed the medical brigade was not known for just sitting around drinking coffee and talking with his staff. Not this general.

In late December 1990, on our final drill weekend of the year, I arrived at the unit early on Saturday morning. I had a full two days of planned activities, plus worship on Sunday, as well as other Army requirements.

As I was walking to my office, I happened to meet Colonel Jim Farr in the hallway. He looked worried, and said, "Chaplain, I need to see you in my office after formation." It sounded like important business to me, and I answered, "Yes, sir, I will be there."

What does he want, I wondered? I told the other chaplains and assistants to begin working on our task list and I would be back soon. I had a meeting with the commander. No one asked what it was about.

When I reported to the chief of staff, he stated, "The commander is waiting for you." I walked in and saluted. Colonel Farr told me to take a seat and listen, but not to take any notes. That seemed a little strange; however, I obeyed.

He looked at me for what seemed a long time. Then he said, "Chaplain, I am sure you have been following the news and the situation in the desert. You already know President Bush is preparing to assist Kuwait. Our unit has received a warning order; we are being called to active duty in a few days."

I knew this was no joke. He was far too serious for that. Besides, there are some things you don't joke about, and this was one of them. Colonel Farr went on to say I would get a lot of "business" when our call-up and planned departure was announced. He said there would be a lot of tears, many reasons why folks could not go, and plenty of fears about how it would ruin their family life or their medical practice. He was correct; we received a lot of business.

I walked out somewhat surprised but not stunned. What I knew was top secret until it was announced to the entire unit. I had a dear friend on Army active duty, the command chaplain at Forces Command at Fort McPherson, Georgia. Colonel Dave Peterson, a godly evangelical Presbyterian, had been my friend for years. Two or three weeks earlier, I had called him and volunteered for active duty for Desert Storm under his leadership.

Dave asked me if I was sure that was what I wanted to do. I had been in the military at that time more than thirty years and had never been involved in combat. My time was running out, and I wanted to be with soldiers who were facing death every day. My desire was to be a combat chaplain.

When I hung up the phone, I was certain my request was granted, and now all it took was paperwork and a few days before I would be departing. All I had to do now was tell my wife. I delayed, trying to find just the right words to say.

When I volunteered, I did not anticipate our total unit would be activated. I was just one chaplain who wanted to get in at least one fight in my military career before I retired. I missed World War II, Korea, Vietnam, Panama, and all others. I did not want to miss Desert Storm. It could be my last chance.

Three days after my initial conversation with Chaplain Peterson, I got a call from him. "Gil, I have bad news for you on your request," where Dave's first words. "Since your whole unit is on alert, and I cannot take personnel from a unit that is being called up. I am sorry, because I could really use you."

Shortly after my conversation with our commander of the 94th General Hospital in Mesquite, Texas, I found myself telling Ann I was leaving, moving out, and would not need many civilian clothes for a while.

"I will be leaving in a few days for somewhere in Europe. I don't where, but our hospital unit is being activated in support of Desert Storm. Our personnel will be the back fill for regular Army troops that are being pulled out and moved to the desert. I don't think we will be gone for more than a year, and it could be much shorter," I said as I held her hand and looked into her pretty brown eyes.

Over the years, I have joked with her a lot, kidding her about things that we always laughed about later. However, this time as she looked directly at me, she knew this was no "cruelty" joke, no joke of any kind. I was dead serious.

"When do you leave?" she asked.

I replied I thought we would not be away until after Christmas and maybe even after the first of the year. That was my honest "not really knowing" answer.

As it happened, I didn't leave until January 3. The night before, Ann and I talked most of the night, with me, the colonel, giving her last-minute instructions about caring for herself, managing money, taking care of Marketplace Ministries, praying for me, and other important subjects.

I was up early January 3; I had slept very little the night before. My duffle bag was packed, along with my Army footlocker. My uniform was heavily starched and black boots shined to a high gloss. We had formation at 0700, and the chaplain is always the first one present, or at least I thought he should be.

I can still remember the silence as we drove east toward the hospital head-quarters. When I arrived there were other soldiers already present, and wives crying as they said their final goodbyes. As I looked closer, I saw husbands cry-ing, too, as they told their wives goodbye. They would be staying home with their children as the wives and mothers went off to war.

As I stated, we had approximately two hundred nurses in our unit, and most of them were married with families. They had signed up to go if needed, and Uncle Sam said they were needed now, so they were going. There were men, women, and children crying everywhere. I will never forget that picture of seeing all those families huddled together and everyone crying. It was hard to fight back the tears myself, yet I told myself I would not cry even as the sun rose and light came.

In formation, we were preparing to march into the gym of Mesquite High School located next door to our military facility. The thirteen buses were lined up and motors running as we marched past them and into the high school. Some fifteen hundred high school students, teachers, and administrators had packed the gym along with the high school band, to participate in our depar-ture ceremony. Our soldiers marched in single file and filled the remaining space on the basketball court.

It was a brief ceremony. The band played the national anthem, and the com-mander gave a few words of appreciation, along with an explanation about why we were going to war in the Middle East. I was to deliver the ceremonial prayer and had given much thought to what I would express to the Almighty. I remem-bered reading about Abraham Lincoln when he left Springfield, Illinois, to go to the White House in Washington, D.C., as president, and his prayer that day on the back of a special train and his private car. I didn't remember all of his words, but I prayed these that he prayed more than 150 years ago: "I am grateful we have a God big enough to go with me and stay here with those we love." That was a part of my prayer that day as we were leaving our families and friends.

When I closed my prayer as the last official part of the event, the crowd of more than two thousand people began singing "God Bless America." We were marching out as the last words of that song were being sung. My bus was num-ber 7, the perfect biblical number and to me a sign that all was well. God would go with me and stay with Ann, a mighty God indeed.

I looked for Ann, as I prepared to board, to share that last embrace. I could not help but recall the personal letter my friend Billy Graham wrote me with a commitment to pray for me, my ministry, and our unit. That meant a lot to me then and every time I thought about it in the months following. I still have his letter framed and in a prominent place in my office.

There she was, rushing toward me. Even though I had already told the Marketplace Ministries board members goodbye, as I looked at Ann, there were Ann's mother, Hattie Mae March, Ed Bonneau and his wife, Barbara, as well as Erma Clifton Williamson, some of my dearest friends and board members. Ed was the first businessman to hire me as his business chaplain in January 1984. Bowen Williamson, Erma Clifton's husband, was an early client, Williamson Printing Company.

The door of the bus closed, and I waved out the window until I could see Ann no longer.

Camp Bullis in San Antonio, a part of Fort Sam Houston and 5th United States Army, was our new home after a six-and-a-half-hour bus ride. We would be there preparing for several days before walking up the steps of a 747, en route to fulfilling our duty in Operation Desert Storm.

After I knew we had been called to active duty, I asked Ann what she would say if I told her I was leaving home, didn't know where I was going, or how long I would be gone. She replied by saying in a loving voice, "Where is the checkbook?"

Well, she got the checkbook and everything else, and I got all my Army gear, in a foot locker and a duffle bag.

We flew to Rhine Main Air Force Base, Frankfurt, Germany, and began to unpack, for we were the back fill for the 97th General Hospital with a thousand beds. All of the medical staff had been pulled out and moved to the sand, Kuwait. Now we were the Army medical services for all the remaining troops and military family civilians.

They didn't pull out the chaplains' staff from the hospital, so we had an abundance of chaplains. Even though I outranked the colonel who was left at the hospital, I was just Army Reserve and that didn't compare with an active duty soldier.

There were nearly seven hundred Reserve soldiers in that hospital, and we did everything the other medical staff had done before they packed up and moved out.

You can imagine a doctor who had been generating a large annual income in his medical practice and now was making much less as a doctor in the Army. Boy, did they complain.

We had staff meeting every week, and the senior staff met with the commander to review the activities of the hospital and solve any problems we were facing. As a senior colonel I always attended those sometimes not so pleasant early morning gatherings.

On one occasion, there were several docs protesting about being gone from their practice so long and losing a large amount of money trying to keep their office open with other doctors stepping in to help them. After two or three doctors spoke, basically saying the same thing, I stood up and asked the commander if I could say a word.

"Sir," I began. "My compassionate heart goes out to all the doctors who are losing a great deal of their income. I feel badly for them; however, when I was called to active duty I was given a raise from my civilian ministry job, and my wife is home right now praying this war will go on for years."

That was greeted by a loud chorus of boos, and catcalls, with "Sit down, chaplain. We have heard enough from you."

Our hospital was prepared to receive three hundred wounded soldiers from the sand every day. We sat up three operating suites in a hanger at Rhine Main. The wounded on a stretcher would be placed on a gurney and rolled from the plane down a ramp right into the operating room. From the time the plane landed until a surgeon was cutting into the body would be ten to twelve minutes.

Close by were eighteen refrigerator trucks. Each would hold forty bodies, which we expected to receive from the battlefield on their way to Dover Air Force Base, Delaware, and process for burial.

Thanks be to God, those operating tables were never used, and neither were the body storage trucks. Desert Storm was a miracle of God, as we only had one soldier die in our hospital.

When I was called up for active duty, no one knew where I was going, and neither did I. It was only after we landed at Rhine Maine did any of us know either. It didn't make any difference; all I knew I was away from home, and away from Ann.

I settled into a weekday and weekend routine of hospital chaplains' work and preaching on Sunday in the hospital chapel. We met some of the finest American troops, all volunteers in the military.

One very special Marine Corps fighter pilot came to the hospital with leg injuries. He was there for quite some time but was improving and looking forward to returning to his unit. I would go by almost every day to visit with him, sometime twice a day if I wasn't all that busy.

On one occasion I began to talk with him about spiritual and eternal things. It was evident he wasn't a follower of Christ but could be categorized as a "seeker of the truth." One morning I looked up in my office and there stood this fine-looking, all-military Marine. He said he came by to talk further about what I said on my last visit with him.

That was the day for which he was born, to be born again as he accepted

Jesus Christ as his Savior. There was an overflowing joy as he told me he was to call his fiancée and tell her about his decision.

He would be leaving soon; however, before he was discharged to return to the sand, and his flying wing, he wanted to be baptized. He asked me if I baptized new believers. "Of course I do," was my response.

The day was set and I asked the chaplains' assistant to prepare the baptistery for that early morning baptism service. That winter in Germany was the coldest the country had in two decades. It was snow window deep at my hospital office on the first floor. Cold, really cold.

I went to the chapel early that morning, and the assistant met me as I came in the door saying, "I have bad news. The water heater is broken and the baptistry water is so cold it is forming ice."

Well, that did it I presumed. No baptism today.

When the Marine arrived, a true fighter pilot who eats nails for breakfast said a little cold water didn't bother him. He wanted to be baptized.

How could an old Army colonel chaplain allow a young Marine captain to get the best of him over a big tub of very cold H2O? Sure, we would have a baptism.

That is the coldest water I have ever felt on my body. I am still freezing just thinking about it. I was shaking so hard I could hardly speak. But you would have thought that Marine was in the Caribbean on a sunny hot day, enjoying the warm ocean surf and warm sand.

When I put him under, all the way, he didn't even flinch. No moans, no fighting, no cringing, and no shivering like me. He was relaxed and comfortable.

After the service, I had to ask him, "Were you cold in that water?" "Cold," he repeated. "I didn't even notice it was that cold; wasn't bad at all." I could not help but wonder if he was in the same water as me. I was shaking so hard I made waves several inches high.

The Marine went back to flying, and I went back to the fireplace to thaw out.

We were gone from home for only seven months, and my only pain was missing my Ann. We lived in the Russian espionage headquarters for all of western Europe, after they had been kicked out. I rode the public transit to work every morning in civilian clothes, changing into Army dress at the hospital.

The Army duty was meaningful; however, returning home was better. I found a soft bed in the crew cabin of the 747 we flew home in. We landed at Lackland Air Force Base in San Antonio, and Ann met me on the tarmac, along with Beverly and Gary Golden and their two children, Celeste and Geoffrey. Three-year-old Geoffrey ran to me and exclaimed, "Uncle Gil, did your team win?" I replied, "Yes, Geoffrey, we won," as I thanked the Lord for my safe return. I was home now and back to the Marketplace.

As I answered the call of my government to go to Desert Storm, Ann answered the call to step into Marketplace Ministries to serve as the liaison between its board of directors and me. She served faithfully, and when I returned I almost did not get my job back. The board wanted to keep Ann. To this day, she serves faithfully as executive vice president.

14

RAILROAD CHAPLAINS SERVING ON THE MAIN LINE

Hearts' compassion covering tracks of cold steel

I am a railroad man.

I was born a railroader and have been one all my life, working five different jobs for three different railroads before I was twenty-four years old. Once a railroader, always a railroader.

Because my dad was a railroad man, he could copy Morse code faster than anyone could speak, and he could send even faster. His hand would move that telegraph key so fast you thought your eyes were seeing two hands banging out dots and dashes, spelling every word.

He would take train orders and write them on thin green paper, almost as thin as tissue paper. He would tie the orders in a train order hoop and rush outside the station, holding up the wooden Y-shaped pole for the fireman or head brakeman to catch as the train passed. If they ever missed, they had to stop the train and walk back a mile or so to get their instructions.

When Dad was working second or third shift, 4 p.m. to midnight or midnight to 8 a.m., sometimes I would go with him to work. As a little boy, I was afraid of those huge steam locomotives that roared down the track toward the station whenever Dad went outside and left me alone in the office with a big, red-hot, coal-burning potbelly stove. It may have been cold outside, but it was glowing red hot inside!

Most of the time, he fixed a pallet for me on a big wooden table, and I would sleep through those mighty loud noises of trains coming through town. I remember him keeping the fire burning as long as I was there.

Those were tough economic times, with hoboes traveling the rails, some of them just out of prison, looking for work and a meal. They were not too proud to steal, and occasionally one murdered a railroad agent and broke into the company safe. However, I felt secure when Dad had his .38-caliber pistol stuck in his shoulder holster.

Dad began working for the railroad when he was eight. He dropped out of fifth grade to help support his family when his father died, and he never went back to school for a formal education. However, don't think he was uneducated. He was self-taught, with Mom's help.

His first job, as a child, was filling switch lanterns with coal oil in a railroad yard. Dad worked all day and then lit the lanterns for night switching and making up trains. It was a dangerous job for any kid today; however, this was in the early 1920s, before most child labor laws had been enacted or even thought of.

Over all those years, he worked his way up from those fifty-cent-an-hour jobs. He made career stops as train dispatcher, chief dispatcher, assistant superintendent of safety, assistant superintendent of a division, and finally, superintendent, which is called general manager today.

I will remember how thrilled he was when he came home one day to tell Les, my mom, that he had been promoted and now would make a thousand dollars a month. One thousand dollars was more money than I had ever seen. I thought if I could ever make a thousand dollars a month I would be filthy rich.

When I was eight years old, we lived in Denison, Texas, a railroad town, about three miles from the KATY's Ray Yards, out northwest of town, down the hill from the old KATY Hospital. I can still hear steam locomotives leaving the yard pulling a long train of cars with a huff and puff, the sound of whistles in dark nights and bells ringing as they came to a crossing near our house. With a cold north wind blowing out of Oklahoma, just ten miles or so up toward Durant, I could smell the coal smoke and occasionally spotted a lighted cinder, like a firefly. Maybe it was my childhood imagination; however, it was real to me.

My dad got phone calls in the middle of the night because of train wrecks. It was my greatest thrill to hear him say on a night when there was no school the next day, "Son, they have called out the wrecker. Do you want to go with me?" Wow, did I!

I would dress faster than a fireman putting on his firefighting outfit to grab the truck as it sped out of the firehouse on its way to put out a blaze. We were off, and I knew for the next several hours, and maybe all day, I would eat in the wrecker dining car and see that huge steam hook do its work in untangling metal engines and railroad cars. My dad was there to find out what went wrong.

One thing is certain, I knew I had to stay out of the way and not be in any place of danger. Dad did not have to worry about me. I knew my way around a railroad accident; I had been there before.

I remember one massive wreck of two freight trains down by Duck Creek, north of town, just this side of the bridge over the Red River separating Texas and Oklahoma. It was a huge stack of twisted steel, like a pile of cordwood going in every direction, splintered and split, torn apart like paper, and crushed as easily as warm butter. When we arrived, as the first rays of light crept up over the horizon, there was that certain smell of death in the calm air that hung over the twisted steel rubble.

I didn't have to ask if any of the crew had been killed. I knew they had, because no railroad man could escape a head-on crash between two freight trains running at fifty to sixty miles an hour. Those engines had reared up like two wild stallions fighting each other. It looked like one had exploded, and steam still hung low over the derailed cars with their contents thrown nearly a hundred yards in every direction from the impact.

Then, I quickly turned my attention to breakfast. I made my way to the kitchen car back down the track away from the work going on untangling the iron puzzle. Eggs and big, juicy steaks with hash brown potatoes and huge "cat head" biscuits; that was the way to start the day. We didn't have many steaks around my house, even though my mom could make biscuits that would match anyone's. The only time I could eat all the steak I wanted was on the wrecker kitchen of the KATY. On occasions like this, I ate more steak than any man, or any boy my age could have.

Dad and I were not the only railroaders in our family; my brothers, all except the youngest, worked on the railroad. It didn't hurt our chances for employment that Dad was well known across the KATY; he had been there a long time and was considered a real railroad man who knew how to run a railroad. Also, the Stricklin boys had a reputation as hard workers who did not complain about any work conditions. We knew how to do real work.

One of my brothers, Jim, followed after Dad. While he was in graduate school, Jim worked as a railroad agent, sending and receiving the same Morse code and copying train orders for the next freight or passenger train coming through his station. Like Dad, Jim carried a pistol, and no one ever thought about something called a concealed handgun license. No, most agents had their own personal protection, which was not concealed, and so did Jim.

You might be surprised to know forty-seven years after I left my last job as a brakeman on a train crew of long-haul freights with the Burlington, Rock Island, and Chicago Railroad, I would go back to work for another railroad. I was seventy-two, and yet I was still a railroader. That new railroad career officially began November 17, 2006, with a major Class 1 railroad.

The concept and idea for this job had been in my mind and heart for many decades. It was born in my days with the KATY as I worked around railroad people, engineers and firemen running steam locomotives and diesels, with conductors and brakemen who did all the real work, according to them.

The desire to implement my new job with the railroad was cultivated by many different situations from the time I was that young boy, with Dad as a railroad official, to the days I sat working in the cab of a diesel engine, or helping floor a new boxcar in a railroad car factory, or seeing railroad accidents.

In the summer of 1950, I was a fifteen-year old high school boy living in North Texas, near the Red River. One day I was with my dad on a "deadhead" train with no passengers, only a crew that was moving cars from Dallas to Denison. We were in one of those non-air conditioned passenger cars. Of course, it was hotter than blazes and the windows were wide open, with coal cinders and smoke filing the air. I knew a bath waited for me when I got home because I had coal spots all over my face, arms, and head, as well as my clothes. I was a dirty sight, and so was the air.

We were approaching Greenville, Texas, when suddenly there was a loud bang. The train's emergency brakes were put in the "big hole," and dust and dirt flew up around the train and into our open widows so thick you could hardly see or breathe.

My dad cried out, "Oh no, we've hit a car."

He jumped up and started running toward the end of our passenger car, opening the door. I was following after him as closely as I could. The train was stopping now as he opened the outside platform door, jumping down on the rocks that made up the railroad ballast, holding the track and cross ties in place. He was running toward the engine, the front of the train. I ran after him as fast as I could.

Even before we made it to the engine, I could see a car wrapped around the steel cow catcher on the front of the massive steam locomotive. As I came to the engine, I saw two people in the car, evidently deceased. Even before the police and emergency crews arrived, the train crew covered the bodies with fine table linens from the dining car we were pulling. I felt sick to my stomach and could not speak.

The engineer said to my dad, "Mr. Stricklin, I am sorry, but I couldn't do anything. He was racing me to the crossing. I tried to stop, but it was too late. I couldn't do anything."

That trainman carried the view of that couple to his grave, even though he really could not have done anything to prevent it. It took that type of train at least a mile to stop.

Dad and I didn't talk much the rest of the trip. Mother knew something was wrong when she met us at the depot as we got off the train. I let Dad tell her what happened. I didn't sleep much that night.

As a chaplain in the military and business for more than forty years, I have assisted in railroad incidents involving employees, employees' family members or friends, as well as railroad employees. Marketplace chaplains helped in these situations long before we formed a specialized group called Railroad Chaplains to offer compassion, condolences, and care to families who suffered loss and sorrow from a railroad incident.

One of those railroad incidents happened in Danville, Illinois, and involved a family member of an employee of the McLane Company, a client we served with a Chaplain Care Team. The single mother was a forklift operator, and she didn't have a pastor; however, she did have a company chaplain who would come to her and her family's rescue.

Her two young children lived in a home located across the road from a railroad track in Danville. It was on a Sunday morning about 11 o'clock, when most church services are beginning and many folks are there for worship.

The young boy, about twelve, and his fourteen-year-old sister walked out of their house and stepped off the front porch on their way to visit their aunt. A train was approaching, and the boy told his sister, "Come on, and let's beat the train so we don't have to wait." They took off in a fast run.

The boy made it across, while his sister was hit and killed. The mother's company chaplain spent hours with the family, helping them deal with their grief. At one point, the mother said something like this: "No one from the railroad came to tell us they were sorry about the accident. Not one person expressed any sympathy for this tragedy and the loss of my only daughter."

The husband and father in a Dallas family walked out of the house to go to work. I don't know if he kissed his wife goodbye and hugged his children, or not. She was preparing to go to work, too, with kids leaving for school and all the hustle and bustle of early morning weekday home activities.

The wife was an employee of a bank that contracted with Marketplace chaplains to care for workers and their family members.

Tragedy can strike anytime, and it struck that family that day.

The husband drove into the path of a freight train at a crossing on his way to work. He never made it to his job that morning; he was killed instantly.

The bank chaplains were called to give help and hope to the family members, friends, and fellow bank employees who were suffering sorrow and loss.

The chaplains, led by a female chaplain, did everything they could to comfort and support the wife, now a widow, her children, and other family members. Just to show compassion, express sympathy, and be present is comforting in itself. Sharing a genuine tear, with a spirit of concern, works wonders in times like these. Add to that the practical assistance planning a funeral, bringing food to the family, notifying friends and other family members of the death, preparing the obituary for the newspaper, all of which makes a huge difference.

The man's widow said nearly the same thing as the mother who lost her daughter: "I wish someone from the railroad had come to tell us they were sad because my husband was killed. No one came to express condolences or sympathy. No one said anything to me about my loss, no one!"

On a Saturday morning in September 2004, a Hammond, Indiana, mother was racing a freight train to a crossing when two trains, going in the opposite directions, struck her SUV, killing her two daughters, ages eleven and eight. The mother died the next day; however, two of her sons survived this horrible railroad incident. She had been rushing to take her children to weekend sports activities and was running late.

The family was not affiliated with a church, just like the great majority of American families today. Consequently, they did not have the services of a clergyman who would officiate at the funerals. Who would help the family plan them? Who would give financial support for the costs of burials? Who would walk through the grief process with the father who lost his wife, and the boys who lost their mother? Who would visit the hospital every week, and often every day, while the boys' bodies were healing?

I tell you who did! Alberto Guang, our chaplain at the PacMoore Company, where one of the family members worked. That's who took on all of the responsibilities and opportunities of caring with compassion.

Chaplain Guang came to the family and planned and performed the three funerals of both girls and their mother. He stood before fifty family members and a few friends to express words of comfort and hope. His comfort, and that of the Holy Spirit, was especially meaningful to the father, who lost his wife and two of his children in a matter of forty-eight hours.

Out of that tragedy, the chaplain became the family's pastor, and even to this day he ministers to family members and their friends who have remained in the Hammond area.

These tragedies were not the fault of the railroad. The deaths were the result of the horrible judgments of drivers and young people. Regardless of blame, there was and is deep sorrow and continued emptiness in the homes of those whose lives were lost.

However, I think we would all agree it would have been a loving, humanitarian expression of sympathy and compassion for someone representing the railroad to have gone to those shattered families to say how sad and heartbroken the entire railroad family was at this tragic loss. Surely the family and friends of those who died would have thought more of the people who run railroads because of their humanitarian expression of love and sympathy.

I promised myself if there was ever a way I could help those people, the families and friends who lost love ones in a railroad incident, I would be the first to volunteer to console. I never dreamed I would have that opportunity.

Legal issues plague our society, and lawsuits drive many actions. Railroads, like scores of other American corporations in the transportation industry, are sued almost daily as money is a driving force in judicial issues and outcomes. I know why most railroads will not go to a family where someone has died in a railroad incident. They may be concerned that showing love will be interpreted as admitting fault, and they may be ordered to pay millions of dollars for their acts of kindness a few months later inside a courthouse before a jury.

Regardless of lawyers, court cases, juries, claims, payouts or dollars, people who are suffering a broken heart, with tears rolling down their cheeks and eyes red from weeping, still need to be consoled, supported, and have hope spread within their hearts so they will heal.

Since November 17, 2006, some seventy specially trained railroad chaplains from near Boston to Seattle and down to San Diego, as well as throughout the whole American heartland of Iowa, Kansas, Oklahoma, Texas, and New Mexico, are doing what I promised all those years ago, reaching out to help hurting and sorrowful people.

Spun off under Marketplace Ministries as a separate subsidiary, a 501(c)(3) non-profit humanitarian caring organization, Railroad Chaplains provides the human touch to giant corporations like Class 1 railroads. Also, we contract with a half-dozen short-haul railroads across the United States from Nebraska to Texas.

There are seven Class 1 railroads in America that have never had chaplains in their 160-year history. No American railroads had chaplain care teams as part of their transportation groups. This new service, Railroad Chaplains, was born out of crisis and has now celebrated years of compassionate caring.

After serving as a chaplain in the Army Chaplains' Corps for twenty-two years and in corporate America for thirty, I know with certainty that having a chaplain deliver the sad news of death, then remain to support the devastated family and friends, is the right thing. You can never go wrong by giving a shoulder for someone to cry on.

That is what railroad chaplains do, sometimes every day and most always every week. When a railroad chaplain is called upon to serve, someone is dead, dying, or critically injured, and a family needs help. I recall reading a July 2006 *USA Today* article about an SUV carrying six Mexican farm workers being hit by a freight train at a rural crossing in southern Colorado, killing all of them. They were immigrants living in a small farm village with a few hundred other Hispanic workers. The story stated that seven hundred dollars was collected from their friends and family members to help ship the bodies back to Mexico for burial. That amount was far short of what was needed.

On that hot July day in 2006, I went to my office and wrote the highest executive of the railroad involved in that accident.

The man who received my letters was the chairman, president, and CEO of this Class 1 railroad. I had heard this individual was a good man, a man who loved his employees and all people. In my appeal, I told him how Railroad Chaplains could express his personal concern and sympathy to third-party families whose loved one had been killed or critically injured in a railroad incident, as well as employees who died of natural causes in non-railroad incidents.

This executive personally called me after the first letter and had his chief legal counsel call me after the second one. In that letter, I exhorted him to take the high moral ground, having railroad chaplains express sympathy and offer caring support in practical ways.

A few days after my September letter, my executive assistant told me there was a gentleman on a call who said he was the chief legal counsel for the railway and wanted to talk with me.

When I answered the call, he introduced himself and told me he was holding the letter I had written to the chairman.

Then I heard the man say, "We want you to come to our corporate office and talk with us about your offer and how we might work together." I was in shock and could only mumble I would be glad to do that.

Between that September telephone call and November 17, when we were officially hired as a contract service provider, we had four meetings, and between one and four attorneys were in each meeting. Our approach to caring for people, offering compassion, sympathy, and love, finally passed the attorneys' legal muster.

Chaplains by their loving spirit and compassionate care for people are thought to have reduced legal claims and the amount of financial payout to those involved in a railroad incident. That is not a reason to hire us. However, a reduction in legal expenses is a by-product of taking the high moral ground and standing tall in caring—because it is the right thing to do. Most people positively respond to love that is extended with genuine sincerity.

Even though the service of Railroad Chaplains has not expanded as fast as I anticipated, the positive humanitarian results, care for thousands of hurting people, make every effort worthwhile. This railroad service has grown from a meager idea in 2006, with five specialized and professionally trained railroad chaplains, to 110 of the best chaplains anywhere. Railroad Chaplains have been carefully selected from a group of more than twenty-eight hundred chaplains already assigned as a part of Marketplace Chaplains USA. Railroad Chaplains are spread out in scores of metropolitan cities and small towns. They are prepared to cover the entire nation, in fact all of North America, on short notice. As long as people make terrible errors of judgment, resulting in death or critically injury in a railroad incident, there will be a need for railroad chaplains.

Those 110 railroad chaplains have been called many times; they are the finest, most experienced, and best trained, most loving and caring people there are. They have gone to nearly three thousand family members across the nation. Those mothers and dads, brothers and sisters, grandparents, cousins, aunts and uncles have lost a loved one to death in railroad incidents, auto accidents, or by natural causes. Many more loved ones were critically injured since we began supporting railroads. Some of those injured will never be the same again, forever carrying scars with them of the incident. You will note there are not many minor injuries when there is a railroad incident. It is usually death or horrible injuries if a person lives.

A suffering family never lives too far away for railroad chaplains to drive or fly as quickly as possible to get to a family. They express deep compassion, often simply "weeping with those who weep." Our chaplains have driven 169,486 miles since 2006 for one reason…to extend loving care to the grieving. That's the only reason!

First, as caring strangers, they have walked into homes and apartments, big and small ones, million-dollar mansions and inexpensive huts, to do the same thing for everyone, give hope to hurting hearts. They have invested dollars to provide food and to meet other physical needs. They have done the things that maids and cooks would have done, like wash dishes, clean house, or prepare a meal. Additionally, thousands of dollars have been spent to pay funeral expenses for those not prepared for the death and the need for burial services.

However, they do much more. They prepare and plan the funeral because most families have never experienced that, at least not under these circumstances. Many families do not have or know a priest or clergyman, so guess who does the funeral? Yes, the chaplain does. On numerous occasions, they have led the entire service or participated in some way.

These chaplains are the same ones who have made hundreds of hospital visits to major medical trauma centers or small hospitals all across the nation. They have stayed with families in the hospital for as long as five continuous days when the loved one was clinging to life. These loving and kind individuals called railroad chaplains have gone back to the same hospital day after day for literally weeks, becoming a cheerleader and prayer partner for the injured individual struggling to regain a normal life.

Railroad chaplains accomplish much more than the initial contact and support. For weeks and often months, sometimes years, following an incident, whenever a chaplain goes to the family, they stay in touch and have made some 3,530 telephone calls to loved ones to check on them and see how they are progressing in gaining a life over sorrow. They have written 2,437 letters and personal notes and sent 1,300 books on working through the steps of grief, plus more than 500 CDs and another 2,600 books and booklets on various topics dealing with the loss of a loved one and how to get passed a broken heart.

Many times the relationship between family members and chaplains goes on indefinitely. Friendship between the grieving and the supporter lasts a long, long time, for healing takes time. Deep friendships, born out of crises, have a way of bonding that is impossible to break.

Of all the people killed in railroad incidents, it is estimated 20 to 30 percent of those deaths are suicide. There is enough sadness in those deaths to break your heart a thousand times. Unless there is a suicide note left, or other certain evidence, officials really don't know how many of those deaths are suicide.

Railroad chaplains are still being called, almost every week, sometimes every day, with requests for help all across America. We have hundreds of stories of railroad chaplains who have been in that special place as God's men or women, at God's time, for His glory and the support of mankind.

No Minister

It was falling dark that cold November evening when a sixteen-year-old girl walked a short distance from her home to the train tracks and waited. It was not long until that freight train rounded the curve with its headlights piercing the darkness. Sometimes a person who has few friends, seemingly no future, and is just down on herself and life makes the worst decision possible. As she looked around her hometown, it was almost a ghost town, nearly deserted. She stepped across the first track and was hit by a fast-moving train with nearly five hundred tons of steel, killing her instantly.

When Chaplain Al Ortiz made his way to the family home, a small wood frame house, the parents were unfriendly, cold in spirit and distant. When he explained that the railway company had asked him to come and express the railroad's condolences and offer the sympathy of the entire railroad family, they began to change. He continued by telling them he was there to help in any practical way possible. Over the next four days before the funeral, their attitude changed completely.

The tent was almost as large as one of those circus tents that once brought lions, tigers, elephants, and performers to small towns all across the United States. Nearly two hundred family members and friends had come to say their final farewells to the young lady.

At the family's request, there would be no ministers there to take part in the funeral service. There was to be no music, no sermons, no words of comfort for her parents, no prayers, and no emphasis on faith or the future. Chaplain Al Ortiz sat toward the back of the tent, with a simple casket at the front.

There were several pictures of this beautiful young girl, a girl who would never live out life, never be married, never love her children, never go to church, and never tell her parents how much she loved them. One of her aunts, whom she had not seen for a long time, stood and spoke. She talked about the separation of the family, how she had not seen her niece and how she now would never have that opportunity again. Another family member said a few words about the girl. Then there was silence. From seemingly out of nowhere, two other family members began strumming guitars and singing, songs of the faith like "Amazing Grace" and other Christian hymns. Some joined in, but not many.

When the songs faded into silence and it seemed the end was near, Chaplain Ortiz walked to the front of the crowd, standing in front of the girl's parents and asked if he could speak. When permission was granted by both of them, he began by expressing his sympathy and love for the family and how sorry he was about the tragic ending of their daughter's life.

The chaplain continued, saying that everyone who knew the girl "must always remember the good things about her life and the good things she did for so many." "Also, in a time like this, you must know God's love that overcame death," he said.

At the end of his remarks, the chaplain was engulfed by strangers, young and old, who thanked him for what he shared in the tent. The tent could now be called "Redemption."

CHAPLAIN

Boskie Boy

Have you ever talked with a loving mother whose twenty-three-year-old son recently had been hit and killed by a freight train, just 150 feet from home? I have! The conversation can only be described as sorrowful, moving, emotional, and heartbreaking, yet not without some hope.

The mother spoke with calm as she described the night of April 19, 2011, after receiving word her son was dead. This fun-loving young man was known by his family and friends as "Boskie Boy," but now he was gone. She told how she, her husband, and their daughter were devastated by the news of his death and how he died. It was more than any human being could stand, without help from others and their faith.

The family had always had a love affair with trains. Even to this day, the mother waves at train crews running the long-haul freights and still enjoys hearing the whistles and bells as a train passes a crossing.

The mother's interest in trains came naturally. Her grandfather was an engineer for the old Northern Pacific, running out of Centralia, Illinois. Even as a little girl, she remembered the black smoke from coal-burning steam engines her grandfather would bring into the station. She never got over that special bond with railroads. She now has a different memory about railroads, one she will never forget; however, her love affair with trains is still there.

Her faith and the assurance of God during the dark days and sad nights were what kept her sane and calmed her mind, giving her peace, she explained.

When asked how this tragic death touched her life and her family, she replied, "Well, it caused me to remember, none of us have many days here, and we need to make the most of them. We need to live well, live full today, and don't be putting things off."

She also said their son's death caused her family to experience a deeper dedication to church, faith, and eternal matters. Her husband was touched with a fresh interest in Christianity and a relationship with Jesus Christ. Their daughter was influenced by her brother's death, as well, and for the good.

Even though the mother began her initial walk of faith as a thirteen-year old girl, it was many years later that her relationship with the Lord became relevant on a daily basis. While working at the Methodist church in Guthrie, Oklahoma, she memorized a Scripture that was on the wall of the sanctuary: "Call to me, and I will answer you, and show you great and mighty things, which you do not know." (Jeremiah 33:3). That verse was written in her mind and on her heart, and it is still there today.

She and her husband had been married since 1986. He was a woodsman, both as a logger and a professional carpenter. They lived in the back woods of

Alaska and could only be reached by pontoon plane. After four years in the fiftieth state, in 2007 they moved to Idaho.

"I felt God sent Railroad Chaplain Dan Blake to offer us comfort and lift our hearts," said Helen. "All of us were touched by this loving man who genuinely cared for us in our time of grief."

Also, in a letter to Joe Mayden, former vice president and general manager for Railroad Chaplains, she told of her family's appreciation for the chaplain attending the funeral of their son, and "for all the prayers and emotional support from all of you."

"Please thank Chaplain Blake for the heartfelt words of love and concern and for making a special effort to be there with us when we laid our son to rest. His presence touched us deeply," she added.

The family had one request they hoped would be granted, and it was. At a time when their hearts were broken and their sorrow overwhelming, they were thinking of others, the members of the train crew on the engine that night that could not stop in time.

"Please contact the engineer who was running the train, and tell him our love and prayers are with him and his family," she wrote. "I am so sorry he had to witness the tragedy and hope and pray it doesn't weigh heavy on his heart. I am sure it must have been a horrible ordeal for him to experience. Give him our love and may God bless him and heal him."

"Our family still lives within a 'stone's throw' from the railroad tracks," she continued. "Every train that passes by our house receives a prayer for all the engineers and crew, that nothing will harm or hurt them in any way."

Not many people pray for railroad engineers as they maneuver those five hundred tons of steel and metal down those rails. However, there is one mother in Idaho who does, and she is making a real difference, even if engineers don't know it.

Railroad chaplains don't perform their acts of compassion for the praise and appreciation of anyone. No, they fulfill their sacred calling to alleviate sorrow, pain, and the feeling of loss and separation.

Regardless of the cause of death, whether by accident at a crossing from a tragic decision of a driver, or by natural causes, the remaining loved ones accepted the love and support offered by railroad chaplains. You could more completely understand the gratefulness of the survivors of an incident if you had been in the homes, hospitals, police stations, morgues or coroners' offices, funeral homes, and cemeteries, standing beside the chaplain and hearing the words of praise and gratitude for the help expressed, with tears in their eyes, by the remaining family members.

"It means a lot to me," said a dear lady in California whose husband had been killed in a crossing incident, "that a big corporate business has the grace to care for people and provide a chaplain to be present with me" during a tragic time.

A sister of a victim in Tennessee sent a card of thanks stating, "Thank you for your spiritual counsel and services at my brother's funeral. Your compassion and kindnesses have meant so much to me during this very difficult time. I am eternally grateful."

Another grieving mother, whose son died in a train crossing incident, expressed her heart to the chaplain assigned to the incident in a small town in Missouri, when she said, "Thank you for your sincere sympathy and for helping us financially pay for the funeral."

A thirty-one-year-old man who thought death was better than life stepped out in front of a fast-moving freight train. Suicide leaves a deep scar of pain that a lifetime cannot totally remove. His mother wrote her railroad chaplain these words: "Thank you for continuing to think of me. You helped ease my pain and get through another day. God bless you all."

You might realize she continues to struggle with her son's self-inflicted death, and chaplains continue to pray for her, even months after the tragedy. She still needs help and support.

Every person who dies or is critically injured in a railroad incident has a family. Every family has a sorrow; every sorrow needs comforting; every human comfort is offered by railroad chaplains.

15

THE VISION

Marketplace Asia-Pacific

"You must come to China. You must come to China."

Following a fellowship dinner with our chaplains and their spouses in Grand Rapids, Michigan, the temperature was dropping and snow began falling as Marketplace president and COO Dick De Witt and I were wrapping up a wonderful evening.

The waiter passed around Chinese fortune cookies for the dessert treat. As we opened the cookies and pulled out the small paper inside, one recorded: "Traveling to the east will bring great rewards." By this time in 2014, I had been traveling to Asia and a part of the Pacific Rim over a four-month period, spending thirty-nine days traveling in South Korea and Hong Kong, along with six cities in mainland China, and Macao, a total of nearly sixty thousand miles. Though I don't put faith in fortune cookies, I had to admit those words were prophetic in nature and truth. We had already seen God at work with a prospect of eternal rewards.

Toward the end of 2010, we began seeking the Lord's vision for global mission impact of Marketplace Ministries International; reaching out to countries of Asia, a part of the Pacific Rim. We began our dedicated efforts of due diligence, looking at part of Asia in which to launch our employee care service, as God directed.

Across the United States we had scores of meetings and conversations with Christian Chinese and Koreans. Also, we had lengthy conversations and strategy planning sessions with Americans serving in that part of the world with the International Mission Board of the Southern Baptist Convention.

My longtime friend, Tom Eliff, leads that organization with Holy Spirit fire and dedication, a true visionary leader for the entire world. His staff gave us much insight on Asia.

The next year we sent Vice President Jason Brown to Beijing to attend a Chinese business leaders' conference and to talk with multitudes of individuals in business and government. He was searching into the possibility of putting Employee Care Givers on the ground in Asia. He returned with a positive report, encouraging us to move forward with plans for that part of the world.

In October 2011, Marketplace Ministries hosted twenty Chinese Christian business owners who had attended a conference in Houston. We brought them to North Texas to see our operation and visit some of our client companies. I shared with our board about that meeting, telling the story of the little Chinese lady who came to me after I spoke to close the luncheon we provided for them at our international headquarters located at the Hope Center in Plano, Texas.

With tears in her eyes and pulling a Chinese interpreter with her, she approached me, speaking quickly in Mandarin these words: "You must come to China; you must come to China. I want my company to be the first company in China to have Employee Care Givers [Christian chaplains] in China. You must come to China." I cannot forget that experience even to this day.

"You must come to China." Her words made an imperishable imprint on my heart and in my mind. I think of them in the middle of the night and during the day. They are there when I go to sleep and when I wake up. They ring in my ears, and vibrate in my spirit. "You must come to China."

I see her tears, hear her voice, and I am moved to a vision, a vision I believed from God to go to Asia, to go to China. On January 27, 2012, I stood before our board of directors for Marketplace Ministries as the chairman. However, today I was standing before them to share my heart and soul, both with a vision from God. At least I thought it was!

I recommended to the board of directors of this ministry in the workplace that we "put out the fleece" for a confirmation from God to move forward with Marketplace Asia-Pacific, placing Employee Care Givers in China and Christian chaplains in businesses in South Korea or other parts of Asia. Also, we had looked at Taiwan, Hong Kong, and the Philippines as possible launch locations of Phase 1 of our mission for souls in Marketplace Asia-Pacific.

The calling for us to begin in China, obeying all of the laws of the land, was strong. I do not know how the apostle Paul felt when he heard the call to "come over to Macedonia and help us" (Acts 16:9); however, I know how I felt when that dear Chinese lady said, "You must come to China. You must come to China." Her call was from God for us to go to China.

I felt we must, too. However, we had a board, and from the board we had an Asia Expansion Committee that was responsible for giving direction for forming an expansion budget, where we would launch, when we would launch, and how we would launch.

After many meetings, much prayer, and visiting with several outside individuals and organizations already working in Asia, the committee still had much to be decided and many questions to answered.

The board had not yet voted its approval or disapproval for us to seek launching this ministry halfway around the world. Even though the concept of a fleece to prove God's will was used only one time in the Bible, that one use made it acceptable for us in the twenty-first century.

What would be our fleece for God to confirm we should move forward, seeking to show His love to workers of the world? It would be through acts of kindness and gospel proclamation, as individuals opened their hearts and minds inquiring about things with an eternal prospective.

What is the fleece we would lay before our Lord? Larry King, our chief financial officer, had put in many hours seeking to design a Marketplace Asia-Pacific budget, and his estimate for sixty months of operation would require at least one million dollars. For any of us, that is a lot of money; however, for the God who owns everything, including cattle on a thousand hills, it was just pocket change.

We said if God entrusts us with a million dollars earmarked for Asia, we would know He met our fleece goal and we would go. The ministry, which does not raise large amounts of contributions, had never come close to one million dollars, and to be honest, I was not certain "we" could raise that much in the year 2012, because it was now January 27.

To reach our goal in 365 days God's people, who have a burning heart for the souls of men, would have to give one million dollars to this Asia campaign and do it in the next 348 days, before the midnight hour of December 31, 2012.

God honors our giving by providing for our every material, physical, and spiritual need, as we put Him first and foremost, above all else. That means our finances as well. That's a promise from God, and He has never broken a promise. Never has; never will!

When I was a boy, on more than one occasion, my mother would pile all five of her sons into an old Chevrolet, with a potato basket overflowing with groceries, homemade rolls, cakes, and pies, and drive out in the country halfway between Denison and Sherman in Grayson County to the poor farm. That was where most of the most poverty-stricken people lived together in the worst conditions.

On these trips, I met many people as we distributed the food as far as it would go. During those times we went to help those down and out, I never met one person, not one, who said he or she was living on the poor farm because of giving away too much money to God and His causes. They were living in poverty because they had squandered their money on things that were not eternal.

I challenged the board to claim with me Psalm 37:25-26. This is what is written there: "I have been young, and now I am old; yet I have not seen the righteous forsaken, nor his descendants begging bread. He is ever merciful, and lends; and his descendants are blessed." I will live and die on those two verses of promise. If we want to be rich toward God, with real joy and a great return on investment, then we must give generously to our Lord and His work.

On July 9, 2012, the total amount committed stood at $642,040. Cash gifts were $335,429, and we still needed $357,960 to positively hear from God through the fleece. The Lord had provided 64 percent of the goal with 36 percent remaining, and 49.3 percent of the days in the year remained. Our board committed a total of $564,000 of the one million dollar fleece goal.

During the eleven months of the active campaign to raise the one-million-dollar fleece goal, there were many unusual and miraculous expressions of generous giving, and God at work in the lives of people. There is one I must share, however, and you will rejoice with me at what God does and how He works to accomplish His plans.

Marketplace Ministries follows a system, set up by our auditors, for opening the mail and accounting for checks and contributions. Two of our staff members open the mail every day and account for all incoming checks from clients, supporters, and all other sources. They are logged and signed off on by both people before taking them to the accounting office.

Only occasionally is there something so unusual a check would be brought to me. However, one day during the height of the campaign to raise one million dollars for the fleece goal to begin chaplains serving in Asia, one of the ladies came in my office and said, "I thought you might want to see this," as she handed me a cashier's check.

A cashier's check is unusual in itself; however, this was more unusual, for it was made out for ten thousand dollars. I looked at the name of the person who had secured the check and sent it to us. Of all things, it was from a neighbor who has lived in our neighborhood for nearly forty years.

How could they do this? Surely they don't have the financial resources to give a gift like this. This is certainly beyond their ability to give; this must be sacrificial giving. There was a touch of sadness, mixed with joy, as I held the check and hoped it did not negatively affect their personal needs and family, their two sons and grandchildren.

Because I was flying out of Dallas early the next morning on ministry business, I picked up my pen and dashed off a quick note of thanks to the couple. I tried to express my sincere gratitude for their extremely generous offering and overwhelming support for Marketplace Asia-Pacific.

Early the next morning, at zero dark 30, I headed for the airport. The day was busy, and the week was long. I was in one meeting after another, speaking to chaplains, meeting with clients, and planning with executive leaders. Only now and again did I think about my neighbors and their generosity in giving ten thousand dollars.

Back in my office, I was going about my duties, as days are always busy. I thank the Lord for health, a calling, an assignment from Him, and work to accomplish. Days run into weeks and weeks into months.

That same lady walked into my office again, holding what I quickly recognized as another cashier's check. She handed it to me with a smile on her face and simply said, "They did it again."

Sure enough, another check for ten thousand dollars had arrived from the same people. That does it. They have given too much, and I am going to call them. I am going to tell them to stop giving, for they have already given above and beyond generously, and they should not give any more. I had never made a call like that before; however, now was the time.

That night after dinner I made my way upstairs to my small home office to place a call to these dear and generous people. I rehearsed what I would say, and how I would say it. "Please don't give any more, for you have already done your part and much more."

I have known the woman of the family for more than sixty years, as we grew up together in a small Texas town just two blocks apart. We belonged to the same church and went to the same elementary and high school, even though I was a couple of years behind her.

"Hello, this is Sunny Stricklin [my nickname growing up]," I said, as she answered the phone. That began a fast conversation about our lives, our families, and God's work.

I told her how much I appreciated their generous support for the cause of Christ in Asia; however, I was calling to say something I had never said before. I told her I was calling to ask them not to give us any more money. They had already done more than they should with their generosity.

I paused, for I did not feel good about what I had just said. I was trying to think what else I could say to express my appreciation and at the same time tell them they should not give additional gifts. They should use their financial resources for their own needs.

She began to laugh.

"Sunny, let me tell you a little secret. Our own family does not even know this," I heard her say, as I listened closely.

She continued, "A few weeks ago we hit oil and gas on our land in South Texas, and today we have more money to give to God's work than we have ever had. We gave to your organization because we believe it will be used to win people to Jesus, and we wanted to be a part of that," were her words as I listened in stunned silence.

Oil and gas on their land? I didn't even know they had any land, but God did! A few days later we got ANOTHER cashier's check, this one for twenty thousand dollars.

When I get to heaven, one of the first things I am going to ask the Father is, "Sir, did you give these dear people that huge sum of money because you knew they would use it to help us go to Asia to win souls for you?"

I am pretty sure I know His answer. That oil and gas had been under that land for hundreds or thousands of years, and they just found it. These dear friends who own the mineral royalties and land are God's people who have a generous heart toward God's work, and they are givers.

The year was rushing by, and each day that turned on the calendar brought us closer to the final deadline of December 31, and that midnight hour. It was now October 10 and commitments and cash stood at $728,270.76. I am not certain how we got seventy-six cents; however, every penny moved us closer to a dollar and every dollar closer to our goal. Cash was $524,584.76, with an additional $217,729.24 needed to hit our target of one million dollars to launch us into Asia-Pacific, with chaplains and employee care givers on the ground showing God's love through acts of kindness, care, support, and human love much like divine love.

Another month ticked by, and it was November 6. We were up to $832,670, anticipating moving on to $883,000 by the end of the month. The end of the year was coming quickly, for we all know between Thanksgiving and Christmas is only a flash in time. Many of us had been led of God to give, and to give sacrificially and generously. I was very grateful for that expression of faith in God's vision and leading for ministry to Asia.

I was still convinced by faith God was in this. He was leading, and the vision had come from Him. We were to fulfill the vision. The first step by faith was to see Him provide the funds for the fleece goal.

Could God do it? I knew He could; however, I did not know with absolute certainty it was His will for us to be entrusted with one million dollars for ministry in Asia. I went back to our board, staff, clients, and general supporters asking them to increase their prayers for this strategic initiative and give even beyond what they had planned to give originally. Beginning with Ann and me, I ask people to give a second gift to help guarantee we would surpass the fleece. I knew many were and would pray with us about this effort and God might impress them to give again, give more; however, that was between each believer and our Lord.

The last month whizzed by, and money flowed in like never before. God was up to something, and we stood on the sidelines to watch and pray. On January 2, 2013, I was able to share these words of Samuel: "The Lord brought about a great victory that day…" (2 Samuel 23:10), for He really had. Only a great God could orchestrate such a great victory for His glory.

Nearly a year had passed when, by faith, I had told our board members, and anyone who would listen to me, I believed a day would come when we would rejoice together under God's banner of victory, when the fleece goal was surpassed.

We join together with the writer of Hebrews in saying, "Through Him, then, let us continually offer up a sacrifice of praise to God, that is, the fruit of our lips giving thanks to His name" (13:15). We shout together with the psalmist, "But You, O Lord, are a God full of compassion, and gracious, longsuffering and abundant in mercy and truth." (86:15).

All praise to God for giving us His grace and pouring out His abundant blessings on our vision from Him to launch the workplace ministry of the King in Asia-Pacific. Additional gratitude is offered to those more than four hundred individuals, client companies, staff, business owners, and generous supporters who gave in abundance to this cause of Christ. The ministry received single financial gifts ranging from $5.00 to $156,000, for a total of $1,140,000.

The fleece goal was surpassed about fifty-six hours before the midnight deadline on December 31, 2012. Our Lord not only confirmed the fleece goal; He far surpassed it by well over a hundred thousand dollars, about 15 percent "above what we could even ask or think" (Ephesians 3:20).

I will never forget it; on the morning we were fairly certain we had gone well above the one-million-dollar goal, I received a telephone call from Noah Kreider, a dear friend from Manheim, Pennsylvania, asking if we needed any more money to reach our goal. I was pleased to say, "No, Noah, God has already given more than what we asked. The goal has been met." That was the second such call that morning, as another businessman in Iowa said he would give whatever amount it took for us to reach the fleece goal. His finances were protected by God for another good cause, and he did not need to give any more than he had already given, for the goal was passed.

Expressions of generosity kept pouring in, which was overwhelming. I had never been a part of something where God's fingerprints were so evident. One of our most dedicated chaplains sent me an e-mail saying he and his wife had not been able to give up to now. However, on the last day of the year they had figured out how they could give the first six months of his salary in 2013 to our missionary effort in Asia. I was pleased to tell them that was a most generous offer; however, we did not need their funds because God had already led many others to give so abundantly; our goal was met, and even surpassed. This couple was blessed by the decision they made, when God knew it was not needed. Yet, they needed to pray through and make the decision they made.

All of us were praising God, as the news spread that the fleece goal was abundantly subscribed and more; praise by many continued all across the country. Our hearts were overflowing with deep gratitude to God and God's generous people. They had been used to achieve Phase 1, the fleece goal for financial assets to begin in Asia and to be able to undergird the work for some time, until it became self-sustaining.

Phase 1, the vision and financial resources; Phase 2, where and when to launch; Phase 3, strategy for implementation of ministry; Phase 4, God-glorifying results. Currently we are completing Phase 2 and seeking to move into Phase 3 before the end of 2014. If the first three phases are successfully reached by the grace of God and His leading, then Phase 4 will come with certainty.

As we sought to gain understanding for Marketplace Asia-Pacific, we needed experienced and wise counsel. We turned to Henry Holley, a man who has been going to China since he was a young Marine in 1945. And, now as the Asian director for the Billy Graham Evangelistic Association, he has made forty-eight trips to China and Southeast Asia. Henry Holley, who has been my friend since 1966 when we both served with Dr. Graham, was the man who led us in our development. He is a godly and good man who loves the Chinese people and has many friends in China. He was a God-send!

We prayed for an extended time that God would lead us to just the right person to lead the work in Asia, if and when the doors totally opened. It was my conviction we must have a Chinese-American who knew the culture and languages, speaking Mandarin as well as Cantonese and other Chinese dialects. I asked God to give us a man who had lived in China, knew the country the way I know Texas, and was called to affect the workers of the world with God's love through acts of kindness.

Over the last years of walking with my Lord and Savior Jesus Christ, I have grown in my understanding of divine providence, His sovereignty. I have come to trust a lot more than I once did, that God controls everything. Whether it is pain or pleasure, God is in charge. He is orchestrating all things in all our lives. If by faith we really believe and trust that, then nothing ever goes wrong. Whatever happens is a part of His will and direction for our lives. If we wait on Him, then He will work out His plan in His time. That is a hard lesson to learn, and even harder to believe and trust in each day, each circumstance.

Bruce Grantham, my dear friend, board member, client owner, and chairman of the Asia-Pacific Expansion Committee, and I were invited to a reception and dinner for Christian Chinese businesspeople. East-West Ministries, effectively led by President Kirk Nelson, launched a Business as Mission in China in 2010 and was developing relationships, along with helping Chinese companies grow into successful economic enterprises.

On that beautiful Texas spring day, I drove out north of Dallas to the backwoods on small winding roads to a beautiful and large home with acres surrounding it, a large tank with blue water, and trees lining the fence line. A lovely tent was raised just outside the refreshing swimming pool, with iced drinks, tables, eating utensils, and the smell of barbecue.

Bruce met me there that Saturday afternoon, and we began meeting the honored Chinese guests.

In one of those quiet moments between shaking hands with new friends and meeting them, Bruce and I were standing off to the side, somewhat separated from the larger group. Suddenly, we saw this distinguished Chinese man walking toward us, coming from where he had parked his car.

For the first time we met Kelvin Wong, a student at Southwestern Baptist Theological Seminary in Fort Worth, who had come to welcome other Chinese to Texas. I liked him as soon as I met him. We shook hands and began visiting.

I did not know for certain then; however, this was God's man, chosen by our Lord, to be the director of Marketplace Asia-Pacific. It would take several months, many meetings, and much discussion before we would offer him the position on September 6, 2013. The position he accepted.

Here was a man who, for more than two decades, was an educated and practicing architect with offices in China. He grew up in Hong Kong and is a third-generation Christian. He and his lovely, musically gifted wife, Alice, along with their two children, came to the United States when Hong Kong reverted to China.

Kelvin sold his architectural business in Hong Kong and moved to California to qualify as architect in the United States, practicing his skills and training with a firm in Los Angeles. However, the future for him was education in seminary and preparing to serve God in a direct and full-time manner. He sensed a call to vocational Christian service. Where and exactly when, only God knew.

When Kelvin finished his degree program after three years of study at Southwestern Baptist Theological Seminary, he had six ministry job opportunities in the King's service. Marketplace Asia-Pacific was only one of them. After much prayer by him and Alice, and all of us at Marketplace, he felt led of God to join our team. That was another red-letter day for this ministry. Another warrior who fights with kindness, compassion, and love had joined the army of the Lord at work.

Between August 2013 and January 2014, ministry representatives made three trips to South Korea and China, visiting nearly a dozen cities, having scores and scores of meetings, and talking person to person to more than 150 Chinese, Koreans, and business executives from all over the world.

Kelvin and I made the first two extended ground-breaking endeavors in Asia. C. G. Maclin, president of Marketplace Chaplains International, and Kelvin spent twenty-three days in Asia in January 2014. We have seven more trips planned in the future, for marketing our service, recruiting chaplains in Korea and employee care givers in China, training them to begin our service, and launching our Employee Care Company in four cities in China, Hong Kong, and two cities in South Korea.

We continue to walk by faith as we seek the Lord's leading and blessings. The doors are opening for our work, and we have obtained letters of agreement from huge corporations and a privately held company. There are other companies considering our services and we believe we will begin in China and Hong Kong with five or six companies and two in Korea. We anticipate a start-up of some 3,000 workers. The ministry first started with only 150 employees in Texas in 1984, and now has more than 150,000, along with than 400,000 family members. We pray, one day, we will be caring, supporting, and loving millions of Asian workers and their families. Everyone needs someone to reach out to them, encourage and help them, extend hope to them, and give a listening and sympathetic ear. All people need to hear of God's love and His salvation, and that includes Asians.

I don't know what God will allow to happen in these countries. We will do our best with His help and blessing, and wait upon Him to show us what blessings He has in store for Marketplace Asia-Pacific.

16

GOD'S PROVISION

Thou hath made me what I am and given me what I have. (Puritan prayer)

Ann and I decided to accept God's call to the marketplace with no guarantees and only one promise: "I will never leave you nor forsake you" (Hebrews 13:5). Launching Marketplace Ministries required opening a bank account. The date was December 27, 1983, and we wrote the check from our personal account for twenty-five dollars to open the ministry checking account. That was the beginning, and in my wildest dreams I never considered God, by His gracious provision, would give us millions of dollars to manage for His glory and reinvest to bring souls from around the world into His kingdom.

What begins microscopic can become gigantic when God is in it. He is the Founder, the Powerful One, the Provider, the Motivator, the Miracle Worker, the Wisdom Giver, and the One who gets all the glory. It is all of God, and no one else.

I am often asked why we did not write the check for a larger amount. The truthful answer is simple and straightforward: That was just about all we had to give. We might have been able to increase that first check by a few more dollars; however, we did not have very much dispensable cash. You recall, we had one son in Baylor University and another who would be there the following year. I was employed in the Evangelism Division of the Baptist General Convention of Texas working with youth evangelism and military chaplaincy.

Really, that twenty-five dollars was more than we could afford to tie up in a bank account with no new income for another month before The Bonneau Company paid the first fifteen hundred dollars for its lone chaplain.

I learned early on money is not the most important in life, for none of us own anything anyway. We are only managers of the financial resources God places in our hands for a brief period of time. I knew we came into this world with nothing, and we will take nothing with us when we depart. Nothing! Empty-handed in and empty-handed out!

My assurance was God would provide, though I didn't know how. I didn't know then and often still don't. Yet, He has never failed, and He never will. If we do our part, God will do His, which is as certain as the sun coming up in the east tomorrow morning. It is absolute, assured, and without a doubt.

What is my part and what is God's part? Mine is to seek His kingdom first, foremost, above all else. What is His part? Adding to me all I need, my daily requirements, my daily provisions. God gives us what we need, for He does not always provide a pension that comes regularly whether we need it or not. If it is a human pension, it is one we have earned, and it will come. God provides when there is a need, regardless of when that is.

However, we are to fulfill Matthew 6:33: "But seek first the kingdom of God and His righteousness, and all these things shall be added unto you." This is the promise Ann and I have built our lives, our marriage, and our family upon, His kingdom first. What is His kingdom? "For the kingdom of God is not eating and drinking, but righteousness and peace and joy in the Holy Spirit" (Romans 14:17).

When God promises to give us "all of these things," what things is He talking about? He is talking about bread, clothing, and the practical things we all need to live in this world called earth, and we do not have to worry about them either. God is in the business of providing our needs, our human requirements, and our self-sustaining items for life. He will do that; however, we are to seek Him and His kingdom before we seek the necessities of physical life. We are to put first the spiritual life and then the physical life will take care of itself.

In our home, we have these words carved in an old heart pine mantel over the fireplace: "Seek ye first the kingdom of God." It is a daily reminder to put the Lord first, first before things, first before money, first before anything except the Savior, Jesus Christ, Himself. If we practice doing that with all our heart, He will take care of everything else, including money to undergird His work inside and outside the church. I have seen the sustaining results of that promise for more than seven decades.

What is the test of how to manage large assets of God's ministry money? It is how you manage money God puts in your hand, no matter the amount. If you are faithful with little, then the Word says you will be faithful with much. As God's stewards, money managers, and overseers of His resources, we will one day give an accounting for what we did with it, how we invested it, spent it, and gave it to causes of Christ. We own nothing and God owns it all is the fundamental principle of money management.

I never considered one day I would be responsible for millions of dollars to oversee, manage, budget, and reinvest in ministry to glorify God and bring men to Him. I never dreamed chaplains would work more than 250,000 hours a year in caring for people and showing God's love through acts of kindness. With a laborer worthy of his hire, those hours would generate millions of dollars in income for His ministry and for the lives of His servants.

I shared with you that in 1984, the first twelve months of chaplains serving in the work arena, our total income was $86,102. It would take ten years to reach one million dollars of income in twelve months. Nineteen years later we are billing well over one million dollars a month. The bigger the income, the bigger the responsibility, and to whom much is given much is required.

I know this is not my money; this is God's money! However, as the chairman and CEO of Marketplace Ministries, I am accountable for its use and care, along with a twenty-two-person board of directors and a finance, audit, and compensation committee overseeing all that I do; they are my governance, as is the Lord.

When Ann and I married in 1958, I entered active duty in the United States Air Force as a second lieutenant. We were stationed at Donaldson Air Force Base, outside of Greenville, South Carolina, about twelve hundred miles from our families. Ann was a recent education graduate from Baylor University. She was in her first year as a school teacher in a poor school district in the mountains north of Greenville. Her pay was $125 a month, while my salary was much higher at $175 monthly.

That was big money to us in that day, and in our budget was figured a tithe. Starting with our wedding in May, we earned a total of $3,026 for the year. I have a record of our giving and income tax returns since 1958. That first year we gave $474.75 to Pendleton Street Church, an Air Force campaign for what was the early version of the United Way received $5.00, and $10.00 went to the Billy Graham Evangelistic Association. Our giving the first year of our marriage was 15.7 percent of our income, a tithe plus, in New Testament giving. We had no dispute about tithing, for it was a part of growing up for both of us, and it was our practice long before we came together as husband and wife. We did not even discuss it except to agree it was what we would do.

However, we did talk about what we called a lifetime giving goal. How much could we give back to God, and His kingdom work, in our entire lifetime of giving? Making just over three thousand dollars a year, the amount of giving to the Lord was not all that much. In fact, the largest amount of money I could even imagine giving over a lifetime was one million dollars, if He chose to place financial assets in our hands to manage for Him. A million dollars is a whole lot of money. I didn't even know if we would ever earn a million dollars between us in our entire lifetime, much less give a million to the Lord's causes.

Then we considered another goal. What if we tithed 10 percent during the first ten years of our marriage, and on the eleventh year we would give 11 percent, the twelfth year 12 percent, and so on the rest of our married life, until we reached fifty years together, when we would give 50 percent. Wow!

We agreed we would try to do that if God supplied the financial resources. After the first ten years of marriage, we found it easy to meet the goals in years eleven through fourteen. At that point, however, with two sons at home and me in seminary graduate school and seeking a second bachelor of arts degree, our goals seemed impossible.

As it turned out, our giving hit its target percentage in sixteen out of the first twenty-five years, not the best record, but at least we had a giving goal. In two or three of those years, we even fell below the standard of 10 percent. Over the next twenty-five years the goal of our giving went from 26 percent in 1983 to 50 percent in 2007, and we hit our target percentage only two times, even though we were giving more than we had ever given, more than we ever thought we would make, much less give. We have been married fifty-five years, and last year we were able to meet and exceed our giving goal, by God's grace and for His glory.

These were years where, even though Ann was no longer working, I had four sources of income: my regular ministry job, Army Reserve duty pay or Army retirement pay, motivational speaking income, and preaching income. I don't ever remember having just one job. In fact, I always had several at any one time for most of my life, even while in college and graduate school.

Making more just means you can give more. God continued to answer my prayer that He would make me a generous person, one who would practice giving generously on all occasions. Corinthians says He made you rich so you can be generous on all occasions. For many years, in my capacity as the senior leader with Marketplace, I refused to accept my total pay package and gave back a portion of my salary to the ministry. Year after year we did not increase our take-home income, keeping the same standard of living we had always had.

We worked hard to get out of debt and pay off our only obligation, our house payment. It was a glorious day when we gathered our family around and talked about getting out of debt, not owing a penny to anyone. We celebrated together by burning our house note and thanking God for His provision. That made a deep impression on our sons and their families, including our grandchildren.

I'm happy to say we have surpassed our lifetime giving goal. Doing so has been an exciting experience achieved for the glory of God.

Please do not get the wrong idea in me sharing this with you. First, we have not sacrificed in our giving. I wish we had, but in all honesty we have not. We have been blessed far beyond what we have given, what we have invested in God's work. We have learned over and over that it truly is more blessed to give than to receive. Also, when you give to glorify our Lord, the Word says He will open the windows of heaven and pour you out a blessing you cannot even receive. He has done that for us, too!

Today, God has made it possible to give away more in one year than I ever made in any of the first twenty-five years we were married. I do not understand God's math. He can provide for you to give when it is difficult to see exactly how it all came about anyway.

God continues to teach me to be "generous on all occasions." I still pray about that, for I want no part of greed or materialism. I want to be a giver, not a getter. I pray daily the Lord will guard me from the "lust of the eyes" which is money, greed, and materialism, and He answers my prayers.

God does have a sense of humor.

A member of our board of directors called me one day and asked me to join him for lunch at a very expensive restaurant in downtown Dallas. I accepted and must confess I knew he would pick up the check.

When you pull up to the double-glass front doors, the car valets descend on you to park your car. They give you a claim check, and you go inside for a delicious meal and good fellowship with a friend.

After a wonderful visit and a fine meal, it was time to go back to work. His office was next door, so he went out the back door. My car was out front, and I started out through the first of two doors that led to the valet station. When I went through the first door I reached for my money clip and pulled off three one-dollar bills.

Immediately, I sensed a voice from heaven saying, "That wasn't very generous." What? I thought that was a pretty good tip. However, I did not want to argue with the Voice, so I went back into my left pocket, pulled off two more bills, and crammed the remaining bills back into my pocket.

The parking attendant saw me coming, so she dashed for my car and quickly brought it up. She opened the door on the driver's side and stood there anticipating my service gift, the tip. I reached out and took her hand, and gave her the five crumpled bills. She politely said in a calm voice, "Thank you, sir."

I got in my car, snapped my safety belt in place, and started to ease away from the front of the restaurant when I heard the young lady shout loud enough for all to hear within a block, "Mister, mister, thanks so much. I really appreciate that!" I stuck out my arm and waved at her as I drove off. She really appreciated that five-dollar tip.

I guessed that amount was sufficient to show that I did thank her. Her voice sounded happy enough anyway.

It was twenty miles back to my office, so it was a while before I got there. When I did, after parking my car, I pulled out my bills to straighten them out, putting them in order and placing the clip to hold them together. As I looked at them, I noticed something strange.

I knew I had had five one-dollar bills, plus some other bills, including a fifty-dollar bill. There was still a one-dollar bill. But that couldn't be, because I had given the girl five one-dollar bills, I thought. As I thumbed through my money, four of the five one-dollar bills were gone, and so was the fifty!

Be careful what you pray for, because God might hear you and answer your prayer! I prayed I would be generous on all occasions, and that day I was; a fifty-four-dollar tip for parking my car. No wonder that young lady loudly cried out thanks for my tip. It was probably her largest of the day, maybe her whole lifetime.

I wonder if that young woman had prayed that morning to the Almighty, telling Him: "Father, I still needed fifty dollars more for my rent this month." If she did, the Lord heard her and met her need from someone else who prayed he would be more generous on all occasions. Both her prayer and mine were answered!

Commitment to Financial Accountability

Some of my learning about managing ministry money came during the years I served on the Billy Graham team of the Billy Graham Evangelistic Association. I was special assistant to Dr. Graham, traveling around the world. I saw firsthand, up close and very personal, the integrity and honesty in Mr. Graham's handling of money, God's money given by God's people.

There was strong accountability and impeccable scrutiny in taking proper care of money, paying bills, being totally open in all aspects of the financial part of ministry. Audits and public openness were a vital part of his ministry, and that is why no mud has ever been thrown on Dr. Graham or his organization in more than sixty years of serving God and man. I would imagine he has been provided several billion dollars, or much more, for his ministry around the world.

During the five years I traveled with the Graham team, from country to country, I could see clearly how finances were processed and accounted for. Being in all kinds of meetings, big ones, public ones, private ones, and intimate ones, I never heard or saw anything that made me question Dr. Graham's integrity, motives, or ministry finances. There never was a question about his honesty, or any hint of greed or materialism.

When we began Marketplace, I thought a lot about the money aspect of the organization, and about my friend, Billy Graham. As you know, in the beginning it was a rather small amount of funds we managed; however, it would grow to be a rather large amount, with fourteen million dollars received in one year. I want the same integrity in our ministry as Dr. Graham has in his, the same safeguards, the same accountability, the same oversight, and the same openness.

We have worked hard to establish that kind of commitment to financial integrity. There has never been a question about our handling of money or any other moral or legal issues. One key on a daily basis is accountability. Someone is checking on everyone, and everyone is being checked on, with the checkers being checked on, too.

Since 1996, Marketplace Ministries has been an active member of the Evangelical Council for Financial Accountability (ECFA), recognized for practicing the highest of standards in financial integrity in ministry. For the past seventeen years the ministry has renewed its ECFA membership, proving it upholds all the requirements for membership, in order to project the ECFA seal of approval in its financial activities.

The largest annual income ever received by the ministry amounted to $14,629,654 in 2012. For the past six years, ministry income has averaged more than $12,500,000. For thirty years, the total annual income of Marketplace has increased over the previous year every year except in 2004, 2008, and 2010. Contributions have increased over the previous year in twenty-six out of thirty years of operations.

Marketplace Ministries has never borrowed money for any purpose and has never been in debt, not one penny. The ministry has paid cash for everything and has closed thirty years of service with all bills paid, ready to start the next year on solid financial footing. The ministry has met its budget every year of operation, never failing to pay all bills for the year with a little left over.

However, red ink has been on the books close to year end. It was fearful on a few occasions in years gone by. In 1987, only four short years after starting up, it looked like there would be debt and all bills would not be paid.

We have made a practice of closing the office between Christmas and New Year's. We laugh and say we don't pay high salaries; however, we give you a lot of paid time off.

I would go to the office every day to check the mail and see if there were any contributions. Also, I would study the accounting books for outstanding bills and other financial needs. As 1987 drew to a close, I knew we must have an additional $35,000 to break even by year's end. We had received only $39,806 in contributions to the ministry all year. We would need almost that much again if we were to close the books in the black, and here it was the last few days of December. Time was running out, and my faith was wavering—not quite running out, but close.

One day I made my way to the office after I knew the mail would be delivered to see if there were any checks. There were three or four envelopes, and I carefully opened them. The first two were very small gifts. Well, any gift will help, I thought, and I was grateful.

I held the third envelope in my hand and looked at it carefully. The return address was Bakersfield, California, and the handwriting had evidence of being that of an older person.

I opened the envelope and there was no note, just a check. I looked at it and thought, wonderful, five hundred dollars will help some; looking again, I thought five thousand dollars. Wow, that will help a whole lot! Looking at it the third time, my eyes focused on the actual number.

It was fifty thousand dollars.

Can you believe that? Fifty thousand dollars came from a lady I did not even know. That would wipe out all that red ink of $35,000 with some left over. The contributions for the month and year just went to $89,806, the largest amount we had ever received.

"Praise God from whom all blessings flow; to God be the glory, great things He hath done," you may have heard me shouting and singing. I wondered if my voice was heard all the way to California; I knew it went all the way to heaven.

I thought about the dear generous lady, whose husband had owned a large company, and when it was sold, he managed millions of dollars. I had never met them before he died.

Sometime later, I learned a client and good friend, Paul J. Meyer of Waco, Texas, told this dear lady about our ministry and what good things we were doing to honor the Lord and telling others about Him. I am convinced the Father nudged her to write that check for a little more than we needed and much more than we deserved.

One day, a letter was placed on my desk. The address was scribbled in pencil and was rather difficult to read. However, it had found its way to our office address. I opened the letter and written were these words: "This is a gift from the widow's mite," and attached was a one-dollar bill.

People give out of their financial resources. The lady in California gave from hers and this unknown saint gave from what he had. I was touched by the note, as well as by the old, wrinkled dollar bill.

If you come visit our national support center and international headquarters, you will see that note and dollar in a nice wooden frame on a stand in a prominent location in the reception area near the front door. I see it almost every day when I enter our office. It reminds me that not every gift is a big one in man's sight; however, in the Lord's sight it is a huge gift.

Every dollar is given to the Lord God, and it all belongs to Him. Our task is to take genuine care of every cent and reinvest it all for God's glory and man's good.

We have a business model for finances, meaning we have a fee for services. We can tell a company owner what it will cost the ministry to have chaplains in the company. We can determine that by doing a cost-study analysis.

At any given time, we are typically owed about one million dollars, and we usually cannot collect a few thousand each year. However, it is a small percent of our total billings. I give you that as background because we do not have to raise as much money now as we did in the beginning.

Our philosophy for direct fundraising is simple. We do not ask for financial help until we truly need it. Usually it's for a specific project, normally a one-time expense. That is our promise and our practice.

I have learned a strategic principle for fundraising. First, I know God is the one who pours out His blessings, and all things come down from above. However, this is the other part of that principle: The one asking must be the first one to give to the cause for which he is asking.

If you as the requester are not willing to give a sacrificial and generous gift, how can you expect others to do so? You must ask all others to join you in this effort, in this giving, in this sacrifice, in excelling "in the grace of giving." People will be open and committed to give to something when the one making the appeal is committed as the first giver.

On occasion, and under the leading of God, you might even share the amount you will give, the amount you are bringing to the coffers as a gift to God and the cause of Christ for which you are appealing. King David did that when he shared with the people what he would give in seeking funds to build the temple. All the leaders told how much gold and other precious stones and gifts to this effort of God they would give. The Scripture records, "Then the people rejoiced, for they had offered willingly, because with a loyal heart they had offered willingly to the Lord..." (1 Chronicles 29:6-9).

The people had joy in their hearts and were stirred in their souls to join the leaders in giving generously and abundantly because of what others had done.

They knew what those appealing for funds to build the temple would do, and the people were inspired to do as much or more by freely and wholeheartedly giving to the Lord's effort to build the temple.

Remember this fundraising principle. You give first, and then ask others to join you in giving, generously and wholeheartedly, as unto the Lord.

Also remember, we do not ask until we really need financial help. We do not ask on the ministry side of Marketplace to build up financial assets to be used sometime in the future, except in the case of endowment gifts to the Marketplace Ministries Foundation. When we ask for financial support, we already know where we will reinvest those funds placed in our hands of responsibility. Often it is for a one-time special project that requires money we do not have in our regular operating budget for the current year.

Mainly we use fundraising efforts to financially undergird ministry expansion. We have done this as we have developed the ministry in forty-five states of the union where we now serve in nearly a thousand cities, a strong base of operations. Our financial and prayer supporters have made it possible by God's empowerment to begin chaplains' service in the Commonwealth of Puerto Rico, Mexico, the United Kingdom, Canada, and soon in Asia. Each time we have first given our personal financial assets, then asked others to join us in an alliance to move the ministry forward to new territories, new cities, new countries, and to care for and witness to new people, the response has been overwhelming.

In 1991, we began to track and account for gifts given by staff members, both chaplains and administrative support personnel. Over all these years, the staff has faithfully and continually supported the financial base for their ministry at work. They give to the place they are called to serve and give generously. It is estimated the workers in this ministry, chaplains and other staff, have given to equal one dollar of every ten dollars contributed to Marketplace.

Not long ago, I was speaking to our chaplain staff in Orlando, Florida. When I travel for the ministry or for a personal vacation, I always seek to have a chaplains' fellowship breakfast or lunch in any city where we have a ministry presence. It is a great time for me to express thanks for their service and hear them relate their ministry experiences blessed by God. It is thrilling to hear how workers are being helped, cared for, supported, and brought to the Savior.

After I finished my talk, I shook hands with individuals and visited with as many as possible. I noticed one lady chaplain who stood at the back of the room waiting to speak with me. She pulled me off to the side where it was more private as she began to apologize for not being able to give cash gifts to the ministry. Then she said, "Mr. Stricklin, I never turn in for reimbursement all the miles I drive, and neither do I request expense payment for the toll roads I drive every week making my worksite visits."

You can't buy that deep dedication and commitment; that is far above money and material things. I could do nothing except try to express my heartfelt gratitude for her and her unselfish support. She will have a greater reward in heaven when she gets home. Her gifts will be recognized by the Father.

In 2007, after we had anchored the ministry in Mexico, our vision was to turn to the United Kingdom, because we had an open door in Scotland. Our dear friend and co-laborer, John Coors, the chairman, president, and CEO of CoorsTek in Golden, Colorado, had a manufacturing plant in Glenrothes, Scotland, where we had a standing offer to place chaplains when we could. Well, could we do that now?

Our chief financial officer, Larry King, did a cost-study analysis to see what it would take to launch a chaplains' ministry in the UK. As we have stated, money is not most important, but money does have something to do with most things that are, and that includes the work of God. Ministry is driven by God's Holy Spirit, and He uses human financial means to help move His work along.

This ministry could not open the third front of national and international ministry of chaplains at work, if it were not for godly and generous donors. We could not have begun in the UK that year or anywhere without the generous support of God's people.

With the financial figures in hand for the King's work, a minimum of $350,000 would be required. Ministry leaders had "faith as a mustard seed" (Luke 17:6) in seeking through a written appeal the $350,000 before the last day of the year. This was to be God's UK Confirmation Campaign, to secure funds to begin a chaplains' care service in the mother country.

When all the funds were counted on that final day of 2007, more had been given than anyone could ask or imagine. The total for this first European effort was a staggering $522,646, given by hundreds of people. Scores gave gifts representing the widow's mite as they gave all they could. Others, blessed with the wealth of Solomon, gave from their abundance with open generosity. Our largest gift was $175,000!

We still have money to continue to invest in England, Scotland, and Wales. God's people by God's grace have provided the financial underpinning needed for His work at home and in other parts of the world.

Even though the ministry began in Canada in 2009, its growth was as slow as the melting snow in April in the Northwest Territory. The funds were barely adequate to pay salaries, plus the other financial requirements. We needed more money in order to send personnel from Dallas all across our northern neighbor's homeland telling the Marketplace story. If we were ever going to expand the ministry base, it would take money, a lot more than we had.

The need was a minimum of one hundred thousand dollars for travel, marketing, recruiting chaplains and training them, and then assigning and supervising them. So, in the beginning of 2010, we started the Canadian Expansion 2011 to raise the needed hundred thousand dollars. We began by asking our boards, then the staff, and finally our general supporters to give for us to expand our reach all across Canada. We asked for only one hundred thousand dollars because we believed that would give us the financial assets needed to enlarge our footprint in Canada.

Some 208 generous people with a spirit for giving to God's work opened their hearts, picked up their pens, and wrote checks for a total of $180,512. One man gave $50,000, which was half of our goal. Many others joined him, giving what they could, and it was enough to pass the goal by more than $80,000. We are slowly and wisely investing those dollars in Canada enlargement, and the results are encouraging.

We have added new clients as well as new chaplains to serve more and more workers and their families in our northern neighbor. God has encouraged us by opening additional doors for ministry to employees. EnCana, headquartered in Calgary, Alberta, is one of the largest gas and oil producers in the world. In 2012, they gave us a contract to place chaplains in Kiwigana Oil Field Camp, about two thousand miles north of Dallas, Texas, and about seventy-five miles north of Fort Nelson, British Columbia. They closed that camp; however, it looks promising to enter another camp in North Grande Prairie, Alberta. We continue to pray for more opportunities with large corporations in Canada, where chaplains will care for thousands of workers and their families.

The Marketplace Ministries Foundation

In 1997, I met a man who wanted to contribute to the ministry. However, he desired to give a capital gift that would not be spent. Earnings from his initial gift were to be disbursed for ministry use. We did not have a venue for that type of giving. That experience led me to sense we needed a foundation for endowed gifts that would be used for Kingdom's work until the Lord came again.

I had already met people who did not want their gifts saved or invested. They wanted us to use them now, and when we needed more they would give more. We had two types of givers, gifts for use now and gifts for earnings off the capital gift to be used continually.

I began to study how to set up a foundation for a non-profit organization, and the Marketplace Ministries Foundation was officially formed in 1997. It became operational the next year in 1998. There is a ten-member board of directors of the foundation, with six of the members serving on the Marketplace Ministries board of directors, as well.

It took five years for the foundation assets to reach one million dollars, while in the beginning of 2014 total assets reached their highest mark ever, totaling more than nine million dollars. Cash contributions for new or previously established endowment accounts grew as well. Today, there are thirty-three endowments in the foundation.

Funds from the foundation are for use of the ministry to obtain its objectives that require financial support. Even though the foundation is open to receive a variety of gifts, there has been one trust endowment given thus far. In 2006, the Aaron L. Colvin family of Dallas gave a gift to the foundation to establish and honor Lieutenant Aaron L. Colvin, US Army combat veteran of World War II.

The gift honoring the former member of the ministry's board of directors came to the foundation at the time of the death of the final member of the immediate family of Mr. Colvin. When Mrs. Colvin died in 2006, following their son Eugene's death, the trust funds began to be dispersed at the wishes of the Colvin family.

Aaron and I were close friends, real buddies, for nearly three decades. Both of us were devoted patriots, both served in the US Army, both churchmen, both family men, and both dedicated Christians. He was a successful longtime Dallas oil man, and I burned a lot of oil in my old Chevrolet station wagon, and Datsun, so we did have a lot in common. He produced it, and I used it.

At age thirty-four, he was one of the oldest lieutenants to serve in a combat unit of the US Army fighting in Europe, and he always displayed his combat infantry badge with much honor. He was leading much younger men when they paid the highest price for our nation's freedom with their blood and lives.

Aaron Colvin was a member of the Marketplace Ministries board of directors for fifteen years prior to his deteriorating health, which caused him to step down from active board participation. He was one of thirteen original board members when Marketplace Ministries was formed in 1984 and served from the first day until 1999.

Even though I spoke at my friend's graveside service, I know I will see him again. He is waiting for me in heaven, and I will join him real soon. Our days are numbered, not numberless. I look forward to our reunion, and what a glorious reunion it will be!

When I think about all the good friends I have met in this ministry at work, seeking to touch the marketplace with God's love, I realize how relationships are much more important than material assets.

An individual can be broke and still be a best friend. Money is not the important issue; how we relate to people, family, friends, and strangers, is what is important.

I never asked our Lord to give me money; I have asked Him to meet needs, and He has. I have asked for wisdom about how to reinvest His assets and where to give to His causes and to His people. He always answers those prayers.

If you would have told me in 1983 God would provide an abundance of money to fund His work at work, I would not have believed it, though I know He could do that and more.

When Ann and I wrote that first twenty-five-dollar check, I did not realize God would use that to prime His generosity pump, that hundreds of others would give additional funds to help underwrite His causes. I can hardly believe it even now. Impossible? Yes, with man; however, not with God.

I simply stand in amazement!

17

NUGGETS OF GOD'S WISDOM IN THE MARKETPLACE

After being a chaplain in workplace America for more than three decades, and military chaplaincy for two decades more, I have learned a few things by experience, trial and error, success, and failure, with God's mercy and grace as my teacher. I have not learned all I need to, so I do not claim to know it all. I just desire to share some of the things God has shown me in His nuggets of wisdom.

Nugget of Wisdom 1: Make the Priority of Your Life the Kingdom of God and Worshipping Jesus Christ

For the kingdom of God is not eating and drinking, but righteousness and peace and joy in the Holy Spirit. (Romans 14:17)

"You shall worship the Lord your God and Him only you shall serve." (Matthew 4:10)

Many times we often think of the kingdom of God as a geographical place, like heaven. Maybe we feel it is a place where there is no sin, no problems, no sorrow or pain, no death, no conflicts, and all is well. That would be heaven, would it not?

However, Paul in Romans 14 is not speaking about the future destiny of true believers of Christ, a place called heaven. The kingdom of God he speaks of is here with us today, and it is carried out by the Christian character traits of righteousness of actions, peace of mind and spirit, as well as complete and satisfying joy, real joy, which is far more than temporary happiness.

It is only when the Holy Spirit lives the Christ life in and through us that we will ever experience the attributes of the kingdom of God here and now. Righteousness, peace, and joy come only from the Christ-honoring life of any individual who wants to experience the kingdom of God. Only the Holy Spirit can produce in us the hallmarks of the kingdom of God: righteousness, peace, and joy.

These are three diamonds in the crown of life; they bring completeness in living, and satisfaction in journeying through this earthly pilgrimage heading home. If you have experienced Christ as your Savior and Lord and are seeking to honor Him day by day, you will one day be at home with our Lord. Until then, you can have His righteousness in living, peace that passes all understanding, and joy unequalled.

When we think of serving our God, many of us become confused and put work before worship. However, Matthew tells us that before we can accomplish effective and efficient service in Jesus' name, we must spend time with Him, time alone in worship, meditation, and prayer. That is the starting point!

We turn to Scripture to see these testimonies from God's best servants, His workers.

When childless Abraham, at the seemingly hopeless age of one hundred, was given the certain promise and assurance of being a father of many nations, of multitudes, he prayed and was alone with God (Genesis 17:1-7).

When Moses received the most impossible human mission ever given to a man to free hundreds of thousands of slaves in Egypt, he prayed and was alone with God (Exodus 3:1-10).

General Joshua; the prophet Samuel; the first prophet; King David; the prophet Elijah; Stephen the martyr; the apostle Paul; the disciple John; and the most significant example of all, the Lord Jesus, all prayed and were alone with God. When Jesus made the most supreme, ultimate decision of self-sacrifice to take your place and mine on the cross, He did it through prayer and being alone with His heavenly Father. While others slept, he prayed, seeking God the Father and yielding His will to the will of His Father.

We can be alone with the Father in the midst of fellow human beings, but we need never be alone in reality because we can spend time alone with God the Savior. The result of this time alone with the Almighty is always more of His voice, more of His vision, more of His power, and more of His praise. How long will it take us to learn and practice this principle of prayer and being alone with God?

The secret of worship as the priority of our spiritual lives is paying the price of prayer and being alone with God. When we do that, surely we will seek the kingdom first and worship will be a priority in our daily lives.

Nugget of Wisdom 2: Pray More Than Anything; You Can Do More on Your Knees Than You Can on Your Feet

Pray without ceasing. (1 Thessalonians 5:17)

You ask and you do not receive, because you ask amiss... (James 4:2-3)

Let it be written for the record, I have a long way to go to reach a powerful and consistent prayer life. God has taught me how to pray, and yet, the evil one sometimes keeps me from prayer, even when I know I should pray and what to pray. Yet, someone has said, "Prayer is the spiritual breath of life, and if you do not pray, your spiritual life dies."

I seek to begin each day in prayer. In those early stirring moments of another day, I begin by thanking Him for allowing me to wake up to a new day, to have an assignment in serving my God and my fellow man, and for physical strength and health to get out of bed with mental alertness and spiritual stability, all by His grace.

I have a ritual of prayer I seek to follow. I have written many of my prayers and pray them from my prayer journal, with my spiritual awareness that God answers prayer. I begin the day in prayer by proclaiming Christ as Lord. "On my face before Jesus Christ, crying out, 'He is Lord.' "

It takes a lot of fervent prayer to cover the needs of more than one half million individuals, individuals with the normal problems, concerns, and crises of life, plus living and caring people called chaplains who reach out to them with compassionate love.

The first work day of the week, Monday, our entire staff meets for Monday morning prayer. We distribute a new prayer list each Monday, a list of ministry needs and clients' needs. There are always at least fifty to seventy-five prayer requests covering everything from death, illness, business crises, on and on go the pleadings for prayer.

The first thirty to sixty minutes of the work week is prayer time, with each team member praying to God from his or her heart of concern and compassion. We ask and often we receive. Prayers are offered for various parts of the world from North America to Europe, and from Africa to Asia. Quietly, staff members slip out of the prayer room to find their way to their work stations for a full day of God's work, after calling on His name with genuine prayers offered from their hearts.

However, there will be a team of prayer warriors who will offer prayers following the prayer request sheet every day of the week. These special prayer saints are spread out from Ocean Beach, California, to the United Kingdom.

These are our paid prayer staff members, with the mission as a prayer warrior for God, with their only task being to pray. These people pray to the Father daily, seven days a week, often many hours a week.

For this role we have tried to find God's special people, people who have physical handicaps, yet their devoted hearts and strong faith spirits are for God and man. They know how to pray, how to get hold of God by faith, believing and seeing God answer their prayers, often miraculously and always powerfully.

These people's lives have been changed because they are on mission for God in a paid assignment for His work, the greatest work anyone can achieve, praying for results and God's glory.

They may be legally blind; however, they can see God and they can pray. They may not be able to walk; however, they walk spiritually with the Lord and they can pray. They may be in constant physical pain seeking relief from a painful burden; however, their pain is laid aside as they pray. They may not be able to talk distinctly; however, God understands them when they pray. Their physical challenges do not limit their ability to cry to God and be heard.

Yes, they can pray, and they do pray. That may be the only thing they can do; however, they can do that well and effectively. Since we began, the prayer emphasis with salaried paid prayer warriors, the ministry has exploded in growth, geographic expansion, and financial stability, increased number of staff and chaplains, and evangelism results with God's protective cover over His work at work.

Breathing power and effectiveness into any work of God demands and requires prayer, consistent, daily, faith-based prayer. These prayers are petitions prayed in accordance with the Word of God, the will of God, in the name of the Almighty, God's son, Jesus Christ.

"When Christians pray, it loosens the hands of God to do great things He does not choose to do when they don't pray," said a saint in days gone by. How true that is, even now.

Over the years of serving God as a chaplain in the marketplace, I have seen blessings of miracles come one after another when God's people prayed. When we pray in the true spirit of prayer, God hears and answers in accordance to His will and plan. We must always close our prayers with those difficult words He told us to pray, "Not my will but thine be done." To pray these words to the Almighty, and mean them sincerely, we must trust He knows best, and because He loves us the outcome will be a wondrous blessing.

I recall praying long and often when things were difficult, money scarce, problems many. No business owners desired chaplains, and the needs of the hurting and dying were overwhelming. Only God could meet our needs and theirs. He is the only One who has the all-powerful resources, whatever the need and whatever the problem or crisis; God is able!

Shamefully, it took me twelve years to apply a paying emphasis on prayer, which illustrates how I lacked God's wisdom. But on January 1, 1996, God impressed on my heart to hire Richard E. Hall of Carbondale, Illinois, to serve as the ministry's first director of national prayer support. His praying would propel the ministry forward by a divine acceleration mighty in results.

It took me three months of consistent pleading with Hall before I finally convinced him to take on this paid staff position, the most important work we had or ever would have. This prayer emphasis, which began eighteen years ago, continues to this day. His stock answer to my consistent invitation to accept the position of director of national prayer support, and be paid for it, was, "I am already praying for the ministry and you. I don't need to be paid." However, I reminded him over and over that a "laborer is worthy of his hire" and that praying was work, important work in the King's service.

Richard Hall had been my friend since we were students at Baylor University in Waco, Texas, in 1955. After graduating and marrying his college sweetheart, Marian, they were planning to be missionary volunteers and enter Southwestern Baptist Theological Seminary in Fort Worth in the fall. However, a crisis struck the newlyweds when Richard came down with the dreaded disease of the 1950s, polio.

For the next fifty-one years, he would be bedridden as a quadriplegic, barely escaping death by living in an iron lung which breathed for him. Even though his body was decimated, his spiritual body was strong, as was his mind. He was flat on his back, unable to move from the neck down except small motion in his fingers, and yet in a perfect position to become a giant of a saint and prayer warrior who would affect the work of God around the world.

With almost no ability to move, weighing less than one hundred pounds and requiring a breathing machine for life support, Hall was obviously weak and frail. However, this man was the most influential co-laborer in this workplace ministry. He was a strong and beautiful person on the inside, the real side of life. For more than half a century, through his prayers, he "loosened the hands of God for many miracles around the world" by the prayers of a righteous man.

Most of us would have complained, become depressed and angry with God, or felt defeated and sorry for ourselves. Richard Hall had only the Lord in his life and a caring wife for twenty-six years, until Marian died of cancer. Richard possibly became God's most powerful praying saint; we will really only know when we, too, get to heaven. This godly man, who thought he answered the call of God to be a foreign missionary, became an individual who influenced every aspect of God's mission both at home and on foreign lands.

He turned his bed of confinement into a bastion of prayer, a cathedral of praise, setting captives free, making blind eyes to see, and binding up the broken-hearted. He was faithful at the task, both day and night, praying when the sun came up and when it went down, praying in the dark night hours, and the bright daylight hours as well. When the final tally of souls is brought into the kingdom, it could be Richard Hall's prayers, simple, pointed, and powerful, were the deciding factor of salvation for more souls than any of us could imagine.

Without a doubt, he is the most influential person this ministry has had in its years of service. Even though we have thousands of staff, chaplains, and supporters in this work of God, our special prayer partners have led the ministry's expansion in North America, Europe, and Asia. Prayers have energized all aspects of this ministry from the time we offered our first prayers in the early 1980s, and the phenomenon continues to this day.

Richard Hall, after faithfully heading up the ministry's prayer emphasis for ten years, heard that great Voice from heaven saying, "Come up hither," on the afternoon of July 30, 2006. It was a bright day in Illinois, and brighter in heaven, when Richard went home. He has made heaven a sweeter place and joins more and more of my friends and co-laborers who are waiting there for us to join them. One day soon we will!

Nugget of Wisdom 3: Be Visible and Available to Love All People

You shall love your neighbor as yourself. (Matthew 22:39)

The greatest of these is love. (1 Corinthians 13:13)

*By this all will know that you are My disciples, if you
have love for one another. (John 13:35)*

We call it the ministry of presence, being with people, feeling their pain, seeing their sweat, hearing their words of sorrow and sadness, wiping away their tears.

We are able to weep with those who weep out of a compassionate heart that comes only from genuine love.

This is the type of love, founded not on human emotion but on divine springs that well up in the spirit, a love that overflows your life, and pours down on the lives of others, and is used by God to extend hope and healing.

Visible and available to all people, the poor and the rich, the educated and the uneducated, the socially elite and the social dregs, the cool and not so cool, black, white, brown, yellow, for love is colorblind, and all need to be loved.

As chaplains, we not only extend the love of God in our hearts; we also extend God's love through acts of kindness. We show God's love with few words; providing support and meeting human needs is clearly God's love in action.

We stand with people when a loved one has been killed in an accident or died of natural causes. We not only stand; we often extend financial support to pay for funerals, because few people have money in their budgets for them. It's another act of kindness that says, "See, this is God's love in action. It is kindness extended by divine motivation."

Our service to people, exhorted by God's love in our hearts, is shown by getting an old car repaired for a single mother so she can get to work and take her kids to daycare. She did not have money for car repairs; we did, and we made a loving investment in her life and the life of her family, showing God's love through an act of kindness.

We provide food for tables and empty pantries, so the family can survive until the next pay day. Getting their electricity turned on, with the bill paid, or getting bill collectors off their backs by making a past due payment on overextended credit are other acts of kindness.

When we extend acts of kindness, it always seems to me, I can hear the words of Jesus saying, "When you did it unto the least of these, my brethren, you did it unto me." We are doing everything we do as if we are doing it to Jesus Himself, for we really are.

Being a chaplain in the marketplace is being a giver and extender of the love of God, and that means "doing unto others as you would have them do unto you." Every day, many times a day, we can show His love to all people. What a joy to be a Johnny Appleseed of love, planting the seeds of God's love in the lives of people, meeting practical human needs, and supporting individuals in crises.

God's love doesn't always involve money, though often it does. It may be as common as being a part of the ministry of the listening ear, giving your full attention with sincere interest to someone's story while looking them in the eye. It may be a sad story, a crisis story, a happy story, an ongoing story; however, it is their story, and everyone needs someone to listen to them sometime.

God gave us two ears and one mouth, so we are to listen twice as much as we talk. That is difficult for some of us; yet, many people just want you to listen and let them tell you their story. They don't even want you to immediately solve their problem; they just want to tell you their problem in detail and with a personal description. What they want from you right now is simple—just listen!

When a Marketplace chaplain pulls into the parking lot of a client company to make a worksite visit, to interact with employees, to check on life in their families, we encourage them to pray that they will be "filled up and overflowing" with God's warm and vital love, that it overflows with every expression they make, a touch, a smile, a nod of the head, a word, looking into an anxious face, or a brief prayer.

Chaplains must always be available, regardless of personal schedules or activities. I will never forget the first chaplain I released from his duties, one of the most difficult things I have done in thirty years leading Marketplace Ministries. I have had to do it more than once.

There was an accident in one of our client companies, and this particular male chaplain was assigned to that company. When we got the emergency call at our office, we began trying to reach the chaplain on his pager. No answer. We tried several times, with no response. We sent another chaplain to the hospital to be with the family as their loved one, the injured worker, clung to life by a tiny thread.

We continued to support the family in the intensive care unit waiting room at the hospital where the employee was taken. Still there was no company chaplain present, even though others were there extending support, care, hope, and prayers.

With chaplains in place caring for family members, I left my office and drove to the home of the AWOL chaplain, the one who did not respond. He was in his front yard finishing up mowing his lawn, improving the look of his home.

When I told him we had been trying to reach him for some time, he said, "Well, I had to cut my grass, so I left my pager in the house." I reminded him chaplains are committed to be available to help people 24/7/365.

Well, he explained he had to cut his grass and that was his priority for a few hours. I then told him about the employee accident at the company and they needed their chaplain, and because he was assigned there, they needed him.

He responded again that he had to cut his grass, and if he had to do it over, he would do the same thing.

I told him to be in my office at 9 o'clock the next morning.

At the appointed hour, I got up from behind my desk, walked around it, and stuck out my hand. "Give me your office key, pager, and chaplains' manual; you are no longer employed by Marketplace Ministries," I told him. "We will send your final check in the mail. You can leave now."

When you promise someone you will always be available to help, whether it is three in the afternoon or three in the morning, you have got to be ready all the time, any time. This was the first time we discovered we had a chaplain who wasn't. Thank the Lord, there haven't been many others; for that we are grateful.

Nugget of Wisdom 4: Be a Servant, Get Your Hands Dirty

...but whoever desires to become great among you,
let him be your servant. (Matthew 20:26)

You are My servant. I have chosen you and have
not cast you away. (Isaiah 41:9)

The Lord told us the greatest of all are not the ones with the largest riches, or the most powerful positions, or even the ones who are most beloved or popular. He said clearly and often that the greatest person of all people is the person who serves everyone else. It is the role of a servant that leads to high esteem, to greatness, to real achievement.

We know a servant is the one who is ardently devoted to others. Often a servant is in a lower status than the one he serves. He takes orders and carries out the wishes of his overseer or boss. The servant is totally under the control of another, doing what he is asked, told, or commanded.

I have discovered there are no practical courses in seminary graduate school, or any university I know about, that clearly teach how to carry out the roles of a servant in the twenty-first century, in the church or outside of it. I know there have been a few times when I took on the role of a servant that I felt no one else was available to join me in servanthood. It was not expected, and neither did I ask to be the servant; it just happened.

About mid-morning one beautiful spring day in Dallas, I got a pager message that there had been a death at the home of the receptionist of a client company I served. I knew the lady, an elderly woman who had worked for the company for scores of years. She was a sweet friend and always greeted the chaplain warmly, with kindness.

I jotted down her home address and jumped in my car to find my way to her small frame house in Dallas. About a block away, as I drove down her street, I could see red lights flashing on two police cars parked in front of her home. I parked across the street and quickly got out. The elderly mother and company employee was lying over the hood of a car parked in the driveway. I heard her moaning, "Bobby is gone; he shot himself. Bobby's gone; he shot himself; Bobby's gone; he shot himself." Bobby was her only son.

He had taken a .357-caliber pistol and put it to his head, pulling the trigger. His body lay on a couch in his mother's home.

I did not know what to say or do. I walked over to his mother, gently lifted her frail body off the hood of the car, and held her in my arms. We both cried bitterly. She finally said again, "Chaplain, my boy is gone. He shot himself."

Neighbor ladies began to arrive, as well as fellow workers from the company. They took her to the next-door neighbor's home, and I went into the mother's house to meet the policemen, a detective, and the coroner. The body was removed out the back door and taken to the morgue.

Four of us picked up the couch, which was soaked in blood, and carried it out to the back alley. We made arrangements to have it picked up and hauled to the dump. The detective and policemen were ready to leave; they had taken the body and the gun.

One of the policemen turned to me and said, "You might want to clean up this room so his mother can come back in the house." For the next hour I used a bottle of 409 and a roll of paper towels to clean the room, making it spotless. It was the most difficult job I have ever done; however, being a servant is not always easy.

I walked with her during the next several days, helping her deal with her grief and manage her sorrow, extending help and hope to her broken heart. My love and prayers covered her, and so did His.

There is no school of servanthood to teach you how to minister in a time such as that. I wish there had been. I need more help in how to help others, and to help me be a real servant.

Nugget of Wisdom 5: Be Sensitive to Others and Their Needs in Their Situation

There are many occasions where every person, especially a chaplain in the marketplace, must call on a tender and responsive spirit to support a person who is in need of help. We may not be able to teach sensitivity; however, we can model it if we have it.

Compassion, love, genuine caring, and having tender feelings for others all lead toward being a sensitive individual, a person who is more concerned about the other person than himself.

Being sensitive to others has a lot to do with empathy for a person who is in a difficult situation. You understand what stress is, and you mentally put yourself in their place, realizing how you would want to be treated, how someone could help you.

One of our chaplains was called by a national railroad client after a teenager had committed suicide by stepping in front of a freight train. As we do in each railroad incident involving death or critical injury, the chaplain offered sympathy, condolences, and practical help in any way possible.

Quickly, the father told the chaplain the family had already buried their son, who was a Muslim. Standing outside the home on the front porch, the chaplain asked the father about his boy, his life, and his interests.

After a few minutes, the father invited the chaplain into their small living room, where he served tea, and they continued their conversation. The father was asked about his religion, as the chaplain showed genuine interest in the Muslim faith.

The father was touched by the questions asked by the chaplain and went into much detail about his religion. The chaplain even found common ground through the prophet Abraham, who was a character in both the Muslim and Christian faiths.

The chaplain lingered in the home for some time, meeting other family members of the young boy who was killed. There was a world of difference between this Eastern immigrant Muslim and an American Protestant Christian in the heart of Texas. Yet, they bonded at a time of great sorrow, and a kindred friendship was created because the chaplain was sensitive to the father, his sorrow, and his religion.

I remember once while serving in Frankfurt, Germany, with the US Army, I got a call from the military police telling me a two-month-old baby had been found dead with what was thought to be Sudden Infant Death Syndrome, or SIDS. I was asked to go to the facility on the post where the mother was at work that early spring morning.

It was one of the most difficult rides I ever had in my life, as the Army driver took me, the servant, to my destination of ministry. I prayed as we drove; there was no human conversation, only a spiritual one. I don't think the young trooper knew what my assignment was, to take the worst message you can ever take to a young mother.

I had learned a long time ago, there is no good way to deliver a death message. However, there is a better way, and that is to be straightforward and clear.

When I arrived, I asked for the commanding officer of the unit, told him my assignment, and prepared some ladies to be nearby; then they brought the mother into the office. When she saw me, the chaplain, she stopped and began backing up saying, "No, don't come near me. No, don't tell me anything. No, please no, no, no . . ."

Standing close to her, holding her hand and calling her name, I said, "Your baby was found dead in his crib a short time ago. Authorities think it was Sudden Infant Death Syndrome." And, before I could say anything else, she began screaming, flinging her arms about, and running around the office and down the hall. Finally, several ladies surrounded her, and we all wept together.

Was I sensitive to this terrible situation? I tried to be, and I did weep with those who wept. What else could I have done? Her husband arrived shortly, and I expressed my sympathy to him, offering my services for the baby's funeral. I continued to pray silently for this broken couple as the father and mother held each other in their arms, shaking with grief.

Ladies from the chapel made their way to the home of this couple, prepared food, and supported them along with the chaplain. It is times like these you wish you could call on God to perform a Lazarus miracle to bring life to a body of death.

It was not going to happen that day, for that couple, even though I wished it would.

Not all cases requiring sensitivity involve death. A young Muslim man was employed in one of our client's plants in Oregon. He regularly read his Quran at break times, usually alone, while other workers sat in their small groups of friends laughing and talking. When break was over, without much conversation, the young man went back to work like everyone else.

One morning when he came to work, he noticed someone had pried open his locker, breaking the lock. When he opened the door wider, he read graffiti condemning his faith, the Quran, and his life. There were words of hate and racism written on the sides of his locker and scattered torn pages of his holy book.

He was devastated and began to weep. He did not have friends among the workforce, and now someone had gone out of their way to show animosity toward him, stating clearly he was not welcome in the workplace, or our country.

His boss said he could have the day off, and they would give him a new locker. Also, they would investigate these acts of hate, for this was not acceptable in their company. The young man walked out into the parking lot, got in his car, and drove away with a broken heart and tears in his eyes.

This young Muslim man did have one friend, one person who respected him as a fellow human being, a creation of Almighty God. That one friend was the company chaplain, for he talked with him every time he made a worksite visit. The chaplain learned about his family and what brought him to America. The chaplain was interested in him and showed a genuine love that reached out past any prejudice or judgmental spirit of any kind.

When the chaplain came to the plant that day, long after the Muslim employee had departed, the first thing he heard about was the act of desecration and words of hate by someone in the company.

The offended employee would return to work in a day or two, and the chaplain was prepared to give him a warm welcome back, along with a special gift. The chaplain had driven thirty miles south to a special bookstore owned by a Muslim to purchase an expensive, leather-bound Quran. It was handled by the store owner, wrapped appropriately, adhering to religious guidelines for touching the book.

At the appointed hour, and on the day the employee was to return to work, the chaplain was waiting for him, with gift in hand. After exchanging warm words of friendship, the chaplain apologized for the hateful acts of others and gave the worker his gift.

The man was stunned with joy and appreciation. He could not believe his eyes as he held the new Quran, a gift from a Christian chaplain. The man could not utter a word; for a long minute he just held his treasure in his hand, staring at the Quran.

Then, with tears again in his eyes, he reached out and threw his arms around the chaplain and said words of appreciation, friendship, and love. "You don't care about this book," but the chaplain responded, "I care about you."

If there ever was a time when a person was sensitive to others and their needs, it was this time. The chaplain had an overflowing, sensitive spirit that produced a bonding love with a worker no one else even liked, much less loved.

The Christian chaplain and the Muslim worker were friends, a friendship that inspired others to consider friendship as well. The locker incident provided an opportunity for the chaplain to express his sensitive spirit to that one in need, and he did.

You and I can do the same in our world of work and life. I pray I will never be insensitive to others, never fail to show I care, and to genuinely hurt with others in their times of pain and sadness.

Jesus always did that, and He sat an example for us to do the same; may we follow His example.

Nugget of Wisdom 6: Receive Permission for What You Want to Do or What Others Want You to Do

This bit of wisdom is somewhat limited in nature, since it has to do with chaplains serving in client companies. However, you may see a connection between what you do at your workplace, as well your church.

When you are involved in secular work or ministry, both of which are sacred if God is in it, then you should remember this idea of getting permission for special activities outside of your assigned task at a particular location.

We perform weddings, with certain restrictions regarding theological perspectives of the chaplain directing the service. In one of our client companies, a chaplain was asked to perform the ceremony for a female employee of a prestigious automobile dealership in a large metropolitan area. The chaplain agreed to her request.

However, she wanted to have her wedding in the showroom of the dealership, making it easy for her work friends and others to attend. They were to have the wedding as a mid-morning event on her day off.

Everything was arranged, except for one thing. The owner of the dealership was not informed, or asked permission for this unusual setting for a wedding. The chaplain made all the other arrangements, including decorations, the wedding cake, punch and coffee, plus helping the bride get out the invitations. However, the automobile dealer was not included.

The day of the wedding came with the chaplain in tux and tails, and the bride and groom dressed appropriately. People buying new cars, or waiting to get their cars repaired, wandered into the corner of the huge showroom to observe the unusual happenings.

One of those individuals who wandered in was the owner. Surprised? Yes, to say the least; he was shocked. The good and godly man was not angry, at least not overly so. However, because he was not informed in any way, he did not have the privilege of being a part of this historic event in his dealership or in making a contribution toward this special occasion. The bride was one of his best and longest-experienced employees, and he would have enjoyed making her day even more special than it was.

The chaplain realized, after it was too late to do anything about it, that he really messed up by not making sure the owner was involved.

You and I should always ask the question, "Who do I need to ask permission of or coordinate with before I do ministry or work that touches others?" This owner would have appreciated that, and the chaplain would have, too.

Nugget of Wisdom 7: Be on Guard to Protect Your Faith and Your Character

There is a stern warning from the apostle Paul in Romans 12:11, "Never be lacking in zeal, but keep your spiritual fervor serving the Lord." (NIV) These are thirteen powerful words of warning, words every follower of Christ must adhere to if he or she is to be in faithful service to the King.

We realize we must never lack zeal, passion, energy, drive, pep, vigor, enthusiasm, and devotion in doing God's work, or any work, and doing it as unto the Lord. There is no place for laziness in life, in work, in doing our duties to God or man.

"Never be lacking in zeal." We are exhorted not even for one day, one hour, one minute to lack passion for Christ and His work, or the work He assigns us, whether on Wall Street, Main Street, or our street. We are never to be lazy in this life. We are warned against having this flaw in our character.

Second, we are warned against allowing spiritual fervor, the fire of the soul, from dying down to cold hardness of the spiritual heart. We are to make sure we cultivate spiritual exercises that keep our hearts aflame, burning brightly in serving the Lord. We know fervor means heat, or hotness. It is a higher temperature that warms our heart and stirs the soul with intense heat, torrid heat.

John the Baptist said he baptized with water, but One would come after him who would baptize with the Holy Spirit and with fire. We all need fire in our spiritual lives; heat that melts away sinful corruption that touches us in this life.

I like this sermon quote from the great English preacher, Charles Haddon Spurgeon: "The love and presence of Christ of a most abiding character, not a love that flames up and then dies out into the darkness of a few embers, but a constant flame, fed by sacred fuel, like the fire upon the alter which never went out. This cannot be accomplished without faith. Faith must be strong, or love will not be fervent." There must be a constant feeding of the flame for it to continue to burn. Faith brings fire, and for a constant flame, there must be constant faith. What happens if the spiritual fire goes out in your spiritual life? It is not good!

Recently, I began observing how many times articles ran in newspapers, whether in the *Wall Street Journal*, the *New York Times* or our local *Dallas Morning News*, telling horrible stories about ministers or church workers who were arrested or charged with crimes. I gathered two or three incidents every day or so for an entire month; it was unbelievable. These were assorted stories bringing ill repute to the blessed holy name and teachings of Jesus Christ.

Most of the legal charges and character failures dealt with illicit sex or money, while others involved murder, rape, bank robbery, worldly and material living, with death as a by-product. Add to that pride, arrogance, and thinking they were better than others, and you will pretty much wrap up the three basic sins the Bible warns us about: lust, greed, and pride.

A minister in a church in Texas got involved with a woman in his congregation, and for his new love, he murdered his wife. It took more than three years for authorities to gain enough evidence to file first-degree murder charges against him. It was his new girlfriend who turned state's evidence against him that got him convicted. He was sentenced to twenty-five years to life for murdering his wife after a long affair with the church member. This whole episode was shown not once but twice on the national television program *48 Hours*.

Story after story was in the newspapers and on television about unfaithful men who claimed to be men of God, serving Him, pointing others to Him, and glorifying Him. All the time, they were charlatans, fakes, and counterfeits using God's name only.

When it comes to money, we all should think twice about any desire for it and be on guard against greed that could spring up in our lives. What does the Word teach about money?

"But those who desire to be rich fall into temptation and a snare, and *into* many foolish and harmful lusts which drown men in destruction and perdition. For the love of money is a root of all *kinds* of evil, for which some have strayed from the faith in their greediness, and pierced themselves through with many sorrows." (1 Timothy 6:9-10).

A state judge in Dallas recently scolded the pastor of a local church, who was found guilty of breaking and entering for theft of ten thousand dollars. The minister stole items including fur coats, designer purses, and electronics from a church member.

"Deplorable" is how the judge described the conduct of the clergy person who stole from a dedicated member of the parish she was serving.

"Police Probe Florida Pastor's Death" was the headline in a New York City newspaper. The story told about a forty-two-year-old minister from Orlando, Florida, the pastor of a megachurch with eight thousand members. He had started the church with just a handful of folks in 1996. The minister became a high-profile church leader through his many television appearances.

The pastor had come out of the drug-infested, inner-city life in Baltimore. He had a dramatic conversion experience at age twenty and often told of his life's struggles with drug addiction and gang life.

Police found him dead in his New York City hotel room.

The evil events go on and on. Almost every day, even now, you read about evil men and women who commit acts of wickedness from their sinful hearts. What a tragedy of immeasurable proportions, which will be completely settled only by the heavenly judgment of our Lord. That will be the final accounting and will be rendered before the highest court of the supreme Judge of any judicial process.

Regardless of who we are, we must be on guard and stand strong against the wiles and temptations of the devil.

The Bible promises those who break the Christian commands of morals, ethics, and godly conduct will be found out, will "have their secrets shouted from the highest rooftops" (Luke 12:3). The *Wall Street Journal*, the *New York Times*, the *Chicago Tribune*, the *Los Angeles Mirror*, and national television are pretty high rooftops, and the message is extremely loud.

We must always remember Hebrews 4:13, "And there is no creature hidden from His sight, but all things *are* naked and open to the eyes of Him to whom we *must give* account."

This is a part of God's wisdom; a day of accounting is coming. That day at the judgment seat of God is for all of us, whether His children or not. Even though this judgment is different for the believer and non-believer, it is still a judgment by God, before God, and one we will all face.

I recall often the pointed words of that great preacher, Charles Haddon Spurgeon (1834-1892), who said, "Better to be sneered at as a Puritan than be despised as a hypocrite."

We are told if we lack or need wisdom, ask God and He will give it to us in generous proportions (James 1:5). God's wisdom stands mountains higher than man's intelligence or knowledge. Wisdom has an eternal value, while man's knowledge is always lacking in some aspect, making it temporal, even if it is long-lasting. I desire to apply the wisdom He has shared with me, and to do it for His glory.

18

INSPIRATIONAL STORIES OF
CHAPLAINS LOVING PEOPLE

An entire book could be written about the thousands of opportunities in which chaplains were good Samaritans to those who were beaten, bleeding, hurting, sorrowing, and suffering on the road of life. I will share a few of these miracles God has done in the lives of people and the life of His ministry at work.

Because I am a grandfather, and have been for many years, I look back on those occasions when one of those girls or boys was in our home for an evening or several evenings. When they were little I enjoyed reading the story of Winnie the Pooh. Surely you remember Pooh, the old stuffed English bear that was alive and talking. He lived in the Hundred Acre Wood, with his friends.

The one who got most of Pooh's corrective attention was the donkey, Eeyore. Now Eeyore always had a black cloud over him, and his personality emphasized a negative approach to life and living. This donkey was always on a downer.

I came across a dialogue between Eeyore and Pooh that spoke to me and touched my heart for ministry. Maybe this encounter will do the same for you.

The scene…

Eeyore is stuck in the river, in the mud, muck, and mire.

Pooh comes by, and looking down on the donkey he says, "Did you fall in the river, Eeyore?"

Can't you just hear Eeyore say, "Silly of me, wasn't it?"

Pooh says, "Is the river uncomfortable this morning?"

Eeyore says, "Yes, the dampness, you know."

Pooh says, "You really ought to be more careful."

Eeyore responds, "Thanks for the advice."

Pooh adds with excitement, "Eeyore, I think you are sinking!"

Then Eeyore pleads, "Pooh, if it's not too much bother,
Would you mind just rescuing me?"[1]

How many people do we walk by every day, maybe some of them even work with us, who are mired in the mud and muck of sin and life, and we only say, "You ought to be more careful; I think you are sinking."

They all think or say back to us, "If it is not too much trouble, do you mind just rescuing me?"

From what I have seen, chaplains are often rescuers, personal 911 first responders to those in need. They are there for most workers who do not have the services of a clergyman, priest, rabbi, or imam, and often become their best friend, like a family member. They are there to help and give hope when no one else will provide a shoulder to lean on or ears to listen.

Many times a chaplain's best and most meaningful support comes at the time of life's worst crises.

The husband of an employee in one of our client companies murdered his wife, then shot himself. Who met the airplane when her parents came to Florida to claim their daughter's body for burial? Yes, it was the company chaplain.

He became a supporting family member to the murdered employee's parents from a faraway state. This compassionate and loving individual knew their daughter at the workplace, so he felt a personal loss as well.

The chaplain was a family aide to those grieving parents, walking with them through all the painful logistics, from the corners' office to the police station, and from the funeral home to arranging the airline details and even leading a memorial service at the company where she worked.

Yes, it was the chaplain who gave hope and encouragement to her parents and her many friends at work and in the community.

After the casket was carefully loaded in the baggage compartment of the wide-body passenger jet, it was the chaplain who said a final prayer, embracing the mother and dad before they walked through security to board the plane.

Oh yes, he did one more thing. As well as keeping up with them after the burial in their home cemetery later that week, the chaplain called their hometown pastor to tell him when the grieving parents would arrive at the airport with the body of their daughter.

That was not the only time that scenario has played out.

Chaplain Lane Park of Dallas, Texas, one of God's best and most effective servants with more than thirty years of caring experience in and outside the

---

1 A. A. Milne, *Winnie the Pooh* (October 14, 1926).

four walls of a local church, was a key senior chaplain leader with Marketplace Ministries. He is retired now.

One summer afternoon, Chaplain Park received an emergency page from a construction employee who had just made a gruesome discovery at his parents' home. This employee's father had murdered his mother and had taken his own life.

After the worker of our client construction company called the police, he called Chaplain Park with the tragic news. Within only a few minutes, the chaplain was holding the worker in his arms as they wept together.

Chaplain Park was there to comfort a heart torn apart by a family crisis, and he stayed close to that family for months. He used his vast experience in planning and performing funerals to plan two more, a husband and wife, father and mother.

Week after week, month after month, the chaplain would interact with that employee at his worksite, praying often for that family and especially the son, and always giving continuous support and encouragement one on one as they visited at work, and in off hours as well.

A pastor cannot go every week to every member's work place to give help and hope; however, if the company has a chaplain, he or she will be there every week, and often every day to extend help and hope, for that is what chaplains do.

Wherever there is a need, a chaplain should be there. Whether the need is in one of the one thousand US cities where Marketplace has chaplains stationed and active or in another of the hundreds of thousands of cities, both large and small across the world, a chaplain must be available.

When a single mom from Danville, Illinois, took her seventeen-year-old son, a cancer victim, to Children's Hospital in St. Louis, Missouri, she found herself alone in a huge city without family or friends. She didn't know any of the one million people living in the greater St. Louis area, and no one knew her or her son.

That is, until the president of the company where she worked called Marketplace's national headquarters, asking for help for his employee and her son in St. Louis. The company where the mother worked was not yet a client of our chaplains' service, but the service was scheduled to start in a few weeks. Times of urgent need and crises don't always wait for contracts to be signed and startup dates to begin, and it was true in this case.

Chaplain Debbie Sandifer, one of four chaplains spearheading compassionate care for St. Louis client companies' workers and family members, found out about the cry for help from the region manager of the company in Kansas City where the single mom worked.

As Chaplain Sandifer put down the telephone, she was heading for her car and a trip to downtown St. Louis to help a mother in need of a friend at Children's Hospital.

For the next twelve days, the mother and Chaplain Debbie would bond like sisters, building a relationship of friendship by tears and prayers. Also, there were many long talks over hot coffee and quick lunches in the hospital cafeteria.

It was Chaplain Sandifer who would chauffer the young boy's mom to her motel after she spent eighteen-hour days in his hospital room, and it was the chaplain who talked with the young cancer patient about his assurance of salvation in Jesus Christ and the home in heaven that awaited him. It was the chaplain who stood across the bed and held his hand, and his mom's, when unbearable pain came. In those times, Chaplain Sandifer's prayers reached the throne of God for relief of physical suffering and assurance of the future.

It was the chaplain and the mother who walked together with the boy through the valley of the shadow of death as far as they could. Every time Chaplain Sandifer looked at the young man, she thought of her own seventeen-year old son at home, a totally healthy young man. She experienced more tears, tears of gratitude, and yet, she could not completely understand how one teenager was dying of cancer while another one was living a healthy life.

It was the chaplain who was there when the boy slipped away from the life of the dying to the life of the living. The chaplain was a part of that solemn moment we all will face one day when the door of death is open for us to go through, either to that new life in heaven or eternal separation from the Lord Jesus Christ.

It was the chaplain who drove four and a half hours from St. Louis to Danville to sit with the mother and family members during the funeral, and to continually extend hope, help, and words of encouragement. If you had seen those two mothers weeping together, holding one another in their arms, you would have had a difficult time knowing which one lost a son to cancer, because love has a way of weeping with those who weep.

Chaplain Debbie and that mother will be friends as long as they both live on this earth. Yet, at one time past, they were unknown strangers meeting in a hospital room; one of these ladies with a need and one of them willing to be used of God to meet that need. That is just what chaplains do!

One of the hardest jobs in America, in my opinion, is a long-haul truck driver. As they log between fifty thousand and a hundred thousand miles a year in those eighteen-wheel rigs, these men and women dodge bad or drunk drivers to make their deliveries. Add to that, these knights of the highway are away from home and family most of the time. These men and women drivers need chaplains, too.

In our client companies who run their own trucking facilities and deliveries, on any one day more than a thousand trucks are on highways and country roads with a professional driver behind the wheel. With that many vehicles on roads, there are bound to be accidents at times.

A chaplain was there when they transported a truck driver to an intensive care unit by Careflight, and he heard the pronouncement by the physician the man had died. It was the company chaplain who planned his burial, held the employee's funeral, and was a source of support and strength for friends, family, and fellow company drivers.

The chaplain is still there with the company and is still the point man for helping people deal with life's problems, which are often life's crises, one of which is death.

It happened on Monday, October 25, 1999. Superstar pro golfer Payne Stewart's Lear jet crossed nearly half of the United States before running out of fuel and crashing in a hay field in South Dakota.

The Federal Aviation Administration said Stewart's jet lost radio contact with the ground not long after taking off from an Orlando, Florida, airport about 9:30 that Monday morning.

A thirty-two-year old Air Force captain from Newport, Virginia, was flying his F-16 Fighter Falcon, nicknamed "Bullet One," on a training mission over the Gulf of Mexico when he was dispatched to intercept the ailing jet and find out what was wrong.

Turning his aircraft northeast at more than a thousand knots, the American fighter pilot soon closed in on Stewart's aircraft. The Air Force pilot saw all the windows of the crippled jet were frosted over, an indication the Lear 35 might have lost cabin pressure and was subjected to subzero outside temperatures. Also, the military pilot saw no signs of life aboard as Stewart's jet continued at altitudes possibly as high as fifty-one thousand feet.

Captain Chris Hamilton could only watch helplessly as he flew alongside the Lear jet over Memphis, Tennessee. "It is a very helpless feeling to pull up alongside another aircraft and realize the people inside that aircraft potentially are unconscious or in some way incapacitated," Captain Hamilton said. "And there was nothing I could do physically to help them from my aircraft, even though I was only fifty to one hundred feet away. That's very disheartening."

The Air Force pilot continued to report he could see nothing but the windows frosted over with ice. Fourteen minutes later, the Lear jet with six men aboard began spiraling down. Radar contact was lost at 1:20 p.m.

In Mina, South Dakota, the plane crashed, nose down, into the hay field at an estimated speed of six hundred miles per hour. The plunge took only about ten seconds from the altitude of forty-one thousand feet.

We all said, what a tragedy, and it was. However, you and I come alongside people every day, and we are much closer than fifty to one hundred feet. We stand next to them or work beside them every day; we can speak to them and hear them; we can even touch them.

Many, maybe most, of these people are going through life being frozen by pain, sorrow, problems, stress, and failures in living. Their spiritual life is frozen, too, without any life and without Christ.

We can share the Lord with them; we can encourage them; we can uplift them; we can support them; we can help them; and we can love them. We can touch them with the warmth of God's love, and they will be blessed and brought to life. That is what they need, and that is what we can do.

Unlike that Air Force pilot who was there beside Payne Stewart and his associates and could do nothing to help them, you and I *can* do something to make a life-changing difference. But often, we don't do anything; we don't say anything; we don't take any helpful action, and we should!

Marketplace chaplains reach out to workers and their family members through acts of kindness. It is kindness wrapped up in compassion and caring that warms hearts and changes lives.

Do you think serving as a chaplain is an easy job? Well, if you do, you had better think again. If you really want to know how difficult the tasks are, just ask one of our Marketplace chaplains.

Ask Chaplain John Lindsey, an Arkansas Razorback who heads up the chaplains' service in Arkansas. He could tell you about burying a company manager he led to Christ as Savior, just 168 hours before the man was murdered in his own home by the blast of a 12-gauge shotgun. What if the chaplain had passed on that opportunity to pull out his New Testament from his back blue jeans pocket and answer the man's questions about life after death? That would have been an eternal tragedy, a tragedy none of us should ever make.

A few years ago, at the Seattle, Washington, Special Olympics, nine contestants, all physically or mentally challenged, assembled at the starting line for the hundred-yard dash. At the sound of the gunshot, they all started out, not exactly in a dash, but with a relish to run the race to the finish and win.

All, that is, except one little boy who stumbled on the cinder track, stumbled not once but two or three times. He sat down and began to cry aloud as he watched the other runners pull away from him.

The other eight children heard the boy crying. They slowed their gait and looked back. Then they all stopped, turned around, and went back to where the crying lad sat…every one of them.

One girl with Down's syndrome bent over and kissed the little boy on the head and said for all to hear, "That will make it better." They helped the boy up, and all nine kids linked arms and walked together to the finish line, crossing it at the same time.

Everyone in the stadium stood, and the cheering went on for several minutes. People who were there are still telling the story today.

Why? Because deep down we all know this one thing: What matters in this life is more than winning. What matters is helping others win, even if it means slowing down and changing our course to show compassion and love for them.

That is what chaplains do in the workplace and hundreds of other places. They pick people up, dry their tears, and get them back in life's race so they can cross the finish line with everyone else.

In Orlando, Florida, where we provide chaplains to Regal Marine, one of the largest and most prestigious privately owned boat building companies in America, our chaplains have dealt with several tragedies and family crises. That is what they do in every one of the client companies we serve every day of the year.

Some time ago, a twenty-four-year old man, one of a company's best and most productive employees, was caught one night breaking into a home. There was a weapon involved, and a young police officer, the first responder to the 911 call, fired on the intruder, killing him instantly.

One of our very best chaplains, Chet Hirshey, who served with us many years and who now is in heaven, directed the funeral for that young man three days after the shooting. A lady chaplain, one of our more than eight hundred dedicated female chaplains, comforted a beautiful young widow, sitting next to her during the service for her husband. The sorrowing wife was trying to understand exactly what happened and why.

Chaplains are involved in teaching volunteer Bible studies when employees request such a gathering. These types of spiritual and biblical events are usually done on workers' personal time before work or during breaks. The ministry usually has well over a hundred weekly Bible studies going on at any one time in our client companies.

Even though I still claim to be a chaplain, like everyone who works for Marketplace Ministries, over the years my role has changed from going to client companies as the primary chaplain to more of an administrator and overseer of my fellow chaplains.

However, I still like the pure chaplain's role best!

I will never forget, not if I live a thousand years, for it so clearly illustrates the separation between the marketplace and the church, a divide that saddens one's heart. A huge number of people don't go to church, and most never will; however, almost everyone has got to go to work, or wish they could.

Where do people learn spiritual truths, and hear the Word of God taught, if they do not attend any church? If they have a company chaplain, they could hear it at work, where they labor and where they earn a living to sustain themselves and their families.

It was 10:30 on a Friday night, I recall, and my congregation was gathering, for I was teaching the Bible study at Williamson Printing Corporation in Dallas before the second shift went to work at 11 o'clock. Jerry and Jesse Williamson, who owned the company, were longtime clients of the ministry, joining us early on. These two brothers were my close friends, as I had known and loved their parents, Bowen and Irma Clifton, for many years.

As I was ready to start that evening, I could not help but look into the faces of those who sat before me, just seven employees, all valuable people in God's sight.

I looked down the two rows of people dressed for work, not in their Sunday best, for they didn't have a church to attend, as well as no pastor.

One of my Bible study participants was an older lady who had a look of despair on her face. It was evident, without judging, she had lived a hard, difficult life. She sat on the front row with an open Bible in her wrinkled hands, a Bible that had been given to her by her chaplain. As I observed this sad lady, it seemed she carried the scars of a sinful life, a life that for a long time had been separated from God. However, she had never done anything to lessen her value to God. She was valuable; a soul is always valuable. She came to study God's Word, and that was a good sign.

There was a big fellow in my group that evening, a huge man who must have weighed 250 pounds or more and wearing a Harley-Davidson black leather jacket. He had a red bandana tied around his head of straggly hair, with a bushy mustache curved down on both sides of his mouth. His arms were as big as my waist. Well, maybe not quite as big as my waist, but close. On one arm he had a tattoo of a naked woman; on the other arm he had "born for meanness." This biker was holding God's Word in his huge hands. He had value, and the Bible he held said so.

The rest of the people in my congregation that night were similar to those I have described. As I stood there before my Bible study students, I tried to visualize those people in the church I attend on Sunday morning, or in any church for that matter. I wondered if the average Baptist deacon or Methodist elder would give them a warm welcome with open arms for morning worship. I still wonder.

There they were at 10:30 p.m., getting ready to go to work on the graveyard shift, yet they chose to study the Word of God before work. I believe if Jesus was here today in bodily form walking among us, He would spend the majority of His time in printing companies, in boat building plants, in old farm houses, and in hospitals and cemeteries with people who don't go to church and yet need His eternal fellowship.

With our Lord spending most of His ministry in the marketplace, it would not be by coincidence or accident but by God's divine, providential intervention of His Son to love people and influence their eternal destiny in the workplace. These are the people who live every day outside the walls of any church and always have to go to work. They all need Jesus, even at work.

In a client company in Dallas, a twenty-four-year-old mother and her husband arrived home after work about 1:30 a.m. As they drove into their driveway and were getting out of their car, a next-door neighbor who had gone mentally berserk came running out of his home with a loaded gun in his hand.

He started shooting, killing the young wife and her husband, hitting him with five bullets. The young woman's brother came running out of their house to see what was going on in the front yard. He was shot, too, and now three people lay on the ground, and first responders were not yet on their way to the deadly scene.

In those early morning hours, we assigned three chaplains to those two families, twenty-four hours a day, for five days after the shootings. Those who were killed never worked for one of our client companies; however, the woman's father did, so we responded with compassionate care for all.

The chaplains were still involved with those hurting families long after the funerals were held and the sound of gunfire had faded.

Most families are not prepared to pay for one funeral, much less three at the same time. You are talking about needing thirty thousand to forty thousand dollars at the least for funeral expenses. This family did not have in their budget a huge amount of money for funerals; in fact, they had no money. Most of us would have difficulty writing a large check for anything, including one for funeral expenses for loved ones.

It was an opportunity for Marketplace Ministries to step up with benevolence funds and help pay for those funerals. We had the joy to invest financially in alleviating the sorrow and sadness of the families and the stress of needed funds.

This ministry does not lend money, and we do not have unlimited financial benevolence resources to cover everyone's expenses in every situation. However, when God gives us money for ministry, we share it with others in need. We do everything we can to help people, and sometimes that involves money.

Again, you never know the day when someone will require the help and support of a chaplain in the work areas of life and everywhere else. You can be assured, without a doubt, that day will come for everyone. Some will have a local church pastor, most will not; the majority will need the service of a chaplain, a minister in the marketplace.

Chaplains are called on to deal with death and crises of all kinds, in nearly every way possible, including airplane crashes, train wrecks and railroad crossing incidents, motorcycle accidents, industrial machine accidents, boating accidents, drownings, and heart attacks. The list goes on: cancer deaths, shootings, drug overdoses, AIDS deaths, automobile wrecks, and deaths by hundreds of other ways, possibly the worst of all being countless suicides, some young and some older people, all leaving the biggest scars of sorrow on those loved ones and friends who are left behind.

Our chaplains cry somewhere every day, along with sharing joyful times with others, fulfilling the biblical exhortation, "Rejoice with those who rejoice and weep with those who weep" (Romans 12:15). After forty years as a chaplain, I have found more people are weeping than rejoicing.

It was Tuesday, August 20, 2002, and Marketplace Ministries was having a gathering of its executive leadership team in Kansas City, Missouri. We move this planning session around to various cities in our regions spread across the United States.

That night we decided to give up the church camp food, where we were staying, and go into town for a "real meal." Maceo Gray, a longtime leader in the ministry, suggested Outback Steakhouse for the best meal we would eat all week, and fifteen of us piled into cars and headed for dinner.

After a delicious meal, three of our ministry leaders were in the car I was driving back to the Presbyterian church camp facilities where we were staying. We went north on the highway back to camp, cut around the Kansas City airport, then turned west for the last few miles out into the country. It was a four-lane divided highway, and there was little traffic. Darkness was falling quickly now; it was dusk, just before darkness closes the day.

We rounded a curve in the road and rapidly came upon a car parked near the side of the highway, with no lights on and the hood up. It was an old, beat-up car. The driver's door was open. When we flashed by, a lone young lady in the car threw up her hands, apparently in despair.

The first thing I thought about was my oldest granddaughter, Allison, who also has long hair like the young lady we passed. Then I thought of my wife, Ann; what if that was her stranded alone on the side of a highway with darkness falling quickly?

I turned around and asked our guys if they saw that young girl we just passed. Everyone had, and one of them said, "Turn around, and let's go back and help her."

I guided the car off the highway and stopped. Maybe we could just back up and not have to go a long distance to find a turnaround area. I am not the best backer of automobiles; however, this was for a mission to help someone in need, and I could back up for that.

When we got close to the car, the young woman was out of her car and walked around to the front of it. Larry Ramsey, the ministry's marketing vice president was riding in the front seat with me and got out to go speak to her. I could see them talk through my rearview mirror.

He came back to announce the young lady ran out of gas, didn't have a gas can, and no one had stopped to help her. We all agreed we would help her, take her to a gas station, get a gas can, and get her going again.

It was dark now when Larry went back and invited her to get in our car, and we would take her to a gas station. I watched in my mirror as this young girl looked at those men in their car and wondered about getting in with strangers. However, both of them began to walk toward our car. Larry got in the back seat, and the stranded lady got in the front by me. With the car's interior lights on, I looked at this young lady very carefully for the first time.

I first noticed she was deeply tanned, not the tan like you get on a beach or sitting around a country club swimming pool. This was the kind of tan laborers get when they are out in the sun for long hours doing hard work. She had a hard and rugged look about her. When we introduced ourselves and I touched her hand with a handshake, her hand was rough, like sandpaper. She was wearing tight-fitting jeans that might have been painted on her, along with an extremely low-cut blouse. She had a worldly look about her.

As we started to ease back onto the highway, in search of a gas station, we all began to visit with our new friend, Angela. We found out she was a brick mason's helper from Houston, Missouri. Her job was to "shake up" mud, cement, stack bricks, and move mason boards to the next location for the brick layers. Hers was not an easy job, to say the least, for I had done that job myself and knew the difficulty of being a brick mason's helper on a construction site. No wonder her hands were so rough and her body so tan!

Someone asked her what she was doing out on the highway at night and where was she heading. Angela replied she and some girl friends had come to Kansas City to attend an all-day Ozzie Osborn concert. She had left the stadium to locate some cheaper food for a late lunch, got lost while she was trying to find her way back to the concert site at Arrowhead Stadium, then ran out of gas.

Dan Shotts, our chief financial officer at that time, asked her how long she had been stranded on the side of the highway. She said she had been sitting there for hours.

About that time, we saw the advertising lights of a major gas station and pulled in. One of our men got out and headed inside to see if we could purchase a gas can and five gallons of gas. He did not realize it, but Angela had quietly followed him into the store and was standing behind our man as he asked to buy a gas can.

The proprietor was listening and observing this young lady with the old guy. When our man realized this new stranger was with him, he quickly began to explain this young lady had run out of gas and we had picked her up to help her out. The man behind the counter evidently believed the story and offered to pay half of the gas can price himself.

Soon we were back on the road, heading toward Angela's car, with a new gas can and fuel for her car in our trunk.

As we drove down the darkened highway with the dashboard lights shining on Angela's face, I looked over at her and asked, "Angela, do you know why four men and total strangers would stop to pick you up tonight?"

She looked at me, for what seemed like a long time, without responding to my question. Then these words quietly came from her lips in a very country brogue, "Well, I'd just guess y'all are some of them do-gooders."

I responded by telling her she was right about one thing, we do follow the One, Jesus Christ, who went about doing good. When we can do good, we are doing as Jesus did.

That led to a discussion about faith in Christ; we talked about salvation and how you could know you were going to heaven when you died, as well as how to live the Christian life here and now. She said her mother was a wonderful Christian and at one time, she had been a Christian, too, but she wasn't living for the Lord now.

She had never been in a confined space with four chaplains, and everyone began to exhort her to turn her life over to Christ anew. After a long dialogue and a continuous witness to this young lady, we drove up behind her car, to her relief I am sure.

We all got out, and after pouring gas in her tank, getting her car running again and giving her directions back to the stadium, we asked her if we could have a prayer for her. There all four of us men, and Angela, with all our heads bowed, car lights shining on us and traffic whizzing by, were led in prayer by Larry. He asked God to bless Angela, that she would turn her life over to the Lord afresh and anew, and she would live her life to honor

Him. When he closed his prayer, big tears were trickling down her face and all of ours.

We then told her goodbye. She was no longer an unknown stranger. She was Angela, from Houston, Missouri, who needed a fresh touch of Christ on her life.

Since then, I have thought a whole lot about that night and our encounter with Angela. That young brick mason's helper was exactly right; we, as Christians, and especially chaplains, are "do-gooders." We are to do good to all people.

There comes a time for everyone, when they run out of gas on the road of life, when they need someone to stop, pick them up, and give them a little help to get going again. That's what we did for Angela that night. That's what our chaplains do for people every day.

We are out there in life as "do-gooders," doing what Christ did, doing good things that are motivated by love for people and love for God. We are there to encourage, help, care for, and love them.

The Bible says in Matthew 10:38 that "Jesus went about doing good." I believe Jesus would be called a chaplain today because that is what chaplains do: they go about doing good.

1. *The five Stricklin boys with mom and dad, Lessie and Gilford Stricklin. Back row Sunny (Gil), Don, and Jim, in lap Charles, and standing right Jerry. The year is 1947 in Denison, Texas.*

2. *Mr. and Mrs. Gil A. Stricklin at their wedding reception at Baylor University on May 23, 1958, in Waco, Texas.*

3. *The first Chaplain, Gil A. Stricklin, is pictured on his 50th birthday, September 11, 1984.*

4. *The first Marketplace office, a 1974 Datsun station wagon that was the ministrys' home office for five years.*

5. *Sysco employee, David Worm and daughter Jana, "The Little Angel."*

6. *The first client, Edwin V. Bonneau, of the Bonneau Company, speaks with the first Chaplain, Gil Stricklin, in the warehouse where Stricklin packed sun glasses to begin his ministry there in 1984.*

7. *In 1984, President David E. Wicker III, of Sysco Food Systems in Dallas, visits with the company Chaplain, Gil Stricklin.*

8. *Renowned Pastor of First Baptist Church Dallas, Dr. W.A. Criswell, laughs with Gil Stricklin at the "Two Incredible Years Celebration" in the newly opened Crescent Court Hotel in 1986.*

9. *Two friends of long-standing and co-laborers for Christ, Cliff Barrows (right) and Gil Stricklin, at The Billy Graham Training Center at The Cove in 1997.*

10. *Ruth Bell Graham, wife of Dr. Billy Graham, and Ann Stricklin visit at The Cove in Asheville, N.C. during the 1997 Marketplace Ministries Gathering of Business Leaders and Friends.*

11. *A portion of the Senior Staff and Chaplains are pictured in the Chapel at The Cove in 1997.*

12. *CH(COL) Gil Stricklin, U.S. Army, in his Dress Blue uniform standing among some of the 400,000 grave markers at Arlington National Cemetery in Arlington, Virginia.*

13. *Lonnie "Bo" Pilgrim, with his favorite chicken Henrietta, was Chairman and CEO of Pilgrim's Pride, with 56,000 employees. In 1990, he hired Marketplace Ministries to provide care for his employees.*

14. *Colonel Stricklin is shown as he boards his bus bound for Fort Sam Houston, Texas, for Army active duty when the 94th General Hospital was called up to support Desert Storm in 1991.*

15. *Billy Graham and his former fellow Team Member Gil Stricklin, visit on March 25, 1994, just down the road from Dr. Graham's home in Montreat , NC.*

16. *The Chaplain and His Lady on the day of Colonel Stricklin's retirement from the U.S. Army at Fort Sam Houston, Texas, in 1994.*

17. *Dr. Charles R. Swindoll, author, pastor, radio preacher on "Insight for Living," and then President of Dallas Theological Seminary is greeted by Gil Stricklin, when Chuck visited Marketplace Ministries International Headquarters in Dallas, 1995.*

18. *Chaplain Dan P. Truitt, Ph.D., the second longest tenured employee of Marketplace Ministries, is shown entertaining the hospitalized child of a client company employee.*

19. *Three friends of 90 year old George Beverly Shea (third from left), Gil Stricklin, Zig Ziglar, and Kurt Kaiser (left-to-right), congratulate Shea upon receiving the Marketplace Ministries Integrity Award in 1999, for "Integrity in Ministry," as soloist for the Billy Graham Crusades.*

20. *Richard Hall, in bed, with Jerry Lilley (background) and Gil Stricklin who fellowship with Hall in his home in Carbondale, Illinois. Hall was the first salaried Director of National Prayer Support for the ministry and was used of God for praying down many miracles.*

21. *Pro Golfer Justin Leonard (center) talks golf with two duffers, Art Stricklin, VP of Public Relations & Charity Golf Fundraising (left), and Gil Stricklin (right) during an early Marketplace Ministries Dallas Golf Classic, where Leonard served as the Honorary Chairman for 13 years.*

22. *The Stricklin men and their wives, (left-to-right) Cliff and Robin, Ann and Gil, Belinda and Art at the Marketplace Ministries Integrity Award Banquet in Dallas in 2004.*

23. *Gil and Ann Stricklin with 102 year old American Beloved Gospel Singer George Beverly Shea at the Marketplace Ministries Gathering at The Cove in 2011.*

24. *A portion of the Board of Directors of Marketplace Ministries in 2011, prior to a Board meeting at the Cove in Asheville, N.C. (front row, left-to-right): Carl Bolin, Gil Stricklin, Ann Stricklin, Dick De Witt, (back row, left-to-right): Del Rogers, Sr., Nelson McKinney, Dr. Calvin McKaig, Jerry Lilley, Will R. Thomas, III, Ed Bonneau, Dr. Charles Tandy, Bruce Grantham and Reverend Ralph McCune.*

25. *CH(Brigadier General) H.D. McCarty, U.S. Air Force, Ret., is shown holding a Lionel engine and caboose of the ceremonial 1976 train celebrating the Bicentennial of the United States. This special train set, plus nine more Lionel electric trains, were donated in 2013, by Chaplain McCarty to the Marketplace Railroad Chaplains Museum at the headquarters in Dallas.*

26. *The Executive Leadership Team at a meeting in Branson, MO, in 2013. (front row, left-to-right): Dick De Witt, Ann Stricklin, Gil Stricklin, (2nd row, left-to –right): Jason Brown, Larry King, Charlie Quackenbush and Art Stricklin, (3rd row, left-to-right): Andy Bunn, George Cotter, Shane Satterfield and Dr. Dan Truitt.*

27. *The Stricklin family on the occasion of Ann and Gil's 55th Wedding Anniversary on May 23, 2013, at the Broadmoor Hotel, in Colorado Springs, CO, where in 1958, Ann and Gil went on their honeymoon. Cal, Robin, Colton, Cliff, Ann, Gil, Allison, Belinda, Ashley and Art (left-to-right).*

28. *The 2014 Marketplace Ministries Foundation Board of Directors (front row, left-to-right and up) are Gil Stricklin, Chairman Will R. Thomas, III, Kyle Hearon, Casey Gurganus, Tom Freet, Patrick Hamner and Mark Lovvorn. (Not pictured, Dr. Calvin McKaig and O.R. "Butch" Smith).*

29. *Although God was the Founder of Marketplace Ministries in 1984, Gil and Ann Stricklin were the human instruments for the beginning.*

EPILOGUE

As I think back over more than thirty years of chaplains doing good works that glorified God and blessed man, I am overwhelmed by the grace of our Lord and the dedication of our chaplains.

God has called out some of finest and most loving, compassionate men and women to serve Him and care for others in the history of the church. These individuals go far beyond the second mile to extend God's love through acts of kindness with unlimited devotion to duty.

By divine providence, His ministry has accelerated in growth and geographic expansion far beyond my dreams or prayers. The door of ministry is wide open, and the cry for help and hope is louder now than ever.

We have only scratched the surface of opportunity and the need of caring for workers across this nation and others. It is overwhelming to think there are two hundred million businesses in China alone, and many more millions around the world. All of those workers need a chaplain-care giver. In thinking about the whole world, that makes the six hundred businesses we are serving seem overwhelmingly small.

However, God has been gracious to us in these years, with more and more Christian business owners desiring to have chaplains to care for their workers and family members. It seems that over the past decades more and more corporate executives are willing to use our chaplains to support and uplift their employees.

The opportunities for business chaplains are wide open, as the fields are "white unto harvest." Marketplace Ministries is just getting started, and the best days of ministry, worldwide expansion, increasing number of converts to Christ, and the greatest glory to God are still before us.

We know people do not have to go to church on Sunday, yours or mine, and realize they must go to work every week day, so we need to have a chaplain at the worksite, to extend help, hope, care, and love. Everyone will need a chaplain sometime, today, tomorrow, next week, or next year; however, life's crises are coming to all of us, and there is that dark time when you cry out for help, needing hope.

It is in those times of despair, with broken hearts and crushed spirits soaked in sorrow, that a chaplain will pick you up and meet your needs to get you back on the highway of life, living with joy and purpose.

That is what Christ does for hurting people, and often times He uses a chaplain as His body of flesh to touch your life with comfort and caring. May one be with you in your hour of crisis showing God's love that meets all human and spiritual needs for now and in eternity.

MARKETPLACE HEROES IN MEMORIAM

Chaplains and board members who are
Marketplace co-laborers now in Heaven

MARY CAROLYN GOODMAN LOVVORN
August 16, 1929—December 14, 2001

Mary Carolyn Lovvorn was one of the kindest and most supportive Marketplace Ministries Board Members we have ever had in the three decades plus of this Christian ministry. She served as an active member for four years before she began her battle with cancer.

Martin Lovvorn, Mary Carolyn's husband, was my life's "biggest cheerleader," the greatest encourager of my preaching and when I was thinking about how to influence the workplace for our Lord. When Martin was called to Heaven at age 54, his wife took his place, becoming an encourager and a strong supporter with her prayers, words of approval, and financial assets.

Mary Carolyn was a happy and holy individual who was a blessing from God for all who knew her and called her friend and fellow believer. All of their family, children Jan, Mark, Linda and Laurie, are active, practicing believers who worshipped at and supported First Baptist Church of Dallas.

The Lovvorns have been family friends of the Stricklins for more than four and a half decades. It was my joy to participate in the funerals of Martin and Mary Carolyn, as well as marrying Mark and Patty Lovvorn. All of the members of their family are very special to us, and have been strong supporters to God's work in the work places of the world. Even now, Mark serves as a member of the Board of Marketplace Ministries Foundation, and has served on the Marketplace Ministries Board as well.

Just a few days before she went home to Heaven, when cancer was taking her life, and while she was still in her temporary home in Dallas, I visited with

Mary Carolyn for 90 minutes I will never forget. It has been more than twelve years ago, and I can still clearly recall her victorious spirit, insightful words, and bright smile.

It was on a Wednesday night, December 5, 2001, from about 5:15 p.m. until nearly 7 p.m. That evening we talked, laughed, cried and prayed as I saw and heard her "heart" for God. She grew weary and I quietly slipped away, the same way she did nine days later.

During our visit that evening I asked Mary Carolyn what she would like to be remembered for the most in her life. She grew silent, and seemingly was in deep thought for a long time, and then said something about not being very good at answering questions like that.

Finally, she spoke, looking across the room at the white lighted Christmas tree in the corner, "I would like to be known as a loving Christian friend, who rightly influenced my family and my friends for my Lord."

She did just that, and still does today from Heaven, as those she influenced here are influencing others, and it will go on and on…through family, friends and strangers alike. It is a part of her eternal legacy, a mark for God that can never be erased.

ANN FORESTER
January 25, 1933—January 9, 2013

Chaplain Ann Forester, the first full time female Chaplain with Marketplace Ministries, joined the Chaplains' Corps in 1990, with joy and devotion to others, effectively serving for the next 18 years, before retiring in 2008. She was greatly beloved by all those who knew her as a friend, as well as those who called her "their Chaplain."

Ann and I were members of the same church, and I well remember the day I visited with her about God's work at work, asking her to join us in this effort. When she came aboard, she gave her total effort to helping and uplifting people by sharing God through her many acts of kindness and love.

During every one of her 6,570 days of Chaplain Service, she touched thousands of lives, workers and their family members, in dozens of client companies in and around greater Dallas. It is estimated she made more than 5,000 work site visits to interface with countless numbers of employees, as well as going to homes, apartments, hospitals and funeral homes to encourage and support both workers and their families.

This dear lady was known for her joyful spirit, disarming smile, and sparking countenance as she met friends and strangers alike. She was recognized as being both happy and holy.

This Chaplain's presence would "lit up any room" as female employees would confide in her during their darkest days, as well as their joyful ones. Her God-given, sincere compassion for people, all people, equipped her to walk beside employees in any circumstance, no matter how deep or hopeless the situation seemed.

Many said it was through her authentic care she exemplified the love of God and guided many to find their hope in Christ as their Savior. Her exceptional Chaplain abilities were recognized in 1996 when she was presented with Marketplace Ministries' highest honor, being named Chaplain of the Year.

Though Chaplain Ann left an indelible mark of love and compassion on the lives of innumerable client company employees and their family members, perhaps her most enduring legacy at Marketplace Ministries will be her role as Chaplain to Chaplains. Many of her fellow Chaplains found in her a skilled and sensitive mentor, especially in the often difficult and challenging early days of their careers. Ask any new Chaplain who joined up while Ann was active in the service, and they will tell you about the best advice and most practical help they ever received in fulfilling their role of Chaplain; most often it came from Ann Forester, their fellow Chaplain.

Chaplain Forester is an all-time servant hero among the ranks of Marketplace Chaplains. God honored us with her life, ministry and presence among us. Now her caring for others on earth is completed, and she is at Home in Heaven.

Do you suppose they have Heavenly Chaplains? If so, Ann is serving among them today, and still doing a superb job.

EDWARD R. SNEED
March 28, 1932—January 9, 1998

Ed Sneed of Denison, Texas, was my friend for more than 50 years, and one of my bosses as a member of the Board of Directors of Marketplace Ministries seven of those years. We grew up in the same neighborhood on West Walker Street in Denison, with his family living just three houses up the street.

His father was a medical doctor in our small Grayson County town, taking out my tonsils and sewing up the back of my left leg with scores of stitches after I failed to clear a barbed wire fence. However, Ed's parents both died very young and his Aunt Ruby reared both Ed and his younger brother Richard.

My mother had five boys and one or two more at the dinner time wasn't a big deal. I guess Ed, and sometimes Richard, ate more meals at our home than they did at their own. Ed was ahead of me a couple of years at Baylor University; however, I visited him more than once before I became a freshman there in 1953. He was then a junior geology major.

This dedicated man of God went on to have an extremely successful oil company business career with Marathon Oil, finally officing in Houston with other company executives.

He and his wife, Ann Gray Sneed, met at Baylor and were married September 3, 1955. They happily spent the next 42 years and four months together, before death separated them. They had a daughter, Susan, and a son David, along with four grandchildren. Monday, January 12, 1998, was a sunny, lazy, slightly humid, mid-winter day, very much like many January days in Houston, Texas. For me, as well as the overflow crowd which gathered at Tallowood Baptist Church, it was a day to celebrate the life and home going of Ed Sneed.

Ed, at age 66, was far too young a "warrior" to be taken off the Battlefield of Life. However, he was gone. It would not be long until everyone there that day would join him again if they knew Jesus the way he did. We were not there to tell him goodbye for the last time for we would meet again.

Ed, who served as Chairman of the Board of Directors of Marketplace Ministries from 1995 to 1997, had worked faithfully as a prayer partner, encouraging friend, and financial supporter since 1991. This godly and good man was just the type of individual any successful Ministry of God would want on their team, even heading the team.

He was equally comfortable whether in a church, at a prayer altar, teeing up a golf ball on a country club course, or talking with a friend, family member or stranger about Jesus Christ the Savior. Ed was the kind of fellow who "fit well" in any circumstance. Most folks would say he "wore well," too.

This ministry leader would take a prospective Marketplace employee out for a round of golf to give me his evaluation about hiring him, and then on short notice would be up early in the morning to go and provide comfort and compassionate care to any Marketplace Ministries employee across town or across the country. His heart made him qualified to be one of our best and most effective Chaplains in his workplace or any place.

I wish you could have known Ed Sneed the way I did. He was a real man, a man's man and man not afraid to poke fun at himself or others when it was appropriate, and that was most of the time. He was the kind of fellow who admitted regularly he would fall asleep on his frequent flights to Dallas for a meeting or working session at the ministry's International Headquarters. He would be awakened from his slumber when the wheels of the airplane hit the runway at Love Field, momentarily wondering where he was and why was he there. When he arrived at our office he was wide awake, prepared to do God's business and do it right and well.

I will remember his words when he accepted the assignment on the Board of Directors, and it spoke volumes about his character, spiritual disciplined life and his humility, for he said, "…I am happy to join you. I'm not much, but if one more person praying will help, you have it."

Ed's wife, Ann, and other family members have given a Legacy Gift to the Marketplace Ministries Foundation establishing The Ed Sneed Memorial Marketplace Ministries Workplace Evangelism Endowment honoring his memory and his love for God's ministry at work. All of his family, and I believe his endowment, which has grown to more than $150,000, is an Eternal Mark that cannot be erased.

Ed is still missed today by me and many others. My thoughts often turn to him, as I am much closer to meeting him again now than when he left us. It will not be long, and I can hardly wait!

THOMAS R. RICHARDSON
CH(LTC)USA, Ret
May 19, 1933—June 24, 2006

"Old soldiers never die, they just fade away" are the words of a ballad sung on the Plain at West Point Army Academy many years ago, and the words used by General Douglas MacArthur as he closed his final speech to the Cadet Corps. However, it is not true for one "old soldier," Chaplain (LTC) Thomas M. Richardson, retired from the U.S. Army.

The first four words are true, and always will be true; however, the final four words are far from the truth. Chaplain Richardson, who I served with in the Chaplains' Corps, was a member of two armies; one was the Army of the Lord, and the other was the Army of the United States of America. He served with distinction, honor, courage and devotion to duty for 64 years in the first Army and 20 years in the second.

He was one soldier who always went "above and beyond the normal call to duty" and was both a prophet and patriot. He was both a Military Chaplain and a Marketplace Chaplain, the first leading to the second.

The obituary of his departure said he was reassigned and promoted to garrison in Heaven on Saturday, June 24, 2006. However, he has never been more alive than he is today. since he left the land of the dying to enter into the land of the living.

I was honored to fly to Albuquerque, drive with his family to the burial site at the Santa Fe National Cemetery, and be a part of the military honors funeral for this distinguished Army veteran.

His memory will never fade, as this Chaplain, both with the US Army and Marketplace Ministries was a special friend for more than three decades. He was admired greatly by all who knew him, and that certainly included me. He was my personal hero and a living example of what a man of God should be.

Mary Jane, his wife of nearly 48 years, their two daughters, Carolyn and husband, John, and Rebecca and husband, retired Navy Commander Jaw Law, along with nine grandchildren, are very special to Ann and me. We have been present as they have grown up and established their own families and homes.

Chaplain Richardson answered God's calls three times to similar but different careers. The first was to be a pastor-shepherd; his second was to serve as a military minister as an Army Chaplain; while the third was to hospital-corporate chaplaincy with Marketplace Ministries. He served in his final career for nine years prior to his life ending illness here.

This man's service was always with love, compassion and sometime tears. He was a man of God, a Good Samaritan, a good Chaplain. His dominant strength was showing God's love through acts of kindness and expressions of care and help. Whether 3 a.m. or 3 p.m., when you reached Chaplain Richardson, you got his whole heart, and all of his human abilities filled with God's Spirit.

When you get that, you have it all. What more does anyone need when they have what Tom gave? Not much, I would say; you have God's love in human form when you can see it, hear it and touch it, and that was Chaplain Richardson in human form.

JERRY D. LILLEY
July 28, 1935—September 26, 2012

Jerry Lilley, who was a member of the Board of Directors of Marketplace Ministries, was my friend for more than 25,500 days. That figures out to be 70 years of life out of the 77 he lived on this earth. I had four brothers, but I tell you the truth, I did not have a blood brother I loved or admired more than my friend and brother in the faith named Jerry Lilley.

This medical caregiver, provider for the poor, Gospel presenter in world missions, and local church leader was one of the most godly friends I have ever had the privilege of knowing and serving with for the King. After 18 months of battling liver cancer, our gracious Lord said, "Enough" and allowed Jerry to come Home to Heaven. At his lake front earthly home in Branson, Missouri, with many family members gathered around him, he said, "Goodbye for now" and entered into another life, an eternal life with our Lord.

Four days later I stood in Branson's First Baptist Church to give the eulogy before 600 admirers of this good and godly man, people from all walks of life. I was pleased to share about our lives together beginning in 1942. The word eulogy in Greek means "praise," while in Latin it means "an inscription on a tomb." It is often referred to as a speech that praises someone or something of high value, typically shortly after someone dies.

I told those present my eulogy was really to praise God for what he had done in the life of Jerry Lilley. We were present to honor the memory of this dear man and beloved friend, for his memory of honoring Jesus Christ was worthy to be honored and remembered.

Jerry was a humble and gentle man, kind beyond description, totally committed to Almighty God and his fellow man. His life brought praise to the Lord, and blessed his fellow human beings. God blessed Jerry abundantly, and he abundantly passed those blessings on to others, sharing his blessings with total unselfishness, free of greed, personal enjoyment or self-centered pleasure.

You already know most high school romances fade as just a passing love, or first love, but usually not a long lasting love. Well, Jerry had his eye on a lovely and smart brunette named Carolyn Harvey. She was his first and only love for his entire life.

Carolyn and Jerry married in Denison, Texas, their hometown, on July 28, 1957. On Jerry's 22nd birthday, he gave himself the present of a wife, and for 55 years they lived to honor God and rear a family together. He always said Carolyn and their life together was the best birthday present he ever received. Their love for God and each other has produced a Biblical relationship as Exhibit A for all of us. This man modeled love for his wife, meeting all Biblical standards for how a man should care for his wife with love, and how a wife is to support her husband. Their daughter, Lisa, and son, Phil, along with their children, grandchildren and great grandchildren, have carried on the faith legacy of their parents. The successful family business, Lilley's Landing, a fishing resort on Lake Taneycomo, is still a project that involves several family members.

For 14 years, rotating off for two one year sabbaticals, Jerry made 41 trips from Branson, Missouri, to Dallas, Texas, to participate in Board meetings, and another nine trips to play in the Marketplace Ministries Golf Classic Fund Raising Tournament. During those 14 years of service, he never missed a Board meeting, even when I begged him not to come when he was ill with cancer.

Jerry drove nearly 25,000 miles in support of this ministry that has led more than 100,000 workers and their family members to Christ. As you would think, he would never accept one penny for expenses for his travel to our meetings and always gave generously to the mission and ministry of Marketplace.

This unique man, Jerry Lilley, Mr. Lilley, as I liked to call him, was a first-class lay minister for Jesus Christ. As a dedicated lay believer, he was committed, and devoted to spiritual matters, to a life of holiness, with godly impeccable character; however, he had the ability and vision for combining the practical application of faith with good works, and always with a bold spiritual application.

Beginning with the spiritual, and extending to the human application of faith at work, he cared for the poor, gave healthcare to the needy who were sick or injured with no concern for money or payment of any kind, fed the hungry, gave clothing to those who were cold and in need of covering for warmth, uplifted the downcast, visited those in prison, and supported the causes of God's Gospel at home and around the world.

These were the hallmarks of his life. Sounds a whole lot like Jesus, doesn't it? Well it was. This man had a deep faith and consistent good works that glorified the Lord and blessed men. Just like Jesus, Jerry Lilley went about everyday doing good.

CHAPLAIN ELBERT SMITHEN
July 17, 1936—December 12, 2013

Elbert Smithen, a 12-year veteran Chaplain with Marketplace Chaplains USA, served in McKinney, Texas, 25-miles north of Dallas. He completed his final Chaplain duties shortly before the end of 2013, when this "Warrior of Love" was taken off the battlefield and moved to Heaven.

This gentle, loving saint had just completed a little more than 50 years of service to the King, with nearly 30 of those years as a missionary in Peru, under the auspices of the International Mission Board of the Southern Baptist Convention. This long time veteran minister had four distinct callings and careers as a local church pastor, an evangelist, foreign missionary in South America, and work place Chaplain, being a minister in the marketplace.

More than 300 family and friends gathered at First Baptist Church of McKinney to sing, pray and praise God for the life of His servant, Elbert Smithen. The Life Celebration Service glorified God, and comforted, Jo, his wife of a half century, as well as family, many friends and co-laborers. It was a cold rainy day outside; however, inside the congregation projected a spirit of warmth with zeal and spiritual fervor.

Scores of workers he served as their personal Chaplain/minister attended the service, many with tears in their eyes. Each of them expressed a beloved spirit for "their Chaplain." A large number of those seated together in attendance at the service on that cold and terrible winter day were employees from Encore Wire Corporation in McKinney. Upward to 75-100 who had been helped and uplifted by the Chaplain had come to say goodbye for now. Those present included the entire Executive Leadership Team, a group men and women Elbert had influenced for good and God.

"Chaplain Elbert was such an asset to me personally and to my Team at Encore Wire," said Daniel Jones, President and CEO of the corporation, one of the companies the Chaplain served. "He was welcomed by everyone, and his work ethic and commitment remain an inspiration to me. Even after he was noticeably sick, Chaplain Elbert was as solid as a rock in his walk with God."

Jones added , he believes (Micah 6:8 ESV) fits the Chaplain perfectly…"He has told you, O man, what is good and what does the Lord require of you, but to do justice, and to love kindness (a) and to walk humbly with your God."

After completing his three decades with the International Mission Board, Elbert did not retire, only changed his "mission field" from the cities and jungles of Peru to the manufacturing plants and commercial businesses in North Texas. Someone in describing Elbert said he "did not retire; he only refired."

He launched his fourth career as a Corporate Chaplain in 2001 and served for the next 12 years. For those years he made hundreds of friends for Jesus as he went about daily showing God's love by performing simple acts of kindness to help people.

Up until cancer took its impact on his physical life, this 77 year old saintly servant, whose energy was not abated, was a hard charging worker in the fields "white unto harvest," and harvest he did.

There have been many Chaplains and administrative workers who have died over the last 30 years plus, since the first Chaplain was hired in 1984; however, none of them will be missed more than Elbert Smithen. All of his fellow Chaplains and ministry leaders look forward to their reunion in Heaven and seeing him again.

It will not be long; life goes by quickly. Our days are numbered, not numberless.

JAMES NEAL JEFFREY SR.
January 22, 1929—May 30, 1991

When I was a teenager, I met James Jeffrey (Jeff) who became one of my dearest friends. He influenced my personality and life more than anyone, including my own family. I loved his wife, Fran White, before he did. She was my Intermediate Class Sunday School Teacher at First Baptist Church in Denison, before she moved to Waco, Texas, to become the Executive Assistant to Baylor University President, Dr. W. R. White.

Jeff was a star football player for the Baylor Bears when he met the President's assistant and married her after his senior year. After a brief stent with the Los Angeles Rams in the NFL, he was heading for the military draft. However, before draft day, he found a running back position on the 12th Air Force football team based at Carswell Air Force in Fort Worth, Texas. His unit was a part of the Strategic Air Command flying the six engine B-36s around the world 24/7/365 during the Cold War with Russia. Jeff wore a football uniform more than he did his Airman First Air Force uniform.

Fran and Jeff had four children, Neal, John, Jan, and Jay, all of them having the athletic ability of their dad and the kindness of their mother. I rode the Katy #6 passenger train to Fort Worth one weekend in July 1953, soon after I graduated from high school. I went to visit the Jeffrey family; however, it was not just any weekend for this weekend turned out to be very special. I was sitting on the sidelines that morning, watching the Bombers workout. Jeff, as usual, was going all out, hitting holes, or rounding end, with power and speed.

When we left practice that morning, we went directly to the hospital. No, Jeff was not injured, but his wife was having their first baby, and the Airman was late. I was at the hospital the day the first Jeffrey, future All-American quarterback, came into the world. James Neal Jeffrey Jr., would be known by college and pro football fans as Neal Jeffrey, quarterback for his father's Baylor Bears, and backup quarterback for the San Diego Chargers. Neal is now serving as a member of our Board of Directors.

After his military playing days were over, Jeff did not return to the Rams, but entered the insurance business. His heart was in God's work, and he became extremely active in the Fellowship of Christian Athletes in Kansas City where he and his family had moved. He was a popular athletic speaker and humorous after dinner entertainer, as well as a church pulpit preacher, speaking hundreds of times annually, as well as keeping up with his insurance business.

His true calling from God was to athletes, coaches, and sports connected professionals and business agents. It was natural the Board of Directors of the Fellowship of Christian Athletes invited him to lead the largest Christian ministry seeking to influence high school and college student athletes for the Christian life. He was extremely successful as the Executive Director of FCA, headquartered in Jeff's adopted hometown, Kansas City.

Jeff and I remained friends over many decades. We did church revivals together, with me preaching one night and he leading the singing. Then we would swap the next night with me leading the singing and him preaching. We drove many miles together, and talked more hours than you could count. All of those hours were "mentoring times" when I was learning something about the Christian life and living it well. Those lessons remain with me to this day.

When I was seeking to know if God was calling me to the workplace in caring for workers, it was Brother Jeff who prayed with and for me. When we moved forward and formed the first Board of Directors for Marketplace Ministries, he served as a founding member of the Board.

He had already taught me how to juggle (not very good), how to speak before an audience large or small, how to tell jokes as a humorist that made people roar with laughter, how to witness about Jesus, how to live for Jesus, and how to be a positive dad and faithful husband.

Even though he was only five years my senior, I loved him as my own father. It was he who inspired me to have a positive attitude in living regardless of the circumstances. I will never forget flying to Houston to visit him in M.D. Anderson Cancer Center, and how he looked and what he said. I remembered how he looked in his football uniform, with strength, health, speed, agility, and power. He was different now for cancer had taken a toll on his body, but not his spirit. Positive, joyful, and assured was Jeff that day, like many other days, for he was heading for Heaven.

He died of cancer May 30, 1991, and began living "Over There." I still miss him; he was a powerful inspiration to me, and still is, as I recall his words, his life, and our times together.

ACKNOWLEDGMENTS

I express my deep gratitude to some individuals who have aided me in the task of writing this book. Of course, to thank some is possibly to forget others, but there are special people I must especially salute for their help and dedication to this writing project.

A special thanks to my longtime friend Chris Ave, who is a brilliant writer and editor for the *St. Louis Post Dispatch* in St. Louis, Missouri. Chris is my son in the faith, as it was my joy to introduce Chris to Christ when he was a sixteen-year-old and a good friend of our younger son, Cliff. He assisted in editing my original thoughts, after I put them on paper. I could not have completed this task without his practical support, and to him I will always be grateful. Chris began and served as the first editor of the *Marketplace Magazine*, then just a four-page bulletin. He got us started in many ways and has been a prayer partner for this ministry since the beginning.

I'm very grateful to a wonderful, God-honoring assistant at Marketplace Ministries, Glenda Davis, who read every word, all one hundred thousand of them, several times, and retyped many of them. She caught errors and gave us her editing expertise. Our older son, Art, a successful author in his own right who serves with us at Marketplace Ministries, also helped with editing the book. Also Linda Triemstra of Gold Leaf Editorial Services edited the book.

Thanks to Dan Truitt, PhD, who helped refine some critical chapters, because he has been a part of what God has done since 1986 at Marketplace Ministries. Additionally, I owe deep thanks to my friend and ministry partner, Marketplace Chaplain Bob Goodrich, who also serves on the staff of RBC Ministries.

The Christian business people who have supported, encouraged, uplifted and inspired me are countless. However, there are a few who stand out in devotion to workplace witness like Paul J. Meyer of Waco, Texas, a generous man in God's work who anchored this ministry in Central Texas; Don Hodges, of Hodges Capital in Dallas, Texas, a dear and devoted friend of God and mine who has stood with me in writing this book and helped get it printed; and Howard and Barbara Dan Butt, of San Antonio, Texas, friends of long standing who encouraged and supported this endeavor. Then too, there are Mickey and Barbara McKenzie of GSC Enterprises in Sulpher Springs, Texas, the Andy Horner family of Premier Designs in Dallas, Texas, the Johnny Bledsoe family of Sturdisteel, Inc., in Waco, Texas, and Fred Caldwell of the Caldwell Companies in Houston, Texas, all of whom have gone above and beyond in support of this ministry.

I saved the most important thanks to last, and it goes to my beautiful helpmate, Ann. She kept me moving forward to the last word and would not allow me to quit when writing became tiring day after day. She gave me her teaching experience to tighten my thoughts and to cut, cut, cut sentences and paragraphs. She put in many hours on the book, just as she has for many years in Marketplace Ministries.

All of us have done this in order that God will receive praise and glory for this written effort, and all others as well. My life's desire is to uplift my Lord and Savior, Jesus Christ, who has worked mightily in my life and to whom I give all honor, glory, and praise every day. When people read this book, may they say with us and the psalmist, "This was the Lord's doing; it is marvelous in our eyes" (Psalm 118:23).